Trapped
in a Closed World

CATHOLIC CULTURE AND SEXUAL ABUSE

KEVIN PEOPLES

Published by
Garratt Publishing
32 Glenvale Crescent
Mulgrave VIC 3170
www.garrattpublishing.com.au

Copyright © Kevin Peoples 2017

All rights reserved. This publication is copyright. Except as expressly provided by Australian copyright law, no part of this book may be reproduced by any process without prior permission in writing from the publisher. Every effort has been made to trace the original source of copyright material contained in this book. The publisher would be pleased to hear from copyright holders to rectify any errors or omissions.

Edited by Cathy Oliver
Cover, design and typesetting by Lynne Muir
Indexed by Kevin Mark
Cover photo: iStockphoto
Photographs by Rob Peoples and Ann Montague

Cataloguing-in-Publication information for this title is available from the National Library of Australia
www.nla.gov.au

ISBN: 978-1-925073-40-9 (paperback)

Trapped in a Closed World is timely, comprehensive and accessible to a broad readership. Peoples' acute insights on beliefs, values and practices that have led to sexual violence and cover-up scandals shows why the Church must stop tinkering with the clergy culture in the vain hope of rescuing it from these historical revelations.

> Dr Jane Anderson, honorary research fellow, University of Western Australia

Kevin Peoples spent three years in a seminary pond, and provides us with a well written account of his own struggle with the cultural murk, while interweaving it with the results of the many inquiries. All great tragedies have a mixture of the good and the bad, and the author describes them both in a book difficult to put down.

> Kieran Tapsell, author *Potiphar's Wife: The Vatican's Secret and Child Sexual Abuse*

Peoples takes a hard look at the toxic culture of the Catholic Church, the madness of seminary training, and the tortured, lonely lifestyle of the clergy. *Trapped in a Closed World* is a serious contribution to the ongoing debate about the future of the institution we know as the 'Vaticanised' Catholic Church.

> Chris Geraghty, former priest and retired judge

Through the prism of his own seminary training, Kevin Peoples enables his readers to see what has gone wrong. Clericalism, misogyny and mandatory celibacy are demonstrably major factors in this unfolding tragedy. This book is not for the faint-hearted, but the Scriptures assure us that 'the truth will set us free'.

> Bishop Pat Power, retired auxiliary bishop, Canberra Goulburn Diocese

A deeply-felt account of a personal journey with faith and disillusionment.

> Ailsa Piper, author *Sinning across Spain* and with Tony Doherty, *Attachment*

Peoples makes a very personal and persuasive case that the institutional Catholic church must reform its closed culture if it is to respond positively to the lessons of the Royal Commission into Institutional Responses to Child Sexual Abuse.

> John Warhurst, emeritus professor of Political Science, Australian National University

I highly recommend this book to anyone seeking to understand how, when, and why the open window dream of Vatican II lost out to the reality of secrecy, clericalism and the protection of the institution's power, identity and reputation at all costs.

> Michael Morwood, author *It's Time. Challenges to the Doctrine of the Faith*

Kevin Peoples has brilliantly combined his experience as a student priest in a Catholic seminary with reflections on clerical child abuse and the Church's cover-up. With insight, humour, and extensive research, he shows that clerical abuse is linked to the history and culture of the Church with its authoritarian structures, misogyny and celibacy. A powerful, compassionate and courageous book.

Iola Mathews OAM, author *My Mother, My Writing and Me: a Memoir*

Peoples describes a toxic seminary and church culture which created clerical egotists who felt comfortable only with defenceless children. He links this to the solid research on the over-representation of Catholic clergy among clerical abusers worldwide and makes sensible suggestions for another Reformation. The book is a page-turner and a heartbreaker.

Helen Praetz, professor emeritus, RMIT University

Reading *Trapped in a Closed World* you warm to Kevin Peoples. That is the sign of a good memoir. He has a good story, knows his material and is a good teacher. It is a page-turning read. He describes the authoritarian style, enclosure from the world and misogyny that pervaded Springwood seminary. He shows how this was a seedbed for clericalism and narcissism; no check for any latent paedophilic inclinations, and a direct contributor to the denial and defensiveness of the church leaders that it produced.

Eric Hodgens, retired parish priest, alumnus of Corpus Christi College

It is essential that truth-telling about what has gone on behind closed doors is not left to abuse survivors alone. Through telling his seminary story, Peoples stands in solidarity with all who have suffered from the misuse of power by what is coming to be recognised as a heretical sect. Peoples shows these discredited leaders, and truth-seekers everywhere, how honest storytelling can be a path to liberation.

James Boyce, author *Born Bad: Original Sin and the Making of the Western World*

A profound contribution to understanding the sexual abuse crisis that has ravaged the Catholic Church. At once sympathetic and forensic, Peoples opens up a secretive world.

Barney Zwartz, formerly religion editor of *The Age*, is a senior fellow with the Centre for Public Christianity

ACKNOWLEDGEMENTS

I thank Chrissy Swearingen, Licensing Administrator, Hal Leonard LLC, for gaining me permission to use Stephen Sondheim's beautiful song, *Send in the clowns.* *

The inspiration for this work resulted from the laughter and compassion of friends on hearing of my adventures as a student priest in a Catholic seminary fifty years ago. They encouraged me to begin.

Thanks to those who read early drafts of what was essentially a memoir: Bill Armstrong, Delia Bradshaw, Father Edmund Campion, Monsignor Tony Doherty, Bill Hannan, John Hird, Iola Mathews, John and Monica Murphy, Margaret Peoples, Pierre and Catherine Rey, Rod St. George, Ann Tuohey and Paul Willy.

Then I read Eugene Kennedy and Viktor Heckler's psychological investigation into Catholic priests in the United States (1972). I began making tentative links between my experience in the seminary and the sexual abuse scandal in the Catholic Church. When the Victorian Parliamentary Inquiry Report, *Betrayal of trust* (2012), rode into town with the Australian Royal Commission into Institutional Responses to Child Sexual Abuse (2013) on its heels, I saw a new direction. Without universal support and with considerable anxiety, I sought to fit my seminary experience into a new, more complex and potentially dangerous framework. My debts here are to Natalie Corke, Father Bruce Duncan, Father Michael Elligate, Chris Geraghty, Father Eric Hodgens, Mark Holden, John Molony,

---

* *Send In The Clowns*
from the Musical A LITTLE NIGHT MUSIC Words
and Music by Stephen Sondheim
(c) 1973 (Renewed) RILTING MUSIC, INC. All
Rights Administered by WB MUSIC CORP. All
Rights Reserved Used by Permission
Reprinted by Permission of Hal Leonard LLC

Ann Montague, Father Kevin Murphy, Michael Morwood, Peter Philp, Bishop Geoff Robinson, Jim Ross, Frank Sheehan and Richard Sipe who gave me advice and encouraged me to be courageous.

I thank two of my old class mates who gave me their time and memories: Peter Donoughue and Father Des Welladsen.

Special thanks to members of my first family, my brother Gerard and sister Peg, who told me old stories, one of which broke my heart but made me determined to see it through to the end – if for no other reason than for our wonderful mother and father, who hid in their hearts their unease at their unpredictable son who thought he should be a priest. Thanks to our two sons, Michael and his wife Isabelle, and Rob and his partner Brian, for all their love, encouragement and technical skills.

My editor, Cathy Oliver, I cannot thank enough. Her structural review turned the work into an organic whole. Thank you also to Kevin Mark for his editorial input and index. Thanks to my friend, Garry Eastman of Garratt Publishing, who once again has agreed to publish a book of mine. To his wife, Lynne Muir, for her creativity, her cooperative and consultative nature and her skills as a graphic designer, I say thank you.

The two people who lived this story from the beginning to the end are my literary agent, John Timlin, and my wife, Margaret, aka *Lover*. Without either of them there would be nothing to say. John, for reasons best known to himself, thinks I can write. His efforts on my behalf have been herculean. This book is dedicated to Margaret. It starts with her and ends with her. She immersed herself in the story to the point that she recently sent me off to the greengrocers with the following instruction: 'Could you please buy me a lettuce, and some tomatoes and celibacy.'

Kevin Peoples
July 2017

For Margaret

The journey of the story, however, is a different journey from the one we actually travel. For the story of our journey is always a fiction; it is always dealing with the past on the present's terms. We tell the story in order to free ourselves from the past so that we can move on, not in order to recover the past, which is merely nostalgia.[1]

Alex Miller

CONTENTS

Acknowledgements   v
Introduction   1

PART ONE: 1964   7

Chapter 1.   A different God   9
Chapter 2.   Seminaries and sexual abuse   29
Chapter 3.   Solo in the bush   46
Chapter 4.   Misogyny   62
Chapter 5.   Catholic Philosophy   75
Chapter 6.   Teaching and learning   88
Chapter 7.   Mister In-Between   101

PART TWO: 1965   113

Chapter 8.   The cultic priesthood takes a hit   115
Chapter 9.   Curtains   123
Chapter 10. Seminaries for young boys   131
Chapter 11. Decade of change   142
Chapter 12. Friends and ghosts   159
Chapter 13. A cultural problem   166
Chapter 14. My narcissistic Church   180
Chapter 15. Undivided heart   190
Chapter 16. I can't go on, I'll go on   199

PART THREE: 1966   **215**

Chapter 17. Ballarat's disgrace   217

Chapter 18. Sisyphus returns   232

Chapter 19. Death   250

Chapter 20. Unlike other men   253

Chapter 21. Begin again   272

Chapter 22. *Deo gratias*   281

Endnotes   283

Index   301

INTRODUCTION

A bus met the Sydney train at the Springwood Station and drove us out of town towards the foothills of the Blue Mountain Range. Singing, surprisingly and suddenly, burst forth from the old hands returning as we rattled through the heritage gates of Saint Columba's seminary. The singing, ironically, introduced a note of seriousness inside the bus filled with shouting and laughter as young men renewed friendships. The new tone, suggestive of why we had come, was reflected in the Latin verse honouring Saint Columba, as we made our winding way up through the trees to the main buildings:

Columba penna nivea
Collo resplendens roseo,
Ioca petit sidera
De claustro mundi luteo.[2]

February 1964. I was about to enter a closed world whose modus operandi dated back to the Council of Trent in the second half of the sixteenth century. Stripped of individual colour, cut off from all worldly contacts, my life would take on a paler hue in an artificial milieu where intimacy and friendships were regarded with suspicion. I was about to live in what sociologists call a total institution. I would learn that the most important members of staff in our seminary were the two Deans of Discipline. I would follow the rules and I would become obedient. I was twenty-seven years old. Academically, I would be instructed, not educated. I would learn that at least three of our clerical lecturers struggled to maintain their sanity, and that our three-year philosophy course would concentrate on a philosopher who died in the year 1274. The Vatican had chosen the writings of their favourite medieval saint, Thomas Aquinas, who would become the standard against which all our philosophical thinking, both before and after 1274, would be measured.

Our bush hideaway would be the symbol of the Church's rejection of the world. We would redirect our young lives to the life hereafter. I did not realise it, but our bus was carrying God's chosen elite, those specially chosen to continue the mission of Christ in his Church. *We* had not chosen to be priests. We were chosen. We were special. Mandatory celibacy would be the visible sign to the faithful and the world that as priests we were set apart, separate from and superior to all other human beings. In the real world I would be a living exemplar of the Church's otherworldly mission. The seminary system was the first stage in a process of learning to be in the world but not of the world.

Trapped is both a personal and public story. My personal experiences as a seminarian at Springwood are important only insofar as they project a spotlight on the major themes, which provide the necessary and larger framework. These experiences help to define the medieval culture in which we were formed as trainee priests; they shape the organisational structure of the story and drive the narrative; and they provide the lens through which that culture – clericalism, authoritarianism and triumphalism, discipline and obedience, celibacy and misogyny – is explored.

Culture is, however, much more than the aspects listed above. Culture determines who we are, the way we think and how we behave. It provides our moral framework. The following two definitions I found useful. The first is by Sister Nuala Kenny, a Canadian paediatrician:

> Cultures are embodied ways of thinking and behaving that shape a people, they are not just major activities and events but the ordinary language, behaviour and rituals of daily life. Cultures are both empowering and limiting as they tell us what to value, how to behave and to whom we should listen. Cultures are highly resistant to change because they generate meaning, security, roots and identity.[3]

A useful second perspective into culture is one by a Jesuit Professor of Theology at the Pontifical Gregorian University in Rome, whose name, for reasons unknown, is blotted out on my copy. It says that 'apart from observable practices and acceptable ways of acting, a culture entails a more concealed set of subjective attitudes often assimilated unconsciously over a long time'.[4]

What *Trapped* does dramatically is link my seminary story with the culture of the Catholic Church, displayed here in all its idiosyncratic glory. My argument is that the culture of the Church is a significant factor when evaluating firstly, the failed response by the Church hierarchy to sexual abuse within the Church and secondly, the causes of sexual abuse by Catholic priests.

The response of Catholic bishops around the world to the sexual abuse scandal was virtually universal. Their aim was to avoid scandal at any price. This meant protecting the reputation of the Church and its clergy at the expense of the rival claims of innocent children. *Trapped* shows how Church culture, especially in the notion of its cultic or sacred priesthood and its pretentious triumphalism, led diocesan bishops to ignore the secular state and the criminality of the sexual offences. Led by the Vatican, bishops around the world turned inward to manage the scandal by burying the issue within the maze of their own secretive Canon Law. Some Church authorities deliberately misused Canon Law to excuse claims of child sexual abuse. Thus, Church culture hindered quick and decisive action by Church leaders against perpetrators. This behaviour was undoubtedly a cultural response.

Insofar as individual clerical abusers are concerned, I argue that the formation of priests in Catholic seminaries left too many young men unprepared for celibate life. Many emerged from their seminary cocoon psychosexually stunted, deprived of normal sexual development. Too many of the newly-ordained entered the world underdeveloped, immature and unable to cope with their priestly vocation in a new modern world following the 1960s sexual revolution. Taught to believe that God had chosen them from amongst men, isolated in artificial all-male, misogynist communities, these young men were deprived of experiencing the cut and thrust of normal, teenage sexual development. Not only did the Church deprive young men of this development, it replaced normality with its sex and sin obsession. Too many young priests entered parish life and the real world as adult-children.

Seminary training of the secular priesthood prior to the Second Vatican Council (1962–65) was grossly inadequate. Candidates were numerous. The numbers in my first year, 1964, were a record high. Diocesan seminaries presumed the unworthy would not have heeded the call. Screening was minimal and little attention was paid to strengths and weaknesses. Emphasis was almost exclusively on intellectual and theological training to the exclusion of human, spiritual and pastoral formation. Spirituality was largely

4 Trapped in a closed world

measured by attendance at public prayer exercises, and human formation was concerned with external behaviour and appearance with little emphasis on interior growth.[5]

Two caveats to my argument linking Church culture to individual sexual abusers are necessary. The first relates to those clergy who are strictly defined as paedophiles. Such priests as are diagnosed as paedophiles in the strict medical sense are not dependent on culture – religious or social – for their sexual offences against children. Paedophilia is a medical paraphilia disorder with no known cure. However, the evidence is that most clerical sexual abuse is not due to priests who are paedophiles. The second caveat relates to priests who were sexually abused as children. These men are more likely to become sexual abusers later in life than those not sexually abused as children. Church culture may well be a contributing factor in these cases, but some individuals brought their personal problems with them into the priesthood. Arguments linking Church culture and the behaviour of individual clerics are extremely complex and demand distinctions. In the end the causes of clerical sexual abuse are multifaceted. These caveats do not diminish my argument that Church culture, especially as experienced in seminaries – the nature of seminary training is a major theme in this book – must be considered in evaluating the causes of individual clerical abuse. Those bishops who chose to protect the Church to avoid scandal over the claims of victims, and the priests who sexually abused, were all formed in the same Vatican-sponsored seminary system.

I do not wish to diminish in any way the scandalous behaviour of Church leaders and the clerical perpetrators of abuse, but merely to state the obvious. The vast majority of priests in Australia – over 90% – are good men who have never sexually abused anyone. Church culture did not lead a majority of clerics to become child sexual abusers. A small minority sexually abused children, and of those, some abused a hundred or more times. The Royal Commission into Institutional Responses to Child Sexual Abuse will release its final report in December 2017. But for a number of years, a joint project conducted by the Commission and the Catholic Church's Truth, Justice and Healing Council has been working on the number of claims of sexual abuse made by victims against Church authorities between January 1980 and February 2015.[6] Their findings are now public. Some 7.9% of diocesan priests who ministered in Australia between 1950 and 2010 had sexual abuse claims made against them. Two dioceses in Victoria – Sale and Sandhurst – had claims of sexual abuse against their clergy at rates of 15.1% and 14.7% respectively.[7] Ireland and the United States saw nothing like this. These statistics are so high that they justify the decision of Australia's first female Prime Minister, Julia Gillard, to call a Royal Commission in 2013, against the wishes of Catholic Church leaders, in particular Cardinal George Pell. Because of the Commission, the victims have been given a voice. We have heard their voices. We have been drawn into their suffering and our hearts have been broken. Justice will be theirs. The cruel facts of clerical sexual abuse, and the craven and misguided actions by bishops, led by the Vatican, must be profoundly disturbing for all those who love the Church, and especially those older lay members of my generation, whose faith in the Church and its clergy has sustained them through all the vicissitudes of their lives. One thing is now clear. The claims against alleged perpetrators within the Catholic Church are certain to be higher than those in other faith communities.

The current crisis in the Catholic Church could have been predicted. It is somewhat surprising that more clergy didn't become abusers. The sexual abuse scandal is a symptom of a much deeper malaise. *Trapped* reveals how young men, deliberately isolated from mainstream society, from families and friends and from all female contact, were formed in the mind of the Church. We were trained to live alone and apart, to act as lighthouses, shining a light in a dark and sinful world. To understand what all of this did to some young men is to begin to understand the sexual abuse scandal.

The Catholic Church now faces an existential threat. Fundamental change is required as the Church faces its greatest crisis since the Reformation of the sixteenth century. In protecting their own first, the clerical class demonstrated to the world – especially to its lay members – that the Church belonged to them. A quick makeover won't do. If the Church fails to act decisively to introduce reforms that humble the Church and capture the humility that was won at the Second Vatican Council (1962–65) – and lost during the papacies of Saint John Paul II and Benedict XVI – then it will become increasingly irrelevant.[8] If those with the opportunity for reform created by the sexual abuse scandal and the presence of a good man as pope fail to grasp the spirit of Christ, who was not a priest, who waged war on the priests of his time, it is difficult to imagine how the institution can possibly recruit new vocations to the priesthood and hold together its already shrinking, practising lay-base. Vocations to the priesthood are in sharp decline around the world. Attendances at weekly Mass in Australia have declined dramatically since the 1950s.[9] In the West especially, the Church will have great difficulty attracting new adherents, especially the young.

Trapped looks at the global phenomenon of sexual abuse in the Catholic Church and analyses research not only from Australia, but in particular from the United States and Ireland. Its focus is limited to secular priests who offended, i.e. not those priests trained within religious orders or religious brothers, e.g. Christian Brothers, whose rates of sexual child abuse were significantly higher than those of priests.

Trapped is deliberately episodic to accommodate frequent shifts in time and place. This style allows for the easy separation of reflection and actual events, of what I thought at the time and what I think now; and importantly, it allows for the dramatic recreation of some of those actual events in the seminary.

I arrived at my medieval seminary at one minute to midnight on a February night in 1964. The old Catholic ways were about to collapse, in particular those related to vocations to the priesthood. I left in 1966. Within a decade, declining numbers would force the authorities to close down Springwood. My time coincided with the reform movement of the Second Vatican Council and the social liberation movements of the 1960s. I missed much, but managed to come down from the mountains in time to witness conscripts for Vietnam burn their draft cards, and one conscript, chased by a plain-clothed policeman, smash his way through a glass door in the café at the University of Melbourne. I had returned to a new world.

PART ONE
1964

I think we should change – how can I say this? Get rid of seminaries.[10]

Dr Michael Whelan,
Catholic Priest of the Society of Mary

Witness at Royal Commission into Institutional Responses
to Child Sexual Abuse

Chapter 1

A different God[11]

One of the most difficult things I must do is dress up in soutane and white clerical collar. Some of the young men around me are enthralled and parade in their priestly attire. I walk down the stairs in my long dress carefully, fearful of tripping, a trapeze artist on wire. In trepidation, I go to join the circus:

> ... But where are the clowns? Send in the clowns
> Don't bother they're here.[12]

I did not want to be a priest, but the weight of not testing a possible vocation lay heavily on me. At the end of 1961, I found myself in a dark corner where the priesthood seemed the only option. I took this as a sign of God's will. My life to that point had resulted in dead ends. I raised the possibility of a vocation to the priesthood with my friend and Young Christian Worker (YCW) chaplain, the then Father John Molony of Ballarat. I cast the option in considerable doubt and Molony said he would raise it with my bishop and his, James P. O'Collins. Bishop O'Collins, who would normally be found in his aviary talking to his feathered friends, told Molony he wasn't interested in a man of twenty-five who didn't know his own mind. Molony, suffering his own purgatory at the time, suggested I approach the Bishop of Wagga Wagga, Francis Henschke, whom I knew and admired. And so it was decided. I would train to be a priest for the Wagga diocese. Molony convinced me that the further I moved away from my old mates and failed adventures, the better. With heavy heart I agreed, but not before asking a young woman to marry me. She sensibly refused, but the action dramatised my ambivalent commitment to the priesthood.

10 Trapped in a closed world

The decision to study for the priesthood was well received at home. The exception was my Auntie Poll, the daughter of Irish immigrants, who at some time in her life had cared for elderly priests holidaying at Koroit in western Victoria. 'Don't do it darlin', don't do it,' she said, while helping my mother sew name tags on my clothing. 'You don't know what it's like,' she said, gripping my arm. 'It's a terrible thing to be old and on your own.' She was speaking from personal experience. My mother interrupted: 'Let him be, if that's what he wants.' Polly turned to my mother. 'You don't know, Ina,' she said sharply, 'you haven't seen them dribblin' down the front and no-one to tell them and keep them clean.' I wanted to agree with her but it was too late for that.

No-one was surprised that I had chosen the priesthood. Some of the nuns at the local Catholic primary school had told my mother, 'That boy will be a priest one day.' They smiled, and she believed them. I was, in many ways, an ideal candidate. I grew up in the old clerical Church where priests did no wrong and their authority was never questioned. Each night our family said the rosary, and if visitors interrupted they knelt and joined in. My father prayed on his knees each morning while making his toast before leaving for work at the milk factory.

We never left the house in the morning without saying our morning prayers. My mother whispered prayers in my ear to Saint Joseph, my patron saint, when I was sick. Mum had a saint for every occasion – Saint Anthony could find anything lost and Saint Jude ensured we passed our school examinations. Saint Gerard Majella made certain that pregnancies resulted in healthy babies. Our Lady of Fatima would save us from communism and convert Russia. The lone wall-hanging in my bedroom went up over my bed in 1944. It marked my First Holy Communion. In the main bedroom at the front of the house, where my younger sister slept, two women resembling Loretta Young and Grace Kelly covered for Saint Thérèse of Lisieux (more commonly known as the *Little Flower*) and Our Lady of Perpetual Succour holding a beautiful child in her arms. In the lounge room was a small plastic statue of The Infant Child of Prague protecting Mum's special requests in writing. We all belonged to sodalities – Holy Name, Sacred Heart, Children of Mary – which guaranteed monthly confession and communion. Pinned to my singlet, wrapped in a small white bag made by my mother, were miraculous medals.

We believed everything that the Church through her priests told us. We read virtually nothing. It was sufficient to belong to the One True Church with sin the only threat to everlasting happiness in the next life. I did the Nine First Fridays, ensuring I would not die without the aid of the sacrament of Extreme Unction, and the Five First Saturdays in honour of our Blessed Mother to save Australia from communism. I lived in a Catholic ghetto populated by nuns and priests, angels and archangels. Throughout the day I uttered aspirations and prayed to be holy. I was not exceptional. It is arguable that never before, and never since, did the Catholic Church in Australia have such a devoted and loyal group of young people as those growing up in the 1950s. In his marvellous autobiographical journal, *End of a journey*, Philip Toynbee comments on the improved quality of the Christian faith. He argues, somewhat askance, that, 'Many thoughtful and good-hearted Christians still believed in eternal hellfire at least until the turn of this century. And we know better? Yes, we know better.'[13] Despite Toynbee's understanding about the existence or otherwise of hell, its flames were still burning brightly at Terang in the middle of the twentieth century. It would be easy to scoff at all this pious plasticity I embraced. I don't. It may have been fairy floss, but in my family the fairy floss was grounded in love and I regret none of it.

I suppose I was an exemplary candidate for the priesthood. In my teenage days I joined the YCW and became a local leader. Eventually I ran my own team. We met in the front lounge room, which was rarely used, lit a candle, read the Gospel and talked about our lives. Then one day, a bemused Auntie Poll asked me, 'What are ye doin', darlin'?' She was shocked when I told her. 'But what is this YCW that leads growin' boys to the front room of a home and lightin' candles and readin' the Bible?'

Catholics, generally, didn't read the Bible. Our priests read it for us. At Sunday Mass they read the Epistle and Gospel in Latin with their backs to us. In their sermons, they explained to us what they had read and what we were meant to believe. The priest was the voice of God. Long before I reached the seminary I had a very clear idea of the power and deference due to the clergy by the Catholic laity.

When I told Polly that we were 'other Christs', she raised her eyes to heaven and muttered, 'Jesus, Mary and Joseph', and advised me seriously to be 'leavin'' all that stuff to the priests'.

Then, in 1959, I became the organiser of the National Catholic Rural Movement, a formal movement of Catholic Action. But informally, the Rural Movement was merely a political front for the dubious practices of B. A. Santamaria, a Melbourne lawyer, whose views on Catholic Action belonged more in the papal court of Pope Boniface in the thirteenth century than in the twentieth. When I realised this I left and joined a new adult form of Catholic Action in Ballarat, but Santamaria and his bishop, James P. O'Collins, closed us down. What was I to do? The priesthood beckoned.

My formation in the lay apostolate was to prove at odds with the formation required in the seminary. My lay spirituality was centred on real people in a real world. I was trained to see the divine in the human. My views were egalitarian and inclusive, derived from my class and my religion. My spirituality took as its base the words in Matthew's Gospel:

> For I was hungry and you gave me something to eat, I was thirsty and you gave me something to drink, I was a stranger and you invited me in, I needed clothes and you clothed me, I was sick and you looked after me, I was in prison and you came to visit me.[14]

I suspect my interest in the words Matthew gave to Jesus was less about any actions I might perform, but rather about the extraordinary identification of Jesus with people in need. In 1964, my world and its people were permeated with the spirit of Christ. The ideas informing seminary life, I would discover, were the very antithesis of my egalitarian and inclusive ideas of the Church in the world. I was about to learn of my participation in a divine vocation, of belonging to an elite group of men specially chosen by God. I was called to be a cleric, celibate and otherworldly. My relationships with others would shrivel to one essential relationship with a distant and remote figure called God. I was to stand alone, to be self-reliant and to seek my reward in an afterlife. The symbol of my rejection of the world would be my celibacy. This would distinguish me from my more worldly brothers and sisters.

Entering the seminary proved as difficult as leaving it. I grew up in a small country town with a population of approximately 2,500. A Year 10 Certificate from the local High School, with majors in typewriting and shorthand, provided me with an office job in one of the two big departmental stores, but was well short of the necessary entry qualifications for the seminary. Bishop Francis Henschke sent all his late (i.e. older men) vocations to Chevalier, the Sacred Heart Fathers' college in Bowral, New South Wales. In my two years there I completed the New South Wales Leaving Certificate with a matriculation pass to University and a First Class Honour in History.

I had provided the necessary documentation to my bishop, namely copies of my baptismal and confirmation certificates, a letter of recommendation from my parish priest and a health certificate. Some have commented that 'testicles were essential'. I doubt that, although it may well be the case.[15] Is it possible that Church authorities, so repressed and punitive in sexual matters, wished to ensure their celibate clergy were making a genuine sacrifice? There was no psychological test, which, following the sexual abuse scandal, is now regarded as essential.

So in February 1964, carrying two old bulging suitcases, held together by long brown straps around the middle, I catch the train at Central Station in Sydney to Springwood, along with a bevy of exuberant young men, whose temperament and general cheerfulness are at radical odds to mine.

I am filled with doubts. Why am I here? I have only myself to blame. I am many years their senior. They fail to identify me as one of their own and when we board the train I sit alone in a carriage up the front. It is only when we leave the train at Springwood and I board the bus to Saint Columba's seminary with them that I show my hand.

I am given a room on the first floor with a window facing out onto the Blue Mountains National Park. Any chance of escape in that direction looks as daunting as it surely did for that earthly trinity of Blaxland, Wentworth and Lawson.

14 Trapped in a closed world

Memory is an issue here. It's not so much the arriving that I remember, but the leaving. I forget the date, but I left the seminary on a Thursday with my friend, Father Bede Heather, a scripture scholar and lecturer at Saint Columba's College Seminary. Bede dropped me off in Sydney and my last words to him were, 'I love you, Bede.' I meant it, but that I told him so says something of my excited state of mind. The month was August, the year 1966. Some events imprint indelibly on the mind. My Spiritual Director, Father Michael Kelly, whom I cannot remember, suggested that I leave during the long retreat. I understood perfectly. I had woken on many a day to learn that one of our number had quietly disappeared, never to be mentioned again. Anyone leaving caused a slight crack in the concrete certainties of seminary life, especially when the one leaving was the deputy head prefect, aged twenty-nine. Best keep it to ourselves, Father Kelly suggested, and go quietly during the long silence. That was never going to happen. My going was not a death – rather a rebirth. I had not failed. I had done what I had to do and it was over. Despite a natural anxiety, I went gently, with no anger, no regrets, but rather a lightness with a sense of hope and expectation. I would not sneak off. I would say goodbye to my friends, and I would drive out into the good world through the sandstone heritage gates more confident than I had been for years.

My room in August 1966 was at the end of a long corridor, at the top of the stairs on the third floor. Anyone walking up the stairs might have seen a flicker of light shining in my room in my last few weeks in the seminary. With lights out, and under the blankets, I read Pasternak's *Doctor Zhivago* – by torchlight.

I recall little about the book apart from two memories. One was my immediate empathy with the poems at the back, which I read and reread under the blankets, and the second is of a good man, Father Len Wholohan. Len was the bursar and one of the two deans at Springwood. Coming up the stairs to his room, Len saw a light reflected on a wall in my Plato's cave, but chose not to embarrass me by knocking on the door. The next day he told me he thought he saw a light flickering on my wall after lights out, but he could have been mistaken. Later, when we said our goodbyes, he wished me well and advised me to continue with my education and to marry a good Catholic girl.

From the top of the stairs I look down and see Monsignor Thomas McNiven Veech. He has come to say goodbye. He waits uncomfortably, shy and awkward, head leaning to the side. I see him now in colours: white hair, red face, black cape and soutane. Veechy is the rector, and in his right hand he carries a white handkerchief like Pavarotti – like Luciano he is an entertainer. Because of him the first book I will read in Sydney is Flaubert's *Madame Bovary*.

Huffing and puffing from his stage in front of our class, Veechy looks through us without seeing. We wait. He makes to begin, but then, as if he has lost his way, he stops suddenly. He turns his head to the left and there is Flaubert, encouraging him: 'Ah, Flaubert.' He then turns to his right and there is Balzac, waiting to be drawn in: 'Ah, Balzac.' He smiles to himself rejoicing in his company and then remembering where he is, he shakes himself and acknowledges us for the first time: 'Ah, gentlemen, this is a book you should read when you are much older.' I am entranced. A man of many colours is Veechy, but is he sane? There is some doubt.

Veechy is gracious and dignified. He has come to wish me well but he also has a purpose. He hands me a short letter advising 'To whom it may concern' that I'm leaving of my own volition. He shakes my hand and wishes me well, urging me to keep the faith. I have kept his letter.

I am aware now of Veechy's capacity to hurt others. Looking back, I suspect I was one of his favourites, but I may be wrong. I was extremely naïve and innocent in my relations with others, always prepared to think the best of them. Because of my religious beliefs, my small-town rural upbringing, my formation in the YCW, and my gentle and loving parents who blessed me with their DNA, my inclination was to believe in the goodness of everyone. Inside my Catholic bubble, I had little to no understanding or experience of the existence of evil in the world. I belonged to a holy people, and Monsignor Veech and I were equal partners in that one body.

A strange man Veechy. Some who knew him better than I would

use much stronger language. Extraordinarily shy, he found talking to his fellow human beings a trial. As his words and meaning faltered, he smiled, blowing out his cheeks and huffing, puffing and guffawing at the absurdity of attempted communion with another.

Veechy and I were both new arrivals at Saint Columba's, although he arrived first. He succeeded a rawer man, Monsignor Charles Dunne, and became rector of Springwood during 1963. Some thought his temperament unsuitable, but the Cardinal Archbishop of Sydney, Norman Gilroy, promoted Veechy from his seminary duties at Manly, a theological college on the water's edge where his office looked out onto one of the most beautiful scenes in Australia. In Dickensian style, Chris Geraghty, judge, author, former priest and seminarian at Springwood and Manly and no friend of Veech, has described his office:

> Being unusually keen and annoying, I would occasionally try to contact him in his lair where he hid under shaded lights and amid phantoms of the past. He had transformed his study which overlooked the vast Pacific ocean in a region blessed with light, with sun and fresh air, into a gloomy, smoke-filled cave. The walls were lined with old books, stained and tattered. The surface of the desk was a mass of old notes and antique papers. An ashtray full of corked tipped butts. A lamp low over the desk spread a yellow light on a soiled blotting pad. The lamp never rested. Even by day, when the world was alive and sparking, the venetian blinds were closed. His room was like a derelict's cave which had been taken over by a solitary grey owl. It was impossible to get past the half-opened door.[16]

It seems we all live in caves! In my first year at Springwood I watch Veechy in his ambulations, white handkerchief in hand, a symbol perhaps of his surrender to a world that makes little sense. He is a solitary man, a man who looks lost, but there is a part of him that vibrates with life, imagination and energy. He chooses to live inside his head, a head filled with the most marvellous characters from plays, poems, history and literature, and every Saturday morning he introduces them to us, his audience, while he struts and converses with them for our enjoyment. Veechy has been a strikingly handsome man in his youth; he now resembles a courtly gentleman, a Francophile, belonging more in the court of the Sun King at the Palace of Versailles in the second half of the seventeenth century, than with students, ants and flies in the Australian bush.

There may be a medical problem. When saying Mass for the community, Veechy at times convulses with involuntary tremors. Is he having some sort of fit or is he in a trance? His words cease and he begins to rock backwards and forwards. He appears possessed.

When I first saw him struggling to control his rebellious body I thought he was having an epileptic fit. The atmosphere within the student body was electric. My mother had such fits and our first reaction was to rush to her side and lay her gently down on the nearest couch or bed. Hence my impulse was to rush onto the altar and help him to a chair. When he began to wobble, the student body held its communal breath waiting for him to fall. But no-one ever moved to help and eventually he would regain control and continue on with the Mass.

Perhaps he is a mystic. Some students think he has visions. Perhaps, like Saint Teresa of Avila, he will float up and land on top of the reredos, a decorative screen at the back of the main altar. Perhaps he sees devils. He was, at some time, the official exorcist for the archdiocese. God knows what he is. All I know is that we student philosophers live ironically together here in our shared isolation, training to be lighthouses, who one day will shine and give succour to a dark and sinful world.

First year philosophy begins in a classroom on the ground floor of the original two-storey sandstone building built in the first decade of the twentieth century. There are sixty of us, the majority straight out of school. Dressed as clerics we are – presenting in our white collars and black soutanes. We sit in desks reminiscent of those at Saint Thomas's Primary School, Terang, in the 1940s. All we lack are nuns, inkwells, and blotting paper and nib pens.

The door into our classroom opens onto cloisters which surround a U-shaped courtyard. In the middle of the courtyard is a concrete path which leads to the relatively new cream-bricked chapel filling up the open end of the U.

18 Trapped in a closed world

My memory is of a warm February day and Father John Walsh. Walshy had been a student at Saint Columba's before becoming a teacher and eventually will be its last Director. Walshy, I will learn, is a finicky and pedantic person. He has a habit of turning up, unwanted, when least expected. Apart from this he is otherwise sane. Some of the students will label him, unkindly, *Mother* Walsh. I was never close to him and I sensed a class difference. He is one of the Deans of Discipline and the choir master – a valuable member of staff.

Walshy's subject is the History of Philosophy. In 1964, I resemble the *Fawlty Towers* character, Manuel, the one from Barcelona – 'I know nothing'. My crash course in Latin has left me inadequately prepared. I have some learning to do, but in these first few months I am incapable of thinking.

Walshy is a man of substance – a serious lecturer, intelligent, interesting and well prepared. He begins with questions and definitions. What is philosophy? What is science? What is the difference? Philosophy, he tells us, is the Queen of all the sciences. Philosophy deals with the fundamental nature of things, such as knowledge, truth, reality and existence. It concerns itself with the ultimate questions, with fundamental principles and it generally advances with the question *why*. Walshy tells us that philosophers are people with ideas about serious matters; they choose their words carefully; they use logic and like to make distinctions.

Science is important but, in comparison with philosophy, limited. I would hear this argument many times in the next few years. Modern empirical science eschews not only God but biblical revelation as a source of knowledge. Science depends on our senses, which in themselves are questionable; it accumulates data that can be measured and tested. The scientific method compares hypotheses, namely intelligent conclusions arising from the data, with experiments and observation. Science relies on evidence and demonstrated arguments to deduce conclusion. The thing about science is that it builds on previous knowledge and any conclusion reached is relative and open to further development or modification. This form of logic Walshy names induction, which is an important notion in philosophy. He is keen to emphasise that philosophy, first, moves beyond the physical world taken in by our senses, and second, seeks the truth of things. With science, truth will always be relative. I listen and understand that philosophy and science are two different branches of knowledge, and that philosophy is more important.

With my limited educational background, I will struggle. I am bereft of science and mathematics, but I cope with these definitions which I note carefully. Problems, however, soon begin when Walshy introduces us to the first philosophers – the Presocratic Greeks who lived six hundred or so years before Christ. Thales thought the physical world of nature was made of water; Anaximander thought that all things came from a single unnamed primal substance; Anaximenes thought all things came from air; Pythagoras thought all things were numbers; Heraclitus thought fire was the primordial element from which all things rose.

At this point, I realise philosophy is going to be a problem. Clearly I am missing something. Either these ancient Greeks were mad or I am mad. Looking out the window into the courtyard I see cloisters, small trees, green grass and a sandstone building. Not a fire or a number in sight.

In the distance I hear the mad male cicadas screaming for a mate. Jesus, Mary and Joseph! A person could become just like them in this place.

There was an ingrained bias against science in our seminary. Our clerical lecturers were obliged to teach us a philosophy that was conducive to the beliefs and dogma of the Catholic Church, and in particular that could, through the use of reason, prove the existence of God. That philosophy, as we quickly discovered, was Thomism or the philosophy of Saint Thomas Aquinas, who died in 1274. I learnt that our philosophical truths were discovered in the thirteenth century, when Thomas brilliantly integrated the reason of Aristotle with the faith of Roman Catholicism. The scientific method, linked to the natural world of material things, was not concerned with faith and could never prove the existence of God. Therefore, not surprisingly, Walshy was keen to point out the comparative weaknesses of science.

I play sport. In my first year I severely scrape my right leg on a hard, dry surface playing rugby. The abrasions become infected and I spend three or four marvellous days in the infirmary, sleeping in, reading F. C. Copleston's *Aquinas,* ignoring the bells and the daily rhythms and rituals of seminary life and being waited on by a young man in my class named Vince whose only qualification in caring for the sick and injured is his kindness, which in this case is sufficient. Each day Veechy climbs up the stairs and comes huffing and puffing over to my bed to see how I am. Perhaps he calls in on every student who enters the infirmary. I don't know. I never feel embarrassed in his company and I suspect he is grateful for that. I didn't know at the time he loved rugby, which may have explained his interest.

The raw physicality of the Australian bush that surrounds us is at odds with our world of magic and mystery that the men at the Council of Trent concocted for us in the middle of the sixteenth century. We are being protected from the same world that we are called to save. God help us. In our febrile atmosphere the danger of neuroticism is real for even the sanest. In my quiet moments in the bush I listen to the screams of cicadas and study the feverish activity of ants. Anything is possible in this mountain retreat in this year of grace, 1964.

I'm discovering that the God in my seminary is not lovable. The God in my seminary is ineffable, cold, distant, masculine, aloof and silent. This is the God of the North African, Saint Augustine. His abode is above the clouds. His preferred mode of interaction is structured obedience. But my God is very different. My God stops for a drink at a well and engages a woman, a stranger, in serious discussion. He seeks out fallen women and tax collectors and enjoys talking and eating with friends around a table. My God welcomes a weeping woman to wash his feet with her tears and dry them with her hair. In my new bush home, we are being purified, cleansed from the world and all worldly imperfections. We are to be polished and honed like white stone. But will our hearts be hardened?

This seminary God has never read the Jewish theologian and philosopher, Martin Buber. We find God as best we can, in the rituals of our days. My God is more feminine, warm, loving and present. Some of those who stand here as his representatives test my faith. We are warned off touching. The only times we students touch is on entering the chapel (apart from hurling ourselves at each other on the rugby field). We walk to the chapel in a line of pairs. The student closest to the Holy Water font offers his wet fingers to the one on his outside. We touch and smile a thanks. Except Bob Donnelly, who thinks Holy Water is a form of medieval magic. There is an unspoken fear of homosexuality. Entrance to another student's room is strictly forbidden. Around the grounds we must walk in at least threes. Particular friendships are anathema. There is an attractive boy in Pre-philosophy. He looks like a girl. We all know it. He is sent home before the year is out. Along with another student, who explains to the authorities they had met after lights out because they needed to talk.

What would Martin Buber make of all this? Buber was interested in real-life experiences, in relationships, in dialogue. But it's more than dialogue as we understand that word today; much more than some communication technique. Buber asked the big question, the philosophical question, 'What is Man?', raised in modern times by the German philosopher, Immanuel Kant. The word 'man' here does not refer to men, to the male gender, but to all people.

The human condition for Buber was an essentially interhuman one. Man's very essence is explained by his encounter with another. But not any encounter. Man is fully human when he reaches his full potential. This potential materializes in a special relationship which Buber calls the *I-Thou* relationship. Man is not some hermit, not some solitary being. To focus on the self is to risk narcissism, and narcissism has the power to destroy one. Man will never find himself by looking at himself in a mirror or exploring the depths of his own heart. When man reaches out with his whole self to another human and the other responds in the same way, then the meaning of life is achieved.

In 1964, I have not heard of Buber. Buber would have regarded our lives at Springwood as stultifying and ultimately destructive, with the emphasis on the individual self. We can never grow and be fully human in our bush home. Neither can we be saved by seeking a direct relationship with some distant God. God manifests himself in our reaching out to others, in the context of those 'truly communicative moments between two subjects who recognise in the other the same subjectivity as in themselves'. God is, therefore, met in the real world, in the concrete realities of two people reaching out to each other in their irreducible wholeness. We might call this love. But in this seminary love is a foreign word and reaching out to others is viewed with suspicion. Loving God should not be at the expense of the love we have for each other.[17]

Some of the best and brightest in our senior class are infantile and immature. How will they cope with their obligatory celibacy? Most are young and came here direct from school – in some cases boarding school. They have spent their adolescence in all-male enclaves. They are encouraged to shun women, the gender that tantalises and tempts. Every natural instinct in their young bodies rebels at that requirement. They are called to be heroic and some will be. But some won't. At least three are obviously gay.

I had been in the seminary for about a month when one of the gay students in the senior class went out of his way to engage with me. I shall call him *W*. He was five years my junior and recognised as the senior intellectual in the college, confident and assured.

We talk and he asks the questions. He brings me out of myself. We are outside the recreation hall (the *rec*) and the mail has just been delivered. I find him prim and sharp but essentially kind. I am somewhat intimidated, out of my social class. 'What a self-effacing man you are', he says, in his posh voice as he walks away. I remember him now and I thank him for his welcome and kindness. His life did not work out. Criminal charges were laid by a Catholic schoolteacher aged twenty-nine. Tried in 2005 under anti-homosexual laws in New South Wales that had been repealed in 1984, *W* admitted guilt, apologised, and was found guilty. The judge sentenced him to the length of time that it took for all to stand, and for the judge to leave the court room. The events in court brought an end to his priesthood. The case became hopelessly mired years later when the teacher sought from the Church compensation which had initially been rejected. In the flood of material that emerged, it became clear that *W* had assaulted others including a young altar boy. One newspaper labelled *W* 'a serial sex offender'. I knew *W* in his early twenties. When he was tried in court he was over sixty.[18]

I am saddened now when I read about *W*. Despite his behaviour, of which I remain uncertain, I am drawn to him in compassion. Yet, we were not close. *W* and I came from different social classes and his being two years ahead of me meant he left for Manly after my first year at Springwood. His one act of kindness to me was fifty years ago and yet I still remember him. I have forgotten much but I hold on to this vivid image of *W* walking away and turning back with a smile: 'What a self-effacing man you are.'

W was educated in a warped seminary system. He gave his young life to an institution that on the one hand nurtured him as a sacred person, and on the other informed him he suffered from an 'intrinsic disorder'. In matters of sexual morality the Church's teachings cannot be trusted. The Gospels are silent on the question of homosexuality. Fleeting references in the Hebrew Bible and the Epistles that some read as condemning homosexuality have been debunked by scripture scholars. Lost somewhere between the Book of Leviticus written in the sixth century BCE and Saint Paul in the first century CE, the Vatican has chosen to ignore modern science. People are born gay:

> It would appear that sexual orientation is biological in nature, determined by a complex interplay of genetic factors and the early uterine environment. Sexual orientation is therefore not a choice, though sexual behaviour is.[19]

The Church's homophobia has continued to obfuscate the facts about child sexual abuse:

> The proclamations by the Catholic Church in the 1990s, which essentially linked child sexual abuse to the issue of homosexuality, are fundamentally flawed and have no basis in empirical or respectable research, scientific knowledge, common social mores or a theology of justice.[20]

Celibacy is difficult enough without the added baggage of being told you are carrying an 'intrinsic disorder'. Mandatory celibacy is cruel and should not be a mark of the priesthood. Despite all the goodwill, the clerical adherents of celibacy today are no longer a majority in some parts of the Catholic world.

Richard Sipe is a former American Benedictine monk who, after eighteen years, left his priestly vocation and practised as a psychiatrist. He is widely respected and has been researching celibacy, sexual abuse and related Church issues for thirty years. Much of his work has been in dealing with the mental health problems of priests and in particular with clerics who abused children. Sipe was present at an audience with Pope John Paul II in 1993. The pope said that neither he, nor any other pope, had the authority to change the requirement for a vow of celibacy in order to be ordained to the priesthood. The current pope, Francis, does not agree, although he too sits on his hands. In May 2014, Francis said that celibacy 'is not dogma. It is a rule of life that I appreciate very much and I think it is a gift for the Church but since it is not dogma, the door is always open.'[21]

Sipe's research found that, at any one time, no more than 50% cent of Catholic clergy in America were practising celibacy. When his findings were presented to the Cardinal Prefect of the Congregation of the Clergy in Rome, His Eminence replied, 'I have no reason to doubt the accuracy of those figures.'[22]

The most recent evidence makes clear that many of the priests ordained in the United States and Ireland, who did their seminary training in the 1960s, found the demands of celibacy virtually impossible to sustain. Many had high levels of psychosexual vulnerability. Clinical data confirms that 80% of those men who received psychological treatment had been sexually active after ordination – primarily with adults.[23] This high level of celibate non-compliance may well have impacted on bishops who failed to act decisively against priests in their dioceses who abused children. Sipe certainly thinks so. Bishops, and clerics above them in the hierarchy, were loath to act directly against their priests, in particular to report them to civil authorities, because their own sexual failures with adults might emerge. Sipe may well be right. He estimates that 60% of bishops around the world entered into a conspiracy of silence to hide the crimes of their clergy who had abused children. I am reluctant to accept this argument without further evidence. It may well be one of the motivating causes in the conspiracy of silence along with the obvious arguments that bishops acted as they did, first to protect the reputation of the Church, second to work within their own legal system, and third to follow instructions from the Vatican.[24]

Celibacy, on its own, is not a cause of clerical sexual abuse. It has to be wrapped within the broader culture of the Church – one element, as Sipe argues, of the clerical/sexual package. Sipe's professional experience led him to conclude that celibacy was one important element in explaining the causes of sexual abuse. Celibacy, he said:

> ... forms a synergism within a homosocial culture that fosters and rewards psychosexual immaturity or regression. Emotional and social dependence, overvalued conformity, a sense of entitlement, assurance of superiority, the arrogance of absolute certitude, and immunity from criticism or personal responsibility for mistakes are constitutive elements of the Catholic clerical culture.[25]

Dr Marie Keenan, a Dublin sociologist and psychotherapist, is more cautious but in general agrees with Sipe. She has worked with clerical sexual offenders in Ireland. Keenan provided a paper to the Australian Royal Commission, a précis of which was read in the opening address by the Senior Counsel Assisting, Gail Furness. Keenan links celibacy within the broader culture of the Church as a possible cause of clerical sexual abuse of minors. Her research suggests that:

> ... while celibacy is not a problem that gives rise to sexual abuse of minors by the Catholic clergy, a Catholic sexual ethic and theology of priesthood, which problematises the body and erotic sexual desire and emphasises chastity and purity over a relational ethic as the model for living, may be.

According to Keenan, attempts by the clergy to control sexual desire and sexual activity 'led to sex-obsessed lives of terror'.[26]

To write this story I read Donald B. Cozzens' book, *The changing face of the priesthood*. Cozzens spent much of his priesthood in American seminaries, many as president-rector. Like me he belongs in the old dispensation, the old Church that ended in the 1960s with the Second Vatican Council. Cozzens was Professor of Pastoral Theology at Saint Mary's Seminary and Graduate School of Theology in Cleveland when he wrote his acclaimed book; he understands the destructive loneliness of the old dispensation.[27]

I gave this story, in manuscript form, to a retired priest friend of my vintage. He made a start but couldn't bear to read it. Too depressing, too many sad memories. Cozzens' thesis is that we all need loving relationships, including priests – close intimates with whom we share our deepest concerns. There will always be times in our lives when we seek out our best friends, especially when we are low and need support. The strongest and bravest need affirmation from other people. Heinz Kohut was a Jewish psychoanalyst who fled Nazi Germany, and who wrote, amongst other books, *The analysis of the self*. Kohut argued that our 'self does not come into being in isolation but is embedded in relationships with others'.[28] Cozzens understands Kohut and Buber. But Cozzens holds on to celibacy. Intimacy in our seminary was regarded as a danger, a threat to the smooth running of the place. We were slowly drained of whatever empathy we brought with us.

Old priests generally tell the truth, especially when it's the habit of a lifetime, as it is with a somewhat eccentric force named Father Bob Maguire. Louise Milligan, in writing her book about Cardinal George Pell, interviewed Bob Maguire, an 82-year-old priest, no friend of the upper echelons of the Church and a magnet for all those needing help and support in inner-city Melbourne. Maguire, a popular personality in Victoria, highlighted the psychological problems faced by many priests in the Church because of their seminary training and mandatory celibacy. According to Maguire, mandatory celibacy does real psychological harm. He told Milligan:

> We priests, we're psychosocially damaged. We're crystallised in adolescence. Of course we are. How could we be any other? We haven't had mature adult relationships. We're stuck in many ways at the age when we entered the seminary. So we have problems. Don't let anyone tell you we don't. Not having meaningful relationships does something to you. It stunts your psychological growth, being celibate, being alone. I'll admit it.[29]

Our seminary system is based on a dreadful misconception of what it means to be human. It thinks we are more than we are. It lacks the warmth of human blood. We are not solitary beings. We are not lighthouses. God cannot be found in artificial structures, but in open and direct dialogue with him through the events of an ordinary life, not in this constructed artifice on the fringe of civilisation. Rules and obedience lead to passivity, dependence and immaturity. Forms and rituals have replaced faith. At the end of this year, 1964, I will be aged twenty-eight, yet I am expected to tolerate a system geared for school boys. Deliberate attempts to turn us in on ourselves, to organise our lives in isolation from each other and the world will lead to neuroticism:

> God is not met by turning away from the world or by making God into an object of contemplation, a 'being' whose existence can be proved and whose attributes can be demonstrated. God is met only as Thou. As I know the person of the other only in dialogue with him, I know God only in dialogue. But this is the dialogue that goes on moment by moment in each new situation, the dialogue that makes my ethical 'ought' a matter of real response with no preparation other than my readiness to respond with my whole being to the unforeseen and the unique.[30]

In the seminary our *ethical oughts* are determined for us. We are called to obey. We are trained for docility.

I was hopelessly wrong about the Presocratics. When Walshy had first explained their philosophical views I thought either they were mad or I was mad. They were not mad. But I was wrong about most things in 1964. It was not the quality of their answers, but the quality of their questions that made the Presocratics important. These extraordinary men looked at their world bursting and teeming with life and asked the question: 'What is its unifying principle?' They assumed there was one. They had asked a philosophical question and ignoring their gods and all forms of superstition they sought answers through thinking. They were giants.

Heraclitus was not merely saying that the world was made of fire. His main point was that the world was constantly changing and all things were held in balance by their opposites. These opposites shared a common structural feature which Heraclitus called *logos* or reason. *Logos* is a very important word in the Christian tradition. This *logos* maintained some sort of balance and regulated the continuity of change. Heraclitus did identify fire as the original and most desirable element, but he thought of it as the physical manifestation of *logos*.

And another Presocratic philosopher, Parmenides, with equal skill, argued the very opposite. Parmenides thought the world was made of one indivisible substance; this meant the world must be static and therefore change was impossible. Ideas such as these have permeated Western philosophy in one form or other.

Bertrand Russell, British philosopher and mathematician, writing about another Presocratic, Pythagoras, argued that he was, 'one of the most interesting and puzzling men in history', and that no other man had been as influential as Pythagoras was in the sphere of thought.[31] Abstract thought was not my forte. But I was learning.

Why was I so dismissive of the Presocratics? In part it was the shock of the new. I had no experience in such questions or thinking in such abstract ways. In part it was the lecturing mode, which failed to involve us in the issues. But the real reason was personal and went deeper. I was not thinking clearly for much of 1964. In those first few months I was distracted and desperately sad. I could see no way out of my predicament, a predicament that I had brought on myself. I was dismayed at my isolation, at the monastic routine, at the choice I had made.

But like the mythical Greek character, Sisyphus, I became resigned to my fate and in my resignation I found meaning. I suspect I knew from the start that one day I would leave but in the meantime I must persist. In my impoverished state of mind I was unable to throw myself into study. I could barely lift myself to converse with other students. I distinctly remember apologising to one for my moroseness. Each day, for much of that year, I crossed off the days on the seminary calendar pinned on the door inside my wardrobe. I was doing time.

Chapter 2

Seminaries and sexual abuse

Buried in a small black box somewhere in my mind is what happened in the seminary. It was never to be opened. I now find it painful to recall many of these events that happened fifty years ago, and wonder why I bother. Twice, I have already stopped writing this story. I received, however, a new burst of energy when I read about Eugene Kennedy. He had died in Michigan and the by-line of his obituary stated: *Ex-priest foresaw the Catholic sex scandals*. Kennedy left the priesthood in 1977, five years after the publication of his landmark study of the American priesthood for the bishops. He wrote the report with his colleague, Victor J. Heckler. Kennedy was a Professor of Psychology for twenty-five years, a public intellectual, an advocate for change in the Church and a syndicated columnist. Kennedy provided me with the stimulus to continue. On first reading Kennedy's obituary, I instantly thought of our senior class of third-year philosophers in Katoomba.

Late in 1964, the student body travelled to the Jenolan Caves, a tourist site not far from Katoomba in the Blue Mountains. It was my first and only day out from our mountain retreat. The credit for this outing belonged to one of our lecturers, Doctor George Joiner, who took pride in organising it each year. We travelled in buses and stopped on the edge of Katoomba. Prefects were allowed out to buy supplies for their year. Ray Liggett took the orders for our first-year philosophers and everyone else stayed on our bus.

I am not a prefect, but in the general excitement I step out of the bus and walk into town. In the main street, I see young men in black suits running and hiding in the entrances to shops. They are members of our senior class

– the third-year philosophy group. They have purchased water pistols and are playing Cowboys and Indians. Shouting and brandishing their weapons, they *shoot* each other with water as they weave in and out of the amazed citizens of Katoomba, who in turn duck and dive to avoid the bursts of water. Following their formation at Springwood, these young men will move to Manly and study theology before being released into the world. A member of the shooters is a young Kieran Tapsell, whose book, *Potiphar's wife* (2014), documents the involvement of the papacy and Vatican bureaucrats in directing bishops around the world to keep the sexual abuse of children by Catholic priests a secret within the Church.

Eugene Kennedy was troubled by what he learnt about the priesthood in America. The sex scandal he predicted eventually reached the public a generation after the release of his 1971 report. In 2002, Kennedy wrote that while the priesthood was not dead, clericalism was: 'It needs to be buried,' he wrote, 'preferably with a Viking funeral in Boston Harbor so nobody can miss the spectacle of its passing.'[32]

Kennedy wanted to bury clericalism – the rule of the clerics, and its superior caste in the Catholic Church. The Church has much to answer for in developing this power elite. Jesus was no priest; Peter and Paul were not priests; the other apostles and disciples were not priests. We have to blame the anonymous writer of the Letter to the Hebrews for linking Jesus with the traditional Jewish priesthood, some sixty years after his death on the cross.[33] Saint John Chrysostom (d.407), one of the early Church Fathers and Archbishop of Constantinople, saw the priest as a kind of 'walking holiness: Though the priesthood is exercised on earth, its acts rank with those of heavenly beings.'[34] By the fourth century, the priest had become a sacred person. This form of clericalism has persisted throughout the centuries, but it sits most uncomfortably with the person of Jesus and his teachings. The Jewish priests were the enemies of Jesus:

> The Priests [sic] were the men most dangerous to Jesus. They had the greatest stake in what he was saying about God's justice for the poor. They had the religious establishment to protect from the Roman imperial overlords. They had to contain any challenge to the status quo, to preserve their own standing with

Roman officials, as the spokesperson for allowed religion. Jesus, by questioning their authority, could upset the delicate balancing act they performed from moment to moment.³⁵

This cultic, or sacred, notion of priesthood, led to an extreme form of clericalism, at odds with the scriptural persona of Christ, and has helped to destroy the faith of many in the institutional Church. It has certainly helped to destroy some of the victims of sexual abuse, both psychologically and physically.

Kennedy and Heckler's (K&H) 1972 research found that seminary training was deeply flawed. After extensive study and in-depth interviews with 271 priests, K&H released their report. They learnt that two-thirds of these men were what they termed 'underdeveloped'. Eight years of training had produced men who appeared lost in a world they little understood, and who, worse still, lacked the skills, maturity and independence of mind to know themselves, and thus make the kind of commitment one might well expect of them. The findings concluded that at least 66% of the study group were emotionally incapable of forming healthy, trusting and non-sexual relationships with others and 74.5% were either underdeveloped or maldeveloped. It was an extraordinary result. K&H divided the priests into four categories. Just 19 of the 271 men were judged to be 'developed', 50 others were 'developing', and of the bulk, some 179 were 'underdeveloped' and 23 were 'maldeveloped'.³⁶ These were the men who sat in dark confessionals and whispered advice to married women regarding the most intimate details of their married life. Complicating this already untenable situation, these same allegedly celibate men represented a Church obsessed with sex and sin.

K&H thought seminary training in the United States was a major issue for the bishops and was the reason for the high level of underdeveloped men. Kennedy argued that seminaries should be made coeducational. Opening up the seminaries would take prospective priests out of their monastic isolation and put them in contact with real people in a wider world. He believed that restrictive psychological conditions in seminaries led to the failure of students to grow as independent and mature people, especially in emotional and sexual areas.

When the sexual abuse scandal became public in the United States, the American Catholic bishops commissioned two research studies from the John Jay College of Criminal Justice, New York, in 2004 and 2011. The first report concentrated on the nature and scope of sexual abuse of children (aged 10 and under – this low age is a matter of some controversy), and minors (aged 18 and under) by Catholic priests and deacons (1950–2002); the second report analysed the 'causes' and context of sexual abuse of minors by priests in the United States (1950–2010).[37]

The published reports from John Jay endorsed the findings of K&H in one important area. They acknowledged the failure of seminary training in the United States. In their 2011 report, John Jay linked seminary training with clerical sexual abuse. They congratulated the American bishops on their seminary reforms after 1985, which they regarded as 'critically important' in lowering the cases of sexual abuse of children and minors in the United States. They regarded poor seminary training as one of the major reasons for the outbreak of sexual abuse after 1960.[38]

The National Review Board (2002), an expert Church panel appointed by the American bishops to monitor the implementation of the *Charter for the protection of children and young people,* produced its own report for the bishops in 2004. The Board also found serious problems with seminary formation. They isolated two main causes for the sexual abuse of minors. The first was the failure of diocesan authorities to adequately screen candidates for the priesthood. The Board wrote that many 'sexually dysfunctional and immature men were admitted into seminaries and later ordained into the priesthood'. The second main cause of abuse related to inadequate training. Seminarians 'were not prepared for the challenges of the priesthood, particularly the challenge of living a chaste, celibate life'.[39]

The National Review Board recommended that in the future, bishops must ensure that candidates for the priesthood be 'mature and psychologically well-adjusted individuals before' entering seminaries. Not surprisingly, the Board would have it that the offending priests brought their psychological abnormalities with them into the seminary. Insofar as the Board was concerned, the major fault of the Church was not to recognise individual pathologies. Dr Marie Keenan argues, however, that individual pathology is insufficient to explain sexual offending by Roman Catholic clergy and alternative interpretations must be explored.[40] Keenan will later argue for cultural factors within the Church as a cause of clerical sexual abuse.

Screening is important and mistakes were made. But not all of the 74.5% of the underdeveloped and maldeveloped priests in K&H's sample – adolescents pretending to be adults – could possibly have been psychosexually damaged *before* entering the seminary. These men are in many cases the products of the clerical system they experienced in the Church's seminary.[41] Available research and clinical experience suggests that seminary authorities are unlikely to 'pick up those men who might come to be accused of the sexual abuse of children'. And there is no evidence that clerics who have sexually abused minors 'have specifically chosen a profession in the Catholic Church so that they could gain access to children to abuse'.[42]

There is evidence, however, that some clerical candidates have been subjected to sexual abuse in seminaries and from sexually active priests, even spiritual directors:

> Corruption of the priesthood is not coming from outside forces; it is specious to blame candidates or culture. Corruption of the priesthood is generated and perpetuated within the clerical system. Corruption does not seep up from the bottom. Corruption is raining down from the top.[43]

In 1960, Richard Sipe began collecting data on what he calls the celibate/sexual practice of Roman Catholic priests. After reviewing 473 priests or histories of priests, Sipe discovered that 10% reported they were approached sexually by a priest during the time of their theological studies.

Sipe also found that 'seventy to eighty percent of priests who sexually abuse have themselves been abused as children, some by priests'.[44] Sipe's statistics are sharply at odds with the John Jay findings. The first John Jay report (2004) collected its information from surveys sent out to all Church dioceses in the United States, i.e. the Church provided the information. No-one was interviewed. The surveys reported that 'nearly 7% of priests had been physically, sexually, and/or emotionally abused as children'.[45]

The significant difference between the two relates to the different methods of collecting data. In private correspondence with Sipe, I queried his extremely high figure of 70-80%. I suggested to him that this fact alone could go some way in explaining why Catholic priests abused children later in life. I also suggested to him if that was the case then I didn't have a reason for writing this book. Sipe strongly disagreed with both my suggestions.

He said that the cause of 'the abuse of minors is multifaceted' and my thesis was 'correct in citing the SYSTEM – the Clerical Culture'. He went on to say that 'the abuse of children is ... very common'. Abuse of children is 'the only sexual activity that Kinsey could not quantify' and it remains 'pervasive in current culture'. Sipe is extremely critical of the seminary system in the States:

> the seminary culture (and all of Catholic Clerical Culture) fosters, selects, and tolerates minor abuse as no other I have studied in the US. The seminary system and clerical culture does not favour growing out of past abuse (do not discount psychic abuse).

A recent report, commissioned by the Royal Commission in Australia, examined this question of child sexual abusers who had themselves been abused. Their literature study concluded there was insufficient evidence to link the two directly:

> There is a lack of evidence to support a *unique* association of childhood sexual abuse with subsequent sexual offending in general. Experiences of physical abuse or child neglect in childhood may be more predicative of sexual offending than sexual abuse in childhood.[46]

Despite that finding, it would be wrong, in my view, to dismiss the link between being abused as a young person and later becoming an abuser. As Sipe said, the causes of sexual abuse are multifaceted and this is one of many.

In an article published in the *British Journal of Psychiatry* in 2001, researchers studied 747 males. They concluded that the risk of being a perpetrator was positively correlated with reported sexual abuse victim experiences. The overall rate of having been a victim was 35% for perpetrators and 11% for non-perpetrators.[47]

In their review of the literature, John Jay (2011) examined one study that found 'the odds of a sexually abused priest offending against children in adulthood were 6.05 times higher than that of the odds of a nonabused priest offending in adulthood'. John Jay concluded, however, that the small size of the sample did not warrant a generalisation of this result. Nevertheless, they recommended to the bishops that the data generally indicated 'that the experience of having been sexually abused by an adult while a minor increased the risk that priests would later abuse a child'.

Marie Keenan's research also indicates a possible link between being abused as a young person and later becoming an abuser. Her research shows that childhood sexual victimisation is one of the strongest predictive variables for clerical men to become repeat offenders. It is possible that while the general literature does not support her conclusion, Keenan believes that priests and religious may well be the exception.[48]

K&H argued that the isolation and strict discipline regime of the seminary system made the integration of celibacy in the lives of the students virtually impossible. The end result of this failure meant that problems associated with celibacy occurred *after* ordination. K&H found that in sexual matters, the majority of the newly-ordained were still in the pre-adolescent or adolescent phase: 'They [priests] look like adults but, on the inside, they still struggle with the challenges of a previous level of development.'[49] Entering the seminary direct from school, young boys missed completely the normal sexual development that adolescents experienced in the secular world.[50] Then, once outside the seminary, feelings of sex were a source of conflict and difficulty, and for many men, coming to terms with their sexuality caused great anguish and pain. Many of these men were vulnerable, i.e. more likely to form relationships with children and young adults than other men. In parish life many priests felt a great void in their lives. Family, and intimacy with women and friends, represented a lifestyle that other adults had. This American study closely relates to my seminary experience in Australia. We were all part of an authoritarian, international organisation headquartered in Rome, and hence all followed the same Vatican system. Perhaps the best and brightest seminarians in America also played Cowboys and Indians in the streets of American towns.

A reading of K&H's findings now makes it clear that a significant cause of sexual abuse of children by the Catholic clergy in the last half of the twentieth century can be traced to the culture of the institutional Church, in particular the culture and manner of its seminary training. The British academic historian and one-time seminarian, John Cornwell, read some thirty national reports on clergy sexual abuse published between 1989 and 2013. Cornwell writes that the culpability of the bishops is usually cited 'but the reports are weak on systemic causes':

> There is a failure in all the reports to recognise the problems inherent in clericalism, clerical formation, and the practice of confession as crucial causes of the phenomenon of clerical sexual abuse.[51]

The chief area where underdeveloped and maldeveloped priests in the K&H study manifested their lack of psychological growth was in their relationships with other persons.[52] Many of the underdeveloped priests had few close friends. Intimacy with other adults was virtually impossible. This problem was exacerbated by the working conditions of priests. Frequently they lived alone and often far from family and friends. Trained to live on the outside of life, too much was asked of these men – and continues to be asked. As Cozzens and Buber contend, we need one another – the human condition demands intimacy. Despite claims to be an authority in these matters, the Church does not understand human nature. Its philosophical understanding of human nature and human sexuality rests on an outmoded and flawed theory of natural law dating back to the Greek philosopher Aristotle (d. 323BC).

If friendship and intimacy are so important, it is an interesting question to compare the sexual abuse of those order priests, e.g. Franciscans, who live in communities, and diocesan priests who live in parishes and frequently alone. Unfortunately the evidence is inconclusive. In America, religious orders living in communities had approximately half the number of clerical sexual abusers as diocesan priests.[53] In Australia, however, the difference between the two was not as great. Some 5.7% of all order priests living in communities had sexual abuse claims made against them as against 7.9% of diocesan priests. It appears that perhaps living in community may have been a factor in lower rates of sexual abuse. But some order priests in Australia had extremely high rates of sexual abuse. Alleged clerical perpetrators from the Salesians of Don Bosco had rates of 17.2%, and for the Marist Fathers – Society of Mary – the figure was 13.9%.[54] More work needs to be done here, especially on the nature of these communities.

Nevertheless, it seems sensible to argue that diocesan priests should not be asked to live alone on the edge of life. This is especially so when there is considerable psychological evidence that sex offenders have higher levels of intimacy deficits than nonoffenders. In John Jay's 2011 study, many sexual offenders (not clerics) reported a lack of close adult relationships, as well as a lack of intimacy in their relationships generally. Just as K&H found high levels of intimacy deficits with their study of priests, John Jay found that incarcerated rapists and child molesters had widespread intimacy deficits. These two groups, namely rapists and child molesters, reported significantly more loneliness than nonsexual offenders and community control subjects, and 'child molesting behaviors [sic] were the best single predictor of degree of fear of intimacy'.[55]

Despite the considerable psychological evidence that sex offenders have higher levels of intimacy deficits than nonoffenders, John Jay argued that the evidence from the wider community did not apply to priests. John Jay compared priestly abusers with priestly non-abusers. They conducted personality tests and clinical assessments that showed no significant differences between priest abusers and priest non-abusers. They concluded that:

> The most significant conclusion drawn from this data is that no single psychological, developmental, or behavioral characteristic differentiated priests who abused minors from those who did not. Most abusers did not exhibit characteristics consistent with paraphilias with specific clinical characteristics, and most importantly, there were very few 'pedophile' [sic] priests.[56]

That is a surprising result, especially when considering the K&H study. The K&H report found there was a significant psychological difference between the developed and the underdeveloped priests, especially in their respective ability to reach out and develop relationships with others. I anticipated a correlation between priestly abusers and the characteristics displayed by K&H's underdeveloped and maldeveloped priests. How then explain what looks like a contradiction? We are dealing with two very different studies. One obvious difference between John Jay and K&H is that John Jay has introduced sexual abuse into the equation. The K&H study in 1971 did not consider sexual abuse. Also, John Jay collected its data from seven different sources, including K&H. That said, I am still uncomfortable with John Jay's conclusion.

⋘

38 Trapped in a closed world

The training of the clergy, prior to the Second Vatican Council, deliberately set out to eliminate relationships, especially those of an intimate nature, but the global sexual abuse scandal has forced the Church to change the way it trains its seminarians. Reforms have worked to overcome the lack of understanding about human sexuality and to concentrate significantly on the personal development of the whole person. Seminaries are no longer the closed societies they once were. But geographical shifts of seminaries from isolated places into the real world and changes to curriculum won't solve the problem. The authoritarian governance structures, misogyny, clericalism and mandatory celibacy of traditional Catholic culture remain as blocks to genuine reform.

K&H's criticism of seminary training was endorsed by the findings of two other researchers. In 1971, when Dr Conrad Baars and Dr Anna Terruwe presented their research paper to the 1971 Synod of Bishops in Rome and later to the US Conference of Catholic Bishops, they cited 40 years of combined psychiatric practice treating some 1,500 priests.[57] They concluded that 20–25% of North American priests had serious psychiatric difficulties and 60–70% suffered from emotional immaturity. This latter group had unresolved psychosexual problems and issues that are usually worked through in adolescent years. Baars and Terruwe warned the American bishops of impending disasters. They argued there was a link between emotional immaturity and sexual activity. They warned the bishops that psychosexual immaturity 'manifested itself in heterosexual and homosexual activity'.[58] This was a critically important finding.

K&H's research appeared in public one year later. They endorsed Baars' and Terruwe's view with their finding that 74% of the priests in their study had unresolved psychosexual problems. They concluded that the sexuality of the clerical majority was 'not integrated into the lives of undeveloped priests and many of them function at a pre-adolescent, or adolescent level of psychological growth'.[59]

It is, however, one thing to be psychosexually immature and another to draw a causal link with the sexual abuse of children and minors. K&H drew no such consequences from their findings. Unlike Baars and Terruwe, they did not mention sexual activity as a manifestation of emotional immaturity, and both groups made no mention of the sexual abuse of children. K&H did say that for underdeveloped priests, sexual feelings were a source of conflict and difficulty, and much energy went into suppressing them or distracting themselves from them.[60] Ironically, at the time of both these reports, the United States Catholic clergy were reaching their peak level of sexual abuse. Some 10% of those ordained in 1970 were sexually abusing children. Did Baars and Terruwe know? The Baars and Kennedy studies were a warning to the Catholic bishops. They should have been terrified but they did nothing.

Other researchers, many years later, make it clear that a deeply flawed seminary training regime has left a percentage of undeveloped priests vulnerable to sexually abusing children. In 2012, in an address at the Santa Clara University, Richard Sipe stated that:

> Seminary training produces many psychosexually impaired and retarded priests whose level of adjustment is adolescent at best. This tends to create a psychic and moral field and situations in which immature liaisons with young children not only become more possible but are psychosexually over-determined because children are actually on a developmental par with these men.[61]

Not all psychosexually immature priests become sexual abusers. Acting out sexual abuse is one thing. Being vulnerable is another. Vulnerability means the psychosexually immature are more open to the likelihood of becoming abusers. Dr David Finkelhood is an American sociologist who has developed a worldwide reputation in the area of child sex abuse. Like Sipe, Finkelhood argues that adults who sexually abuse children may experience 'emotional congruence' to children or adolescents, i.e. when an adult's emotional needs are not fully mature he may relate better to children than adults. This can be a particular problem when the abuser has a 'blockage' in attaining or maintaining adult relationships.[62] Emotional congruence can lead to sexual arousal and thus become a motivator to the sexual abuse of children.[63] And we know from the K&H study that a majority of priests in their study were emotionally incapable of forming healthy, trusting and non-sexual relationships with others.

It is the case that Catholic seminaries failed to form many of their seminarians into psychosexually mature adults. If I am correct, my cultural argument is that higher rates of clerical sexual abuse will be found within the Catholic faith than from within other faith communities. I assume here that other faith communities have very different seminary systems to the all-male celibate systems sponsored by the Catholic Church. I am almost certain that other faith communities will have lower levels of clerical sexual abuse in Australia than that which exists in the Catholic Church.

Patrick Parkinson is the Professor of Law at the University of Sydney, and has worked with the Australian Catholic Church in assisting the victims of sexual abuse. He has twice reviewed the Church's program *Towards healing*. Parkinson puts the challenge facing the Church bluntly:

> Which culture will prevail – the culture of faith and commitment to the carpenter who walked the shores of Galilee and the streets of Jerusalem two thousand years ago, or the culture of corrupted power? Will Catholic Church leaders, into the future, be lords and princes, or will they be servants? How will they hold one another accountable?[64]

In his Smith Lecture in 2013, Parkinson sets out to explain sexual abuse, not just in the Catholic Church, but in all faith communities. There is, however, an initial problem, which Parkinson is quick to acknowledge. While sex offenders are found in people of many different theological persuasions, it is the case that very limited research evidence is available concerning child sexual abuse by priests or ministers in faith communities other than in the Catholic Church. A recent report commissioned by the Australian Royal Commission and published in September 2016 found that most of the available research concerns Roman Catholic clergy. Very little literature exists on other religious denominations and almost none on religious non-Christian institutional settings.[65]

Nevertheless, Parkinson argues that what little evidence does exist suggests that rates of abuse are much lower in other faith communities than in the Catholic Church. His conclusion is endorsed by others. Geoffrey Robertson, QC, contends that the emerging facts from around the world show that the sexual abuse of children by priests in the Catholic Church is at a level considerably above any other organisation.[66] Parkinson is meticulously careful and fair. He quotes, first, what he calls a 'substantial and systematic' study over a 40-year period from within his own faith community, the Anglican Church of Australia.

Parkinson acknowledges this Anglican study is not a complete census. Taking a conservative estimate of 10,000 clergy serving in parishes where incidents of child sexual abuse were reported, Parkinson concludes that the proportion of clergy accused of sexual abuse appears to be well under 1%. Parkinson insists that this is no more than a 'rough estimate'.[67]

Parkinson then compares this finding of 1%, rubbery as it may be, with a study of priests ordained between 1940 and 1966, from a particular Catholic seminary in Melbourne. The clergy from this seminary had a 3.7% rate of conviction of sexual abuse against children. And further, the percentage of those from the same seminary, ordained between 1968 and 1971, who were convicted of abuse against children, was 5.4%.[68]

It would be good to know how these figures match with figures from the general population. Parkinson says they are much higher. It is no easy matter, however, to feel confident about figures relating to the general population. Unfortunately, there are no reliable baseline data on levels of men offending in the general population in Australia. Parkinson draws on a study completed in England, which found that between 1% and 2% of the male population could be expected to be convicted for some form of sexual abuse over their lifetime.

It may well be the case that sexual abuse of children is much higher than first thought. The incidence of child abuse needs to be distinguished from its disclosure. An Australian academic study completed in 1988 surveyed 1000 female students. A similar study was carried out with boys. Nearly 28% of the women who responded reported some form of abusive sexual experience before the age of 16. The survey with the boys found that 9% of boys who responded to the survey had been sexually abused in childhood. Based on these figures, it is reasonable to conclude that at least 1 in 4 girls and 1 in 10 boys have experienced sexual abuse in Australia before the age of 16. Similar results were found in the United States.

As well as the figures from the 40-year Anglican study, and the Melbourne seminary study above, Parkinson also quotes figures from the Victorian Police who gave evidence in 2013 to the Parliamentary inquiry in that state. The police identified all criminal convictions for sexual abuse of minors in Victoria between January 1956 and June 2012. Significantly, the number of victims in the Catholic Church was exactly ten times higher than that in the Anglican Church. Parkinson says this is only partially explained by the greater size of the Catholic Church in Melbourne – the Anglican Church is about 70% of the size of the Catholic Church in the two Archdioceses, as counted by number of parishes.[69]

In a comparison of allegations in the Anglican and Catholic Archdioceses of Melbourne respectively, Parkinson found a further indication of higher rates of abuse in the Catholic Church. Since 1996, the Catholic Church recorded complaints of abuse against 331 children that were dealt with under its complaints procedures against priests and religious. Of these, 310 complaints were substantiated. In the Anglican study for the Archdiocese of Melbourne, since 1990, complaints of abuse were registered for just 44 children in the archdiocese.[70]

A year after his Smith Lecture, Parkinson told the Victorian Government's Parliamentary Inquiry into the handling of child abuse by religious and other organisations that:

> If you compare the statistics, I would say conservatively that there is six times as much abuse in the Catholic Church as all the other churches in Australia combined, and I would regard that as a conservative figure.[71]

Following the release of the data by the Australian Royal Commission in February 2017, Parkinson may well be correct. In 2012, Sipe reported that religious in the Australian Catholic Church had offended at a rate six times greater than that of all the other Australian churches combined. Perhaps Sipe read Parkinson's transcript. If Sipe is correct, then such a failure cannot simply be attributed to the crimes of individuals, although individuals are ultimately responsible for their own moral failures. Individuals go to jail, not the Church. Clearly, there are systemic issues here. We will know more in December 2017 when the Commission makes its final report.

Sipe argues that it can be stated with reasonable certitude that a higher proportion of Roman Catholic priests abuse minors than do a group of men of comparable age, training and profession. Sipe maintains that one of the main reasons for the high levels of abuse in the Catholic Church – and he comes to this conclusion after years of working with clerics in the field – can be found in Catholic training for the priesthood, which leaves too many men psychosexually immature. Sipe also contends that the 'clerical culture attracts, cultivates, promotes and protects psychosexually immature men'.[72]

The role of the Vatican in providing both help to their bishops and to civic authorities has been disingenuous in the extreme. One of the most disturbing points made by Gail Furness, Senior Counsel Assisting the Australian Royal Commissioners, was her references to the continuing failure of the Vatican to provide information to the Commission.[73] In general, the Vatican has tended to downplay the numbers of its clergy involved in sexual abuse. In 2001 the then pope, John Paul II, gave Cardinal Joseph Ratzinger (later Pope Benedict XVI), Prefect of the Congregation for the Doctrine of the Faith (CDF), 'exclusive competence' for dealing with world-wide sexual abuse by Catholic clerics.[74] The truth is that Ratzinger had been involved with the sexual abuse issue well before 2001. According to the Catholic theologian, Hans Küng:

> We cannot ignore the fact that the system devised to conceal clerical abuse misbehaviour and then set in motion all over the world was led by the Roman Congregation for the Doctrine of the Faith, led by Cardinal Ratzinger from 1981 until 2005. Under Pope John Paul II, reports of cases were already being collected by the Roman Congregation under the cloak of strict confidentiality.[75]

From 2001, Ratzinger ordered all Catholic bishops to direct preliminary investigations into claims of abuse to his office. Ratzinger's letter stated that the Church had jurisdiction in cases where abuse had been perpetrated with a minor by a cleric, and the right to judge each case in secret. The letter spoke of penalties for bishops and those investigating the allegations, and threatened excommunication to anyone who breached confidentiality.

Theoretically at least, Ratzinger should have known more about the extent of global sexual abuse in the Church than anyone else. We can't be certain just what Ratzinger read or how many bishops obeyed his instructions. Nevertheless, Ratzinger confidently told the Catholic News Service in 2002 that less than 1% of Catholic priests were guilty of the sexual abuse of minors.

Ratzinger believed the enemies of the Church were conspiring with their lies and exaggerations against the One True Church. He went on to criticise the media in the United States for its manipulation of the facts and its planned campaign against the Church.[76] Ratzinger was wrong. The first John

Jay Report in the United States (2004) put the clerical abuse figure at 4.3% of all priests active in the period from 1950–2002. The Center for Applied Research in the Apostolate (CARA) found that 5% of diocesan priests in the United States from 1960–1996 received complaints of allegations of abuse. In the same period, 2.7% of religious order priests received allegations of sexual abuse. It is now likely that these figures are underestimated. The Church in the United States now accepts a percentage of 5.3%. Sipe thinks it is more likely to be somewhere between 6 and 9%.[77]

Some clerics and their lay supporters, stung by what has happened in their Church, argue that Catholic sexual abuse is no worse than in other churches or civic institutions. The statistics suggest otherwise. The argument is ill-conceived and avoids the fact that something dreadful has happened in their Church. The sexual abuse of one child is one too many. Criminal acts have occurred. Innocent children have been violated. Popes have behaved deviously. Much has been conducted in secret. Bishops have avoided the truth to protect the Church and perhaps themselves. Abusive priests have been moved from parish to parish. In many cases some victims have lost their lives; others have had their lives ruined. Those Catholics, with energy to spare, who believe their Church is no worse than the rest, should direct their attention inwards and argue for essential Church reform. If the Church is to be saved it will be by its critics. These defenders of the faith who regard all criticism of their Church as treachery, might start by demanding greater accountability and transparency from those making decisions that impact on the faithful. They could demand that the Church rid itself of clericalism, misogyny and the notion of papal infallibility, which is a formidable barrier to any reform. It is difficult to make changes when previous mistakes can't be acknowledged! Optional celibacy, women priests and the election of local bishops by the laity would be a promising start.[78]

In February 2016, when Cardinal George Pell gave evidence from Rome to the Royal Commission, he dismissed the idea of structural change in the Church. The problem, said the Cardinal, was not structural but *original sin*. Pell saw the sexual abuse scandal in the Church in strictly personal and religious terms. For the Cardinal, we are all born in original sin. The problem for him, therefore, relates to individuals in the Church: 'I think the faults overwhelmingly have been personal faults, personal failures, rather than structures.' And besides, according to Pell, the Church can never change its structures for they are 'divine', tracing their history 'back to the New Testament', to the Church's understanding of what it means to be a pope or a bishop. Pell thus dismissed the twin ideas of either a structural or a cultural problem in the Church.[79]

In the recent February 2017 hearings before the Royal Commission, there was considerable discussion and questioning among the commissioners, archbishops, bishops and expert Church witnesses about structural reform and governance issues in the Church. Much of it was a waste of time. Pell is correct in acknowledging the link between structural change and ideology. Structural and governance issues in the Church must be preceded by theological reform. Within all institutions, structures and governance issues flow from values and ideas, not vice versa. Totalitarian regimes develop structures that protect their power. Democratic regimes work within structures that curtail their power. The Church is no different. Its culture and structure follows its understanding of itself.

Chapter 3

Solo in the bush

In 1964, sexual abuse is far from my mind. It is the monastic setting that troubles me. My seminary is dominated by the bush. This is not the bush waiting for the settler's axe and green pastures. This is wild, torn and uneven, heaved up from eons past. It offers no solace and stretches out behind and on both sides as far as the eye can see, grey and silent, rough and indifferent, uncompromising and alien. It belongs in another time to another people. Yet I am drawn to it. If I walk straight into it perhaps I will uncover both its mystery and my own in being here. But as in most things I am ambivalent – even about the bush. I feel its otherness, and deep down I fear it. When we were kids my father took us children into a gentler bush. He was cutting wood for the winter fires. 'Don't wander', he warned, 'kids get lost in the bush.' I knew that from my school reader. I had bad dreams of being lost in the bush.

In the front of our seminary buildings, reminiscent of a rich man's mansion, and where we are forbidden to wander, is a green circular lawn edged with a road for vehicles to turn and drive back into the world, and, if I remember rightly, a water fountain in the centre of the lawn. A pointed tower, more Arabic than Christian, sits three floors above the squat block of stone with its Romanesque entry into the courtyard. These are signs of civilisation. The Irish poet, W. B. Yeats, in his *Meditations in time of civil war*, knew these signs: an ancestral house with a water fountain 'where Life overflows without ambitious pains'; but we live at the back, deprived of any such signs.

D. H. Lawrence came to Australia in 1922. He was overwhelmed by the:

> terror of the bush. [He] looked at the weird, white, dead trees, and into the hollow distances of bush. Nothing! Nothing at all.[80]

Like Englishmen before him, and like me, Lawrence sensed something menacing in the Australian bush. It was, he felt, waiting for something, but no one knew what. The bush, he said, was 'biding its time with a terrible ageless watchfulness, waiting for a far-off end, watching myriad intruding white men'. Lawrence was also fearful of Australians, and on the great questions of life, he thought Australians had nothing to say. He wrote of the great Australian emptiness, with its 'fascinating indifference', and its 'physical indifference to what we call soul or spirit', with 'no inside life of any sort: just a long lapse and drift'.

I am a drifter, and unlike the owner of Yeats' ancestral house, I am filled with ambition and pain, doing God's will, waiting for something to happen, waiting for a sign, waiting to make up my mind. And yet gathered here in this seminary, named after a sixth-century Irish monk who made his home on the island of Iona, Scotland, we live a life modelled on the monastic lives of the saints and monks of medieval Europe, reading our Latin, praying our liturgy, pondering the thoughts of Plato, Aristotle and Thomas Aquinas, training to shine like lighthouses in a dark world. We are not nothing. We are not indifferent. We are people of the soul and spirit. What would Lawrence make of us?

We Catholics are a people set apart. In the old dispensation, before the virtual collapse of vocations to the priesthood in Australia, in the decade before the Second Vatican Council, Catholics live in a separate universe. We run along parallel lines to the rest of the community. We have our own tracks, trains, train drivers, stations and station masters. Our trains have a direct route to Heaven and we only pick up Catholics. I am studying to be a train driver. I belong to an institution apart from and superior to the world. We have our own culture, our own set of laws, and our own jurisdictional system. We are an international body and our allegiance is to the pope in Rome. We are a law unto ourselves. When the sexual abuse scandal breaks, this cultural triumphalism will come back to haunt us.

Our lives here are ground out of a stone called routine. We move in centuries' old rhythms according to electronic bells which determine our days. There is an ancient bell-tower, which from memory chimes out the *Angelus* at midday aided by a first year student hauling down on a rope. Our days split into three: study, prayer and recreation. We rise at 6.00 am and enter the chapel sometime before 6.30 am. Meditation occupies our minds until Mass begins at 7.00 am. We have no serious training in meditation, but I am reasonably competent and give it my best shot. For much of my life I have carried on an interior monologue with a personal God who loves me and lives somewhere within me and who, if the seminary had had its way, would disappear into the distant blue.

After Mass we walk quickly back to our rooms, make our beds and generally clean up, gather together our books for classes (no coming back if anything has been forgotten) and are drawn by another bell to gather in pairs outside the refectory for breakfast at 8.00 am. No talking. The *great silence*, which began after late evening prayers the night before, continues until after breakfast.

Classes begin at 9.00 am but there is generally time for a quick walk before they commence, hopefully with company that is pleasurable. That depends on the luck of the draw. One must not deliberately avoid the company of any one student and seek out a smiling face. At 11.00 am we take a fifteen minute break. Classes resume again and finish just before dinner, not to be confused with lunch. Before dinner at 12.45 pm, the main meal of the day, we proceed in pairs into the chapel for an examination of conscience.

Immediately after dinner is one of the best times of the day. We wander down to the *rec* hall built by previous students, collars off, soutanes undone, scungy t-shirts, some of us positively louche-like, and wait for the head prefect to come with the mail from loved ones, which he delivers frisbee-like into the raised welcoming arms of children at a circus. I always read my mail in the jakes (toilet) because they contain pink cuttings from *The Sporting Globe* with the football results from Victoria, which of necessity I keep to myself. Sport, recreation of some sort (hobbies) or Father George Joiner's working parties fill in the early afternoon until we meet again in the chapel for spiritual reading at 3.45 pm. Study follows and then another visit to the chapel before lining up for the evening meal at 6.30pm. A short walk after eating and back to the chapel for either rosary or benediction before private study at 7.30 pm. Finally, after a short evening walk at 9.15, we head back to the chapel for night prayers when the *great silence* begins again and lights close us and the day out at 10.00 pm.⁸¹ And the next day... And the next... And the...

I suspect the seminary was much more civilised in my time than under the previous rector. Veechy was strange but his predecessor Monsignor Charles Dunne, whom I never met, appears brutal. When Geoff Mulhearn, a serious asthmatic, arrived in 1956, he told Charlie of his illness. Geoff came 'fortified with an abundance of medication to protect him against the harshness of the climate, the mountain frosts and the unheated study halls'. Charlie told Geoff: 'If you have one attack of asthma in this place, it will be your last. You will be sent straight home. Do you understand?' 'Yes, Monsignor,' was the reply.[82a]

Dunne was born in 1897 in Victoria and was educated by the Jesuits at Saint Patrick's College, East Melbourne. He graduated from the University of Melbourne with Honours in English in 1922 and for much of his teaching life at Springwood taught English and Latin. Doctor Daniel Mannix (1864–1963), Archbishop of Melbourne, ordained Dunne to the priesthood at Saint Patrick's Cathedral in Melbourne in 1927, despite Dunne having completed his studies for the priesthood in New South Wales at Springwood and Manly. It is not clear why Dunne studied in New South Wales and not Victoria.

Apart from the last two years of his life – he died in 1965 – Dunne appears to have spent the whole of his priestly life teaching at Saint Columba's, Springwood. From 1928–48, Dunne served as Professor, Dean of Discipline, Bursar and Vice-Rector (1940–48), and in 1948 he became Rector, a position he held till his retirement from the seminary in 1963. He was appointed Monsignor, Privy Chamberlain to His Holiness Pope Pius XII in 1951, and in 1960, His Holiness Pope John XXIII conferred dignity of Domestic Prelate on Monsignor Dunne.

Dunne sexually abused young girls. In his book of his time at Springwood, Chris Geraghty writes in all innocence that 'Charlie Dunne liked me. He also liked my father, and my little sister, Colleen.'[82b] Dunne could not be trusted with young girls. Some thirty-five years after Dunne died, Bishop Geoffrey Robinson, appointed by the Australian bishops to lead their response to revelations of sexual abuse of clergy and religious brothers, received a visit from a 'mature woman' who told him that when she was in her early teens she was sexually abused by Dunne. These events occurred in the early 1960s. She also told Robinson that Dunne had sexually abused her younger sister. Robinson has told me that neither woman had approached the police or the *Towards healing* program; nor was he given any details of the nature of the abuse. The women appear to have made no official complaint to the Church and neither sought compensation. It is apparent that the accusations against Dunne were not pursued. I am absolutely confident that the 'mature woman' was telling the truth. There may well be other cases.[83]

Seminary rules were at the centre of my life under Veechy, but Dunne took them to another level. Every student in the college was given a rule book but that didn't stop Dunne reading large slabs of it aloud to the students every Sunday in the chapel. On one occasion, a scrupulous student asked one of the spiritual directors a question: 'Is breaking a rule a sin, Father?' Father Frank Mecham replied that breaking the rules deliberately and perhaps constantly could amount to a mortal sin and eternal punishment in hell. For the already neurotic this was bad news indeed.

Coughing and nose-blowing in the chapel was outlawed under Veechy, and enforced by one of our lion tamers, Dean of Discipline, Father John Walsh (Walshy). We were frequently warned not to cough during Mass, especially so during the holiest part of the Mass, the Consecration. I was a big cougher, but managed to stifle the noise with a handkerchief over my mouth.

Dunne had a fetish about nose-blowing in public, especially during any of his conferences in the chapel. He would explode in anger, demand the student stand, castigate him in public, and forbid him to ever blow his nose in the chapel again. Seminarian, Domine Geraghty, was left-handed and Dunne noticed him cutting bread with his left hand. He called him in and told him bluntly that left-handed people could not be priests. Geraghty quickly became right-handed. Communion must be distributed in the right hand.

Stuttering and stammering students were made to suffer under Dunne. He insisted that stuttering students had to take their turn in reading to the student body during lunch, despite their terrible humiliation before their peers. It was difficult enough for the best readers to be heard in the refectory. Stuttering becomes worse under pressure. I stuttered myself as a small child and know how the pressure builds as words choke in the throat. As some students could barely utter a sentence, embarrassed listeners, the majority in their teens, would break out in barely controlled titters. Dunne could have called a halt but he allowed the public ridicule to continue.[84]

Paul Crittenden, academic, philosopher and priest till he resigned in 1983, travelled by train to Springwood from Sydney to complete his secondary schooling in 1951 aged fifteen. Crittenden, a brilliant student, was there under the guidance of Monsignor Charles Dunne for four years, but, unlike Geraghty, is more measured with his views about Charlie:

> Whether as Rector or lecturer, he was a strict disciplinarian, given to pronouncing terse judgments in quiet but absolute tones. He had a full head of gingery hair, and a puffy face with small, piercing eyes. He looked for much of the time like a smouldering volcano forever on the point of eruption. As Rector he occasionally struck fear among the ranks; but in many ways his disciplinary performance was an act that was relatively benign and even entertaining.

There is a studied coolness about Crittenden. He aims for balanced estimates by heading in one direction then strategically withdrawing to consider another. For example, his view of Springwood when he first arrived was that it was 'quite strange', a modest enough judgement, but then he equated the regime with a detention centre by claiming it was 'run on the lines of a borstal'. Borstals were detention centres in the United Kingdom run by HM Prison System for serious delinquent young people. A few sentences later, Crittenden concluded that, nevertheless, 'Springwood, whatever the faults of the system and the times, remains in memory as a place of innocence and youth, infused with a spirit of generosity and hope'.[85]

In a recent publication, twenty-three ex-students of Springwood (1961–63) have written of their time at Springwood. Some few of the writers chose not to comment about their lecturers. Of those who spoke about Charles Dunne, only two made comments that might be construed as even slightly positive, namely that he was 'both feared and respected' and that he was a 'gruff old bugger'. Dunne was a cruel 'martinet' who denigrated and humiliated students until they were submissive. An 'acerbic bully' with little or no respect for the dignity of others, he seemed to delight in embarrassing and ridiculing students in a most public way. One ex-student wrote he never 'discerned the least sign of Christ-like compassion nor the joie de vivre one might reasonably associate with belief in Christ's Resurrection'. Dunne oversaw a system that diminished some of the best human qualities that many of the young men brought with them to Springwood. Inevitably this:

> produced a mindset in many that this was the way in which power should be exercised. Perhaps their experience helps explain the continuing authoritarian behaviour of many clergy today.[86]

Charles Dunne represented the Cardinal in Sydney and followed the seminary system outlined by the Vatican. He was probably as much a victim of this antiquated seminary system as we students were. Nevertheless I was fortunate to miss his leadership by half a year. Dunne was undoubtedly 'a bad joke', but it seems to me now that no two of us experienced our isolation in exactly the same way. Along with our suitcases, we each brought our cultural and class histories, our family traits, our individual temperaments and our life experiences to Springwood. All of these combined to determine how we reacted to our immutable routine.[87]

The seminary system is an all-male caste of clerics and would-be clerics. Women are to be shunned. Mothers in particular, family members and all loved ones are to be shed. Our Manly seminary in Sydney is where we will study Theology. Apart from geography both seminaries are much the same; both seminaries are under the control of Cardinal Norman Gilroy and some of our lecturers have arrived from similar work at Manly.

In his first year at Manly Seminary in 1958, Domine Geraghty asked the dean, Father Paddy Murphy, for permission to go home for his sister's Confirmation. The answer was a firm *No*. When Geraghty, aged nineteen, queried Murphy, he replied, 'We think you pay too much attention to your family, that you are too close to them.' Frank Devoy arrived at Springwood as a nineteen-year-old in 1961. During his seminarian years, four of his brothers were married. When Frank was refused permission to attend the first three, his family wrote to Cardinal Gilroy requesting his intervention. No permission was granted.

The God of my institution is an all-demanding God. Just as Jesus did, we are called to reject our families:

> A crowd was sitting around him, and they told him, Your mother and brothers are outside looking for you. Who are my mother and my brothers? He asked.[88]

Ah, Jesus. Did you really say that?

So we slip out of our old earthly skins and put on our new clerical skins. Like young snakes we leave the old to rot and dry in the hot Australian sun. We take on a new mother who will love us and care for us, the Blessed Virgin Mary, represented by our male authorities. Once when a student returned to the seminary having attended a family funeral he was called to Charlie Dunne's office. He was accused of being away too long. The young man's explanations were pointless. Quoting the Bible, Charlie admonished him saying, 'Let the dead bury the dead.' Then he added, 'Everyone out there is dead except us. Let them look after all that. You have a higher calling.'[89]

We must learn to live without women, for they are the great temptation. But I will not reject them. When travelling back to boarding school in Bowral and to this seminary, I begin with the morning train in Terang. On leaving the station, I move quickly from one side of the train to the other. Waiting with white handkerchiefs in the vegetable garden next to the railway tracks are the women in the Green family, relatives on my mother's side, led by Auntie Poll. I then race to the other side of the train and my tearful mother stands in the middle of the road waving her handkerchief. Then quickly back to the other side where Mum's sister, Beryl, in her pink dressing gown, is waving goodbye. In Melbourne I stay with Mum's sister, Anne. She watches me from her front gate as I walk to catch the tram in Commercial Road. When I left the seminary, Anne told me that each time I left she went inside and had a 'little cry: I knew you didn't want to go, darling,' she said. I thought I never let on.

Mary, the mother of Jesus, is our model of womanhood, as she is for all Catholics. But for us, isolated here in the bush, contemplating our celibate future, Mary, the virgin, is the perfect fit. Mary, immaculately conceived (i.e. born free from original sin), assumed into Heaven (i.e. no earthly grave, but taken up body and soul into the sky), impregnated by the Holy Spirit miraculously (i.e. no sexual intercourse), gave birth while still remaining a virgin, will remain ever a virgin. In keeping with our vocation, we are called to love a virgin.

In 1964, I did not query the Church's teaching on Mary. I reject it completely now, but, sadly, I note the recent 2003 edition of the *Catechism of the Catholic Church* (n.510) has this to say regarding Mary:

> Mary remained a virgin in conceiving her Son, a virgin in giving birth to him, a virgin in carrying him, a virgin in nursing him at her breast, always a virgin.

In our seminary we pray to the Virgin Mary at midday. We are called to love her as she loves us:

> My soul magnifies the Lord
> And my spirit rejoices in God my Saviour ...

But Mary has taken wings and joined the angels. Mary is a Goddess. The Church has desexed her, dehumanised her and destroyed her as a model. She is no longer believable as a human being. But in 1964, I believed.

Now I prefer other images of the mother of Jesus. The Russian communists put Raphael's painting of *The Sistine Madonna* on display before returning it to Dresden in 1955. They had stolen it during the Second World War. Vasily Grossman saw it and was entranced.

Take note, Church. Vasily destroys your misogyny with his majestic words, but at the same time he celebrates the spirit of Mary, the mother of Jesus, the wife of Joseph. Vasily was a war journalist. He accompanied the Red Army from 1941 through to the end in Berlin four years later. Despite the suffering and insanity all around him, he never lost hope, and he never stopped loving. Vasily Grossman is not a Catholic, not a Christian. He is a Russian Jewish writer, who knows what it means to be human. Vasily's mother was murdered by the Nazis in 1941. On the twentieth anniversary of her death in 1961, Vasily wrote a letter to his Mama:

> ... And you don't need to worry about my spiritual life: I know how to protect my inner world from things around me ... I cried over your letters because you are in them, with your kindness, your purity, your bitter, bitter life, your fairness, your generosity, your love for me, your care for people, your wonderful mind. I

fear nothing because your love is with me and because my love is with you always.[90]

Vasily knew about mothers and their love for their children. He saw something in Mary that Pius IX, who defined the dogma of the Immaculate Conception of Mary, could never have imagined in his wildest dreams. When Vasily saw Raphael's Madonna, he saw into the soul of Mary.

Vasily had walked into the murder camp, Treblinka, in July 1944 with the Russian army as they advanced towards Germany. He had looked into the face of Raphael's Madonna in the spring of 1955 in Moscow and had seen Mary holding her small child up and out as if offering him to the world. In her face he saw the face of every woman who goes to meet her fate with a child on her breast. In the sad face of her child, Vasily had seen the sign of a cross, a cross the child would one day carry.

In the painting, Mary is a slip of a girl, a teenager in bare feet. Her beauty is the beauty that lives in every woman: 'in the cross-eyed, in hunchbacks with long pale noses, in gold-skinned Asians, in black-skinned Africans with curly hair and full lips.' What Grossman saw that day was the 'visual representation of a mother's soul' and in seeing it he saw 'something inaccessible to human consciousness'. This Madonna is the soul and mirror of all women. What is human in her will live forever. The Hitlers and Stalins of the world may kill this woman, but the human in her will live forever.

Vasily had met this Mary before:

> in 1930 in Konotop, at the station. Swarthy from hunger and illness, she walked towards the express train, looked up at me with her wonderful eyes and said with her lips, without any voice, 'Bread' ...

He had met her again in 1937:

> There she was holding her son in her arms for the last time, saying goodbye to him, gazing into his face and then going down the deserted staircase of a mute, many-storied building. A black car was waiting ...

Vasily's Mary is of this earth. Vasily's Mary, like Raphael's Mary, belongs to all of us and is one of us:

> We live in a troubled time. Wounds have not yet healed, burnt-out buildings still stand black. The mounds have not yet settled over

the shared graves of millions of soldiers, our sons and brothers. Dead, blackened poplars and cherry trees still stand guard over partisan villages that were burned to the ground. Tall dreary grasses and weeds grow over the bodies of people who were burned alive: grandfathers, mothers, young lads and lasses. Over the ditches that contain the bodies of murdered Jewish children and mothers the earth is still shifting, still settling into place. In countless Russian, Belorussian and Ukrainian huts widows are still weeping at night. The Madonna has suffered all this together with us – for she is us, and her son is us.[91]

Yet I persist. Each night I rule a line through the day. Sacrifice and suffering are central to my understanding of Catholicism. Jesus has died and suffered for our sins. I am called to share in His suffering. To be a priest requires courage and strength. But I am alone. We are all alone.

In our bush monastery we do not share our doubts, misgivings and loneliness with each other or any of our private thoughts with anyone. Courage and strength beyond the call of most humans is required. I have answered the call. I am in a long line of those willing to die for their faith. Each day at dinner the Martyrology is read aloud for our edification. Thank God it's in Latin. Our heroic forbears, men and women, were sliced, cut, hacked, raped, beheaded and some eaten by wild animals. I get the drift but the details go over my head while I slice the stale bread which we fill up on before the main course arrives. We are always hungry.

Sacrifice and suffering are reminders of my journey, a journey through time in this seminary. I learn of Pascal's wager. Pascal was a seventeenth-century French mathematician and philosopher. He argued that reason could not prove the existence of God. Therefore, one should take a pragmatic view and believe in God because the rewards, if God does exist, are great. On the other hand, to choose not to believe in God, and if in fact God does exist, then the loss is unimaginable and could result in eternal damnation. Pascal is advising all to play safe just in case. I'm no gambler on the existence of God, but I am something of a pragmatist. My gamble seeks an answer to a different question: how do I best serve God? Should I serve him as one of his elite priests or should I serve him in the world as a lay man? On my good days I stand with Saint Paul: 'All I want is to know

Christ and the power of His Resurrection and to share his sufferings by reproducing the pattern of His death.'[92] My parents, my loved ones, my own hopes of a family are to be offered up as my small sacrifice. Against the sufferings endured by Christ on the cross, my celibate offering is as nothing. So I persist. And yet ...

On many days I have this recurring image of a small boy. In 1958 I worked on a dairy farm near my home town. Pat and Maureen have a growing family. Bernie is three. He follows me about their home and the farm. Sometimes he walks up the paddock with me to bring in the cows. We walk slowly. I hold his hand, and up the hill I carry him on my shoulders. He talks continuously. I tell him he's as handy as a piece of string. When I give him something to do he says, 'Handy as a piece of string.' Later, when Maureen is having a new baby, Bernie is sent to one of her sisters in Yambuk, a small town near Port Fairy. I have begun collecting money from farmers for Santamaria's Rural Movement. I'm working in the Yambuk area and decide to call in and see Bernie. I round the corner and a team of children are rollicking on the green lawn in front of their house. In the group is a little blonde kid. He sees my brown, low-slung Peugeot 203 coming down the road. Immediately he runs to the car. I stop so that he doesn't run into it. I get out and he runs into my arms throwing his arms around my neck. He holds on tightly. That he loves me there is no doubt. Celibacy is strangling me. Too much is being asked.

On Good Friday, the senior prefects lead us down the long road in front of the seminary to the heritage sandstone gates where the bus brought us in some months earlier. No priests accompany us. This is a rare event when the student body appears to be in left in control. We make for the Grotto with its statue of Mary and head off the road into the bush. The Head Prefect, Brian, a tall, fine young man, reads the prayers and we make our way through this indifferent bush recalling the sufferings of Jesus on his way to Calvary. Previous students have cut the fourteen stations out of the bush. I remember happier Easters.

58 Trapped in a closed world

Second and third-year philosophers study at night in their rooms. First–year inmates study in a classroom. I share a desk with David Adams (not his real name). A prefect sits on guard at the front. David has a rocking knee over which he lacks control. He doesn't rock and roll like Veechy, but his right knee, leaning against the old desk already askew, makes writing difficult. Like riding a bucking horse, the desk and I are in a perpetual pig-root. David and I are reasonably good mates. He has come straight from school, a serious young man with blonde hair. Like me, David is in the choir and enjoys singing. In second year, we teamed together to do a rendition of *Bill Bailey* in a concert performed for staff and students.

Some few years after I left Springwood I called in to Manly to meet some of my old friends. I was invited to have a cup of tea. David arrived to have a drink and I welcomed him warmly. He looked at me and said, 'You're using my cup.' And that was all. He never said another word to me. The seminary did strange things to some people.

I resemble T. S. Eliot's J. Alfred Prufrock. I am torn in two. The prophet and the lover. The outer and inner man. The spoken and unspoken word. One identity displayed. Another hidden. Like Prufrock I have a question I dare not risk: 'Why am I here?' And another question: 'Why do I stay?' How easy it would be to disturb the universe and float them out on the mountain air. But how should I begin? To simply say, 'I'm leaving?' There is time, but not this time.

Like Prufrock I measure my days. Not with a coffee spoon, but at night I mark each day off with a cross. For what purpose? My vocation, my indecision, pin me to the wall.[93]

Red gravel roads radiate out from my window on the first floor of our accommodation block and disappear into the thin wilderness of the Australian bush. Nothing is flat, nothing even, everything ragged. This is hotch-potch country, untamed, arrogant, at odds with our seminary symmetry. Rocks and stones balance precariously on edge clinging to trees and undergrowth. We see lizards, who belong in ways we don't, rush for cover when they hear us coming. Escarpments rise above deep gorges and valleys. We are not the first to live here. This is Aboriginal land, ancient land, much older than Christendom. There is evidence here of the lives of Indigenous people. Eugene Stockton is a young priest on the staff. He goes out in his spare time looking for Aboriginal caves and art. On one occasion I fancy I've made a discovery of early Aboriginal art. I tell Eugene and he appears surprised. He'll check it out and get back to me. 'It was nothing,' he tells me later. Eugene comes from around here and is two years older than me and already has a doctorate. He becomes famous as an archaeologist and will later find artefacts thought to be 40,000 years old – the oldest human occupation in the Blue Mountains. When Eugene leaves for Rome midway in the year to continue his studies, he comes to the *rec* on a Saturday night to say farewell. He tells us that life and the priesthood are really about love. I raise it with Domine Donnelly, our brightest. 'That's what they all say when they drop their guard – or when they are leaving,' he assures me.

What is real? The seminary is a grand stage play featuring participants who dress up and play their roles. At times the make-up comes off and we experience the real. I want to believe Eugene, but my life here is more about obedience than love. On Wednesday evenings our spiritual director, Father Ted Shepherd, addresses us in the chapel. From the time I was a small boy I enjoyed being in church at night – the high roof-line of Saint Thomas's, the timber that curled up and met at its apex and disappeared in the dark, the flickering candle lights on the altar, the colour of the vestments of celebrant and altar boys, the rattle and swing of the thurible, the smell and smoke of incense, the voices from the choir in the loft. The warmth of it all with loved ones.

Ted enters from the side, genuflects and kneels to pray. He then moves to the chair and sits at a small wooden table inside the altar rails. The old hands sit down the back. Pre-philosophers and first-year philosophers up the front. We sit together in our tribes. Ted encourages us to love God. He is a good man. But I am unmoved. These are mere words. I feel no warmth. The seminary God is too abstract. Perhaps I am not the best to judge any of this. I feel so alienated that my thoughts are not to be trusted. What is real in this place is our presence. What is real is the felt fear authorities have of our relationships with each other. Their lack of trust. Love and friendship threaten the very essence of this place. Love demands freedom. Love is lived in the fullness of our lives. It is lived in the present. We are confined within the rules. If we reach out to others we break the rule. If we do not experience the love of friends in our lives, then we can never understand God's love for us.

One of my friends in first year is Domine Ian Fox. I meet Foxy after breakfast, before our class begins. We walk together, which is forbidden, but we meet coming out of the bush and there is no one else around. When we get closer to the main buildings we will join another group of walkers. Foxy is a member of our impromptu singing group, which meets in the ablution block in the evening before private study. Foxy is a delightful happy young man, fair-headed, stocky and short, who bounces along next to me like a young pup chasing a rubber ball. His dad has a dance band back in Sydney and they play on a Sydney radio on Sunday nights. Foxy has been brought up with a spring in his step and a song in his heart.

'Kev, what sort of a singer are you Kev, I mean, how would you describe your singing voice?'

He pants along beside me, barely able to contain himself.

To Foxy's dismay I take a long time to answer. I'm thinking of the time my Auntie Anne's husband, Albert, took me to a well-known singing teacher in Melbourne to see if I had a voice. I'm doing National Service training at the time and rigged out in slouch hat and khaki. Sitting at his grand piano is a distinguished grey-haired gentleman. On a desk nearby are photographs of some of his past successes. Patricia Kennedy, a famous Australian actress of stage and screen, smiles at me and I know I'm in the wrong place.

'Come soldier,' he demands, 'open your mouth wide and bring it up from down here, right down, not in your throat, but from your diaphragm.' He pats his diaphragm – low down.

'I'm a lyric baritone, Foxy.'

'A what, Kev, a what? A lyric what?'

'A lyric baritone, Foxy.'

'Shit, Kev. A lyric baritone. Impressive Kev, impressive.'

I can see Foxy is flummoxed.

'Well, what do you think I am, Foxy?'

'Well, Kev, I'd say you're a crooner, Kev, a crooner.'

'Like Bing Crosby?'

'That's it, Kev, that's it.' He's cruising now, back in rhythm. Is he thinking of his dad?

Foxy's dad is a crooner.

The bush surrounding us is like an old, old man, wizened and drawn. When I can, I join company with this old man, along one of these red gravel roads, but not looking for ancient signs like Eugene Stockton. I look for different, more recent signs. Clinging to the trees are the abandoned shells of cicadas. On the red ground black ants scurry in frantic busyness. If I walk far enough I can hear farm noises. I hear a man shout away in the distance and a dog barking. There is another world and I am comforted.

Chapter 4

Misogyny

Our Church is triumphant and patriarchal. In celebrating both we necessarily exclude women. We are encouraged in myriad ways to live without them. There are, however, nine women working here in the seminary. They are members of the Sisters of Our Lady Help of Christians. They wash, cook and clean for nearly 190 males. These women stand on the bottom step of the Church's hierarchical ladder. They dedicate their lives to care for us. Forbidden to converse with them, we never manage to meet with them, to thank them. They live in a convent at a respectable distance from the rest of us. One of the sisters drives a car and sometimes we meet her coming along the road up from the front gate. We all wave and to our great joy she waves back. That is the extent of our communication.

We were pampered little petals. For nearly three years in the seminary I never swept a floor, cooked a meal, washed my undies or ironed a shirt. Women's work. Would it have been any different if I were at home? I doubt it! My loving mother anticipated my every need. In general, life in the seminary was physically comfortable.

The Sisters of Our Lady Help of Christians recruited an attractive young woman into their ranks when I was there. Because of my age, I suspect I was chosen by the authorities to become the student liaison person between the nuns in the kitchen and the students. This involved my entering the kitchen and meeting the sister in charge. I could not help but notice a very beautiful young woman who kept to herself in the background. There was some talk amongst us. I was not the only one to catch an occasional glimpse of the new nun. I see her now. She is in the kitchen. Her back is to me. A blue veil drapes down her back. I discover she comes from near Warrnambool in the Western District, not far from Terang. One of our lecturers, Father Frank Mecham, has made a practice of visiting her family and giving them a report on her welfare. When this happens Frank invites me to his room at night and tells me he's driven through Terang. My heart pines for her and Terang. She comes from my country. I feel I know her. If she smiled at me would I reach out and grasp her hand?

On a glorious, nondescript afternoon our male world is suddenly disturbed. I'm painting a fence for Father Noel Carroll, our novice master, when Mary descends. Not the virginal Queen of Heaven variety, but Mary McMahon, radiating the female heat that drove mad the scholarly Saint Jerome (d.420 AD). Mary's dad, Tom, was the Terang station master and her mum, also Mary, produced this magnificent young woman who has somehow made her way to Springwood on a non-visiting day, conquered the six miles out of town to Saint Columba's, and then, once inside the heritage gates at the road, slipped through the defences to the front of the main building and entered the courtyard without being challenged. She is an apparition. She meets a student and asks demurely if she can see Kevin Peoples. I see her now in my dreams. Her short skirt is above her knees, her hair has streaks of grey, her eyes, always beautiful, have long eyelashes, and dark pencil shades highlight the blue.

Our leader, Monsignor Thomas McNiven Veech, Francophile and secret lover of Emma Bovary, is called to engage the enemy. A young woman has breached the wall and is in the courtyard, Monsignor, and asking if she may see Kev Peoples.

What I remember now is the miracle of her coming, her physical presence, her beautiful female presence. She was a few years younger than me; we had never been more than good friends and we had not met for some years. Over the years I dream about this day. I ask her to take me home with her and with a shy smile and a flicker of eyelashes she always answers, 'Of course.'

After she left, Monsignor Veech, red of face, huffing and puffing, reminded me that visitors were welcome on visiting days. She must not do this again. He could have turned her away. I have since learnt that Mary later followed her partner, named Kevin, to Macau where he tragically died in a mud slide. I have not seen her since that afternoon, but she lives on in my dreams. On that glorious afternoon she reminded me that life was worth living and why one day I would leave.

At Springwood when a disoriented tradesman happened to knock on the double doors at the end of the polished corridor near the statue of St Joseph, a fellow student who had grown mad with scrupulosity, answered the call and recited to the visitor the college rule as set out in the tiny, green book.

'The unauthorised intercourse of students with externs inside or outside the College, is forbidden' [Rule 16 (a)].

He told the bewildered man: 'Students are not permitted any intercourse with externs.'[94]

Faced with [Rule 16(a)], Mary would have smiled demurely and replied, 'Of course.'

In 1956, the Von Trapp Family singers had been invited by Cardinal Norman Gilroy to sing for the seminarians at our senior college in Manly. It was an embarrassing mistake. The rector, Monsignor Jimmy Madden, said no. No nubile women permitted on seminary soil. But it was too late. They were famous international visitors and the Cardinal had invited them. Their coming was said to have greatly upset the lads, some of whom left the seminary soon after the visit.

Then in 1958, Monsignor Joseph Cardijn, the international founder of the YCW Movement, arrived in Sydney accompanied by Miss Maria Meersman, Vice President of the International YCW, aged thirty-five. Following the Von Trapp visit, her presence was a further embarrassment for the seminary. Shivers went through the rector, Monsignor Jimmy Madden, and his staff. Father Kevin Toomey, the National Chaplain of the Australian YCW, was in the official party which met Cardijn and Meersman in the Manly grounds. Toomey had arranged for Australian young leaders of the YCW and the National Catholic Girls Movement to spend time with Cardijn and Meersman. Consequently, he had invited Betty King, the National Secretary of the Girls Movement, and two other young female leaders one of whom was Shirley Carroll, the Melbourne Secretary, and one other young leader from Brisbane. Toomey arrived at the door of the seminary with his young workers and was confident that Madden would be forced to admit all of them as members of the official party. He was wrong. Meersman could enter but the young women were singled out and refused permission. Their male counterparts from Victoria, Bill Armstrong, a Victorian Regional Staff member, and Jimmy Wilson, the National Secretary of the Australian YCW, were welcomed. The three young women were instructed to wait in the car park. At the end of proceedings lunch was served to the official party in the refectory. Maria Meersman was, however, refused permission to eat with the men. She was shown to the front door and eventually found the three young women in the car park. Shortly after, Monsignor John Leonard, the chaplain of the Sydney Archdiocesan Catholic Youth Organisation, came out and gallantly escorted the four females down into the centre of Manly for lunch.[95]

Sixty years on, Catholic women are still sitting in the car park. Some have given up and driven away, others are still there working for change while others are happily putting flowers on altars or on their knees praying for the Church to never accept gay marriage or women priests.

Misogyny and Catholicism are synonymous. Women, sex and sin have been an unholy trinity throughout the two millennia history of the Church. Not that the idea of misogyny came from Jesus or his group of married men.[96] Misogyny is all man-made and the traditional arguments for the exclusion of women from the priesthood and other positions of authority have no theological validity.[97] The scandal of sexual abuse by Catholic clergy fills the daily press and television screens. Misogyny was an integral part of my seminary culture and it is one necessary causal factor when considering the sexual abuse by Catholic clerics whose psychological and emotional development was often stunted and damaged in all-male seminary enclaves celebrating clericalism.

In 1994, Bishop Geoffrey Robinson from Sydney was appointed by the Australian bishops to a leadership role in responding to revelations of sexual abuse of clergy and religious brothers. For nearly twenty years Robinson has been intimately involved with this issue and during that time managed to offend those higher authorities who were ultimately responsible for protecting the good name of the single-sex Church. Robinson's argument is that 'the exclusion of women from all positions of influence in the Church has been a significant causal factor in sexual abuse...'.[98] In summarising the submissions received by the Royal Commission, Gail Furness, Senior Counsel Assisting, said that the lack of women in positions of leadership was identified by many as a relevant factor in the failure of the Church to act decisively against clerical sexual abuse.[99]

The exclusion of women in the Church has led to a cultural neurosis. It has fostered a warped environment in which abuse 'will more easily occur' or which 'can compound the problem by contributing to a poor response'[100] Robinson is not saying culture is all. He is far too knowledgeable, wise and cautious to claim too much. The causes of sexual abuse are multifaceted. Misogyny and celibacy go together. Just as misogyny is one causal, contributing element in a complex network of causes, so too is celibacy. There are some causal factors that are common to all offenders and others that are particular to each individual offender. But in between the two there is culture. Culture as a cause must not be dismissed. The cultural values that prospective priests imbibed in Catholic seminaries, especially those values relating to sex and sin, were for some of the ordained a potential danger to women and children.[101] The Catholic cocktail of a cultic priesthood, sacred and supreme, specially chosen by God, misogynist and celibate, was a mix beyond the control of too many men.

It is impossible to believe that any female bishop, or any woman assisting her bishop as a consultor, on hearing rumours, gossip or allegations of the raping of young children by priests, would have been strongly inclined to readily accept priestly denials. It is difficult to imagine a woman admitting in public that she was not particularly interested in the issue. The childless male leaders of the institution seriously misjudged the loyalty that Catholic parents have for their children. Women, in positions of authority, would not have made the same mistake.

Tom Keneally, Australian author, agrees with Bishop Robinson. Men without women become neurotic. Keneally is arguably Springwood's most famous student. In 1953, the boy from Homebush, winner of the Booker Prize for *Schindler's ark*, arrived in Springwood to study for the priesthood. Fifty years on, Robin Hughes interviewed Keneally for the *Australian Biography* project. The words spoken in the interview have been left in their original state. Some of the views below are also taken from the recent biography of Keneally by Stephany Evans Steggall (2015).

The rector of Springwood in Tom's time was Monsignor Charles Dunne, whom Geraghty labels a 'monster' and whom I name a sexual abuser of young girls. Unsurprisingly, Keneally's relationship with Dunne was not warm. He was, said Keneally, an 'emotional bully; a sour and unlikeable' man who, 'needed a wife to say, "Stop being a silly old bugger"'. While Dunne knew little about wives, and even less about marriage and love, that did not stop him from giving advice to his students. Drawing on his own twisted sexual morality, Dunne told the young men in his care that 'People only marry for lust'. He did not believe that the marriage bond could provide love or affection.[102]

Authority and obedience were big issues for Keneally. Absolute authority, exercised by men like Dunne, 'corrupted them'. Keneally, an anxious young man, found Springwood 'very hard' with a 'fascist' level of obedience. Authority, exercised by religious superiors like Dunne, hid behind the claim their voice was the voice of God.

Keneally told Hughes that Springwood was a closed community of males who regarded themselves as above those outside the seminary. Priests, specially chosen by God, have a calling above those in the wider community. The all-male caste led Keneally to believe that 'men who lived without women became pernickety in a particular neurotic and self-centred way…' Blowing of noses was out, along with books, newspapers and radios, and letters home must be left open. Bells must be rung without the bell slewing around inside the steel! Dunne became 'enraged' when bells were not rung properly.[103]

Mandatory celibacy was an issue for some students. During the fifties, tuberculosis was a health problem and x-rays were compulsory. Some of the young men fell instantly in love with the young nurses who came to Springwood and asked them sweetly to breathe in – hold it – and out. And out they went. According to Keneally, after these annual visits a few young men made their way down the long track to the heritage front gates and bolted back to Sydney.

Despite the demands of mandatory celibacy, the seminary system provided no coping strategies. While sex and sin dominated moral theology courses, the difficulties surrounding the celibate life of a priest were rarely if ever mentioned. Keneally now believes that the failure of seminaries to provide programs that educated and prepared young men for the challenges of the celibate life in parishes may well be linked to the sexual abuse scandal in the church. Keneally believes that isolating young men in seminaries was 'emotionally stunting'. The seminary, he told Steggall, 'was a good – or bad – breeding ground for paedophiles. Not that they [seminarians] would go there intending to become paedophiles.'[104]

But the general impression gained in reading Keneally's interview with Hughes is that mental health issues were equally as important as celibacy issues. A dramatic and passionate man, Keneally told Hughes that Springwood was 'a very Stalinist place' and dangerous to one's mental health. 'Crack-ups' or breakdowns affected both students and professors:

> ... when you have a lot of silence and a lot of obsessiveness and the boys who kept the rule best, the rules of silence, the young men who kept the rules of silence and the rules of everything best were most likely to um, crack up. And when they did they were looked upon as having somewhat failed and were sent into the community. And their parents were left to carry the bill ...

It wasn't only some students who cracked-up:

> ... one of the professors had a nervous crack-up in there. A very brilliant philosopher. A man who would have been an academic in the outside world. He had a doctorate from Leuven in Belgium. And um, we began to notice that he was, had lost it because he was looking at a picture of St Jerome in the hallway. And when we'd troop in there to breakfast, have breakfast in silence he'd be there. When we'd troop out he'd be there. When we went to class he'd still be there staring at minute details of this painting of St Jerome ... it was the early indications that there's something unnatural about an all-male cast[e].[105]

Keneally moved to Manly seminary after Springwood and left just before his ordination. Known as Mick in the seminary, he was an obsessive character and over-scrupulous; the emphasis on obedience caused him serious problems and in the end the seminary system caused him to 'crack-up'. After seven years he went back to Homebush feeling a failure. When he asked the rector of Manly, Monsignor Jimmy Madden, for a reference it was refused.

The problems he experienced in the seminary have made it difficult for him to remain a Catholic.

Misogyny developed very early in Christianity. The earliest example is the pastoral epistle, *1 Timothy*, written by an anonymous author sometime possibly between the end of the first century and the beginning of the second.[106] Misogyny in *Timothy* has its source in the mythical story of Eve in the Garden of Eden and the patriarchal society in which he wrote. By the end of the first century, women were subordinate to men in at least one community in the early Church:

> Let a woman learn in silence with full submission. I permit no woman to teach or to have authority to teach or to have authority over a man; she is to keep silent. For Adam was formed first, then Eve; and Adam was not deceived, but the woman was deceived and became a transgressor.[107]

Tertullian, one of the early Fathers, who died around the year 240, broadened Timothy's negative view of women; not only was a woman responsible for the origin of sin, but she was sin:

> You are the devil's gateway: you are the unsealer of that (forbidden) tree: you are the first deserter of the divine law: you are she who persuaded him whom the devil was not valiant enough to attack. You destroyed so easily God's image, man. On account of your desert – that is, death – even the Son of Man had to die.[108]

According to Augustine, Adam and Eve in the Garden of Eden, before the fall, were perfect. Following their fall, sin came into the world. Their sin was passed down to all future generations. How? Augustine argued that:

> every child born into the world has sin passed onto it by its copulating parents and is thus doomed to eternal damnation. Sex is the means whereby original sin is transmitted …[109]

Sex became unsavoury. Women were damned – a temptation and a distraction, a mere vehicle bringing sin into the world, and sex is forever associated with women and sin. To avoid female temptation, Origen, the first great Christian theologian, so feared his sexuality that he castrated himself in his desire to give himself wholly to God. That would have excluded him from our seminary!

Hatred of women in the early Church quickly centred on Augustine's theory of original sin. Augustine made women responsible for the fall and placed female subordination in creation *prior* to the fall: 'For we must believe that even before her sin woman had been made to be ruled by her husband and to be submissive and subject to him.'[110]

Embedded in Christian dogma from those early days, and persisting to this day, is the notion of male superiority and female inferiority. Augustine thought the 'body of a man is as superior to that of a woman as the soul is to the body'. John Chrysostom thought the female sex 'frail and frivolous'. Women were not only 'defective', their bodies were unclean. The biblical scholar, Jerome, wrote that:

> ... for our salvation the Son of God became the Son of Man. Nine months he awaited his birth in the womb, undergoing the most revolting conditions there, to come forth covered with blood.[111]

Jerome, who translated the Greek bible into Latin, lived for some time in the desert as a hermit. But he had problems concentrating on spiritual matters:

> I often found myself surrounded by bands of dancing girls. My face was pale with fasting; but though my limbs were cold as ice my mind was burning with desire and the fires of lust kept bubbling up before me when my flesh was as good as dead.[112]

Jerome was seriously disturbed. On one occasion a young woman sought advice from him on Christian virtue. Jerome replied thus:

> What will you do, a healthy young girl, dainty, plump, rosy, all afire amid the fleshpots, amid the wines and baths, side by side with married women and with young men? Even if you refuse to give what they ask for, you may think that the asking is evidence of your beauty. A libertine is all the more ardent when he is pursuing virtue and thinks that the unlawful is especially delightful. Your very robe, coarse and sombre though it be, betrays your unexpressed desires if it be without crease, if it be trailed upon the ground to make you seem taller, if your vest be slit on purpose to let something be seen within, hiding that which is unsightly and disclosing that which is fair. As you walk along your shiny

black shoes by their creaking give an invitation to young men. Your breasts are confined in strips of linen, and your chest is imprisoned by a tight girdle. Your hair comes down over your forehead or over your ears. Your shawl sometimes drops, so as to leave your white shoulders bare, and then, as though unwilling to be seen, it hastily hides what it unintentionally revealed. And when in public it hides the face in a pretence of modesty, with a harlot's skill it shows only those features which give men when shown more pleasure.[113]

I fancy, having written his letter, Saint Jerome left his room and took a very cold bath.

The early Fathers of the Church contrasted the fallen Eve with the ethereal glories of Mary. As Eve descended, Mary ascended. The Fathers isolated the 'culprit responsible for humanity's aggravated sexuality, and with collective venom, they pinned the blame on Eve'.[114] Insofar as the Fathers were concerned, women brought sin into the world.

Men were identified with spirituality and goodness, and women were linked with carnality and evil. Women were as big a problem in the fourth century as they were to us seminarians in the twentieth century.

Regarding the status of women Thomas, the Angelic Doctor, writing in the thirteenth century, was little better than Clement of Alexandria, Tertullian, Origen, Augustine, Jerome and John Chrysostom. According to Thomas:

> Only as regards nature in the individual is the female something defective and manqué. For the active power in the seed of the male tends to produce something like itself perfect in masculinity; but the procreation of the female is the result either of the debility of the active power, of some unsuitability of material, or of some change effected by external influences, like the south wind for example, which is damp, as we are told by Aristotle.[115]

Damp or not, whatever way the wind blew, women were a problem for the Church and so was sex. The early medieval Church did its best to enforce total abstinence on married couples. Sex was forbidden while a woman was pregnant (with no contraception, this was much of the time), menstruating or breastfeeding; it was forbidden during Lent and Advent, on Ember days and also on Sundays, Wednesdays and Fridays. It was forbidden before communion. This left a small window of opportunity for the faithful 'which did not fall into any of these forbidden periods'.[116]

The early Fathers of the Church were products of their time and place. The views of pagans, Greeks, Romans and the Jewish authors of the Hebrew Bible provided the cultural backdrop for the extreme views of these early Christians. The stand-out exception was Jesus. In his teaching and actions, Jesus rejected the patriarchal culture of his time.[117] Plato and Aristotle thought that the 'power of sexual passion ... distracted men from reason and the search for knowledge'. Aristotle went so far as to describe a woman 'as a mutilated male'.[118] Jewish women were forbidden to enter into particular areas of the Temple in Jerusalem that were available only to men. There are frequent references in the Hebrew bible to women as 'unclean'. And the Romans had no concept of equality between the sexes.

The long history of antipathy to women and the supremacy of celibacy has led to the relative devaluation of the family and marriage as a vocation. In the early centuries of the Church, clerics quickly developed liturgical ceremonies for most of the sacraments, but not marriage. Couples, if they bothered, were married in the presence of a witness not necessarily a priest. Marriage was a mutual and private affair, essentially secular. Priests were not needed as witnesses. This system, known as spousals, endured well into the eighteenth century. If a marriage did take place at a church it was normally enacted in the porch. Karen Armstrong, a recognised scholar in such matters, contends that until the Reformation 'it was thought holier to be celibate and marriage was not considered a valuable Christian vocation'.

Marriage was not officially recognised as one of the seven sacraments until the thirteenth century. The question is this: if marriage didn't involve sex and reproduction would the Church be interested? As an institution, marriage is always evolving, and marrying for love is a very modern idea. Politics and class have degraded and determined the nature of marriage for much of its western history. Women were expendable and used to extend power, gain property and stabilise dynastic arrangements. As a valued institution, marriage and the family are very new in Western society.[119]

The Council of Trent in the second half of the sixteenth century summed up the relative merits of marriage and celibacy, and the previous fifteen hundred years of Church history in one of its Canons:

> If anyone says that the married state excels the state of virginity or celibacy, and that it is better and happier to be united in matrimony than to remain in virginity or celibacy let him be anathema.[120]

This anachronistic view was still being taught to student moral theologians four hundred years later! Life-long virginity had a 'special aureole'. Marriage was instituted by God for the 'allaying of concupiscence as for the procreation of children, but the state of virginity is the higher and nobler state and absolutely more pleasing to God.'[121] Throughout the history of the Church, marriage as an institution was tarnished by its poisonous link with women and sex. Insofar as the magisterium was concerned, marriage was acceptable only if its primary aim was the procreation of children. Despite the welcome addition of 'conjugal love', this same view was endorsed by the Council Fathers at the Second Vatican Council:

> By their very nature, the institution of matrimony itself and conjugal love are ordained for the procreation and education of children, and find in them their ultimate crown.[122]

No-one should be surprised that such views would emerge from a Council composed solely of celibate males, and with a long history of misogyny and an antipathy to marriage. Despite its hypocritical support for marriage in the current debate about gay marriage, the institutional Church has been, from earliest times, a half-hearted supporter of marriage between a man and a woman. Its continued support for the supremacy of celibacy as the nobler state, and for an all-male priesthood is a visible and dramatic reflection of its misogyny and clericalism.

The Church's misogynist views expressed in this chapter are shocking and have no place in a modern church. They are, in part, responsible for the sexual abuse scandal. In Australia, 95% of alleged perpetrators were men.[123]

In the United States, prior to the Second Vatican Council, some 70% of those priests against whom allegations of sexual abuse were made were trained in misogynist seminaries like mine.[124] For young men, cut off from the wider society and the company of women, the misogynist views of the Church were designed and destined to create a psychologically unhealthy environment. Little wonder then that young men, some of whom had entered the seminary as young as 13 or 14, entered parish life psychosexually immature. The Church had denied them their right to develop socially and psychologically.

The final word on misogyny and original sin should be made by Tatha Wiley, a female theologian. Wiley has argued that male theologians have:

> used the doctrine of original sin to denigrate women, blame them for evil, and prohibit them from full participation in the life of the church. By deeming female subordination a divine punishment, instead of exposing it as human bias, the doctrine reinforced a cultural ideology of male superiority.[125]

Chapter 5

Catholic Philosophy

At Springwood, we were students of philosophy, but there was a problem. Holy Mother Church was at odds with modern philosophical ideas. We were to be taught Catholic Philosophy, which looks like and is an oxymoron.

The impetus to teach Catholic Philosophy came in 1879, when Pope Leo XIII (d.1903) wrote his encyclical *Aeterni Patris* or *On the restoration of Christian philosophy*. It was the pope's third encyclical following *On the evils of society and on socialism*, written in the first year of his papacy. Leo was an aristocrat and shared with his class a hatred and fear of Liberalism and Socialism. The pattern of his early encyclicals highlights the Church's and Leo's alienation from the world outside the Vatican. Leo colluded with ultra-conservatives in the Vatican, against the better judgement of some Italian bishops, to use diplomatic pressure to bring down the new State of Italy. Leo's constant threats to leave the Vatican kept the states of Europe, especially those with significant Catholic populations, on a knife edge. Leo, however, did not move outside the Vatican walls for twenty-five years. He was a better pope than his predecessor, Pius IX, whose sanity at times was doubtful, and better than the pious saint who followed him, Pius X, but he is, nevertheless, grossly overrated.[126]

Leo's encyclical was attempting to hold back the tide of modern thinking and science, which had begun three hundred years earlier with Copernicus, Galileo and Descartes. For Leo it was all a question of truth. The Church not only possessed the truth but was the truth, and Leo, in a long line of popes, was defending it and its thinking.

The situation for the papacy was exacerbated in the nineteenth century by the ideas of the Enlightenment, which had led to the French Revolution in the late eighteenth century and the growth of Nationalism in Italy. For the men of science and the Enlightenment it came down to a critical issue – the separation of Church and State. The same men believed in freedom of speech and freedom of religion. For the popes these were the modern evils.

In 1870, Leo's predecessor, Pius IX (d.1878), had been forced to flee his palace as the forces of Liberalism and Nationalism stormed Rome and set up the unified state of Italy. After the creation of this new state, the popes became prisoners in the Vatican by locking themselves in. To save the Church from what he saw as the modern evils, Leo XIII returned to the thinking of Saint Thomas Aquinas (d.1274). These world events, which had imploded around the papacy, were, in part, directly related to why we were cut off from the world and stranded on the foothills of the Blue Mountains, and why the Church in her wisdom insisted we learn her philosophy as a weapon against modern philosophy. The Church was at war with the modern world and I was learning to be a foot soldier.

At Springwood, Thomas Aquinas was my favourite philosopher. He came from an aristocratic family, the son of Count Landulf of Aquino near the monastery of Monte Cassino. Thomas was the youngest of seven brothers, who were all disturbed when Thomas chose a mendicant order to join, namely the Dominicans. The family argued that if Thomas was to be a monk he should be a proper monk in a proper abbey, i.e. with the Benedictines, where he could at least become the Abbott of a monastery. The Dominicans decided to move Thomas, an extraordinarily silent young man, out of Italy and settle him in Paris away from his intervening family. Along the way to Paris he was kidnapped by a group of men, including at least two of his brothers. He was imprisoned in a castle and instructed to change his mind. Thomas, however, just sat and thought until his brothers unleashed an unholy weapon, by way of a painted courtesan, who would, they supposed, take his mind off thinking and onto more pressing matters. Thomas was furious. Moving with uncharacteristic energy, he grabbed a red hot branding iron from the fire and charged at the screaming woman who fortunately managed to get out the door just before Thomas rammed the burning brand into it.[127]

It took centuries for Thomas's work to become Thomism. Initial reaction by some Church authorities to his work was cautious, even negative. There was anxiety about linking the works of Aristotle with Christian theology and philosophy. For some centuries his work faded into insignificance, especially between the fifteenth and the seventeenth century, when the term *Scholastic*, referring to the earlier school of thought, became a term of abuse.

But Thomas was brave and positive. He was an innovator, a synthesiser, a scholar who took in ideas from near and far, from centuries past and from the twelfth-century renaissance. And he made them new. Thomas's God was not the narrow, sectarian God I met at Springwood. He was a very big God, *being* itself. Every living thing, everything in nature participated in this ground of *being* from where it obtained its existence and its essence. Thomas, working away in his medieval monastery, saw a world which was God-filled. For him, theology and philosophy were one. God was not the static and distant unmoved mover of Aristotle, but a dynamic, vital creator who lived on in his creation, which was continuous. God is *being*. God does not *have* existence as we do. He *is* existence. But Thomas was no pantheist. We are parts of a bigger whole.

When Thomas looked at nature outside the window in his cloister he saw God. Thomas took Plato's Forms out of their ethereal and eternal environment and gave them to his creator – the God who had embedded them in all created things. What every particular thing was, whether it was a person, a cow or a dog or a tree, it received its *whatness*, its essence, from God. And the same was true for its existence. Everything, through its essence and existence, was intimately connected to everything else and to its creator.

But in our bush home, we were adrift from the world. We had stopped looking, stopped seeing. We had now a ladder of being, and at the top looking down were the pope and his cultic priests.

Because of the intimate connections of all things, Thomas declared a new basis for the dignity and potential of man. Within human nature lay the potential for actively moving towards perfect communion with God, who was the source of all development toward perfection in nature. For Thomas, in loving one another and the natural world, we were drawn towards a loving God. Ah Thomas. What would you make of us?

The first great thinker to seriously challenge the Church's medieval paradigm of philosophy was Rene Descartes (d.1650), French philosopher, Catholic, mathematician and physicist. Before Descartes, the Church virtually owned

Western philosophy. This was hardly surprising as philosophical thinking in the West developed within the religious orders in the early Middle Ages and culminated in the significant achievement of Thomas Aquinas in the thirteenth century. Aquinas drew on the Greek philosopher, Aristotle, and his Arabic interpreters. He set out to reconcile Aristotle's metaphysics with his Christian faith. In the process he synthesised faith and reason. What was required, he argued, was balance – a central idea in all Aquinas's thinking – the truth, he said, stands in the middle. Too much reliance on faith could lead to irrationalism. Too much reliance on reason could lead to scepticism.

By the time of Descartes in the seventeenth century, Aquinas's achievement was a distant memory. The philosophy enunciated by religious scholars, such as Abelard and Anselm in the eleventh century, and John Duns Scotus and William of Ockham, two Franciscans in the fourteenth century, led to the school of Scholasticism. This was the philosophical title given to the philosophy and theology dominated by Thomas in the thirteenth century.

But by the time of Descartes in the seventeenth century, Scholasticism was fragmented, buried in legalism and mental abstractions, and lost in a world of its own. It was a period of decay and the Scholastics lost their philosophical credibility. In the transition to a new modern world a vacuum developed, and there was a real question as to whether truth itself was any longer possible. In this context, Descartes set himself the task of identifying knowledge that provided absolute certainty.

Descartes' contribution to both philosophy and science was considerable, but of significance for the Church was the importance he gave to reason, at the expense of faith, and the way he dismissed Scholasticism. Descartes began modern philosophy, broke the dominant clerical link between the Church and philosophy, and destroyed the unity between faith and reason developed by Thomas. Descartes gave God a role but it was equivalent to moving furniture back stage. Descartes began the process of moving from a God-centred world to a human-centred world.

The first thing Descartes did was to place human reason at the centre of his philosophical thinking. Descartes:

> ... enthroned human reason as the supreme authority in matters of knowledge, capable of distinguishing certain metaphysical truth

and of achieving certain scientific understanding of the material world. Infallibility, once ascribed only to Holy Scripture or the supreme pontiff, was now transferred to human reason itself.[128]

Next, Descartes posed a serious problem for the Church in the way he went about philosophy. His approach was distinctly original. Ignoring the Church and the various forms of Scholasticism, Descartes began a new paradigm. He decided to think for himself, always a threat to the papacy, and his first step was to doubt everything. He concluded that the only thing he could not doubt was his doubting. Everything else could be questioned. This led him to postulate his famous, *Cogito ergo sum*, i.e. 'I think therefore I am'. It didn't sound much but it changed the world and terrified the prelates in Rome, who spoke on behalf of God and who appeared to be left out of the equation. But Descartes was no sceptic. His method was indeed sceptical, but his belief in rational thinking, based on the method of mathematics, led him to argue that a disciplined and critical rationality could overcome the untrustworthiness of information about the world given by the senses and the imagination.

Descartes was also a believer. The existence of God was important for him. God became the guarantor of certain knowledge. Truth was possible because God existed. Descartes's God was a good God and His goodness, said Descartes, was the guarantee that man's cognitive powers, used responsibly, would lead to truth. Descartes's philosophical approach upset the Church then on five main counts: his rejection of Scholasticism, his sceptical method, his emphasis on human reason and on the individual, and the importance he placed on experience.

At the beginning of the twentieth century both Leo XIII and Pius X believed that a radical scepticism had replaced the apparent certainties of Aquinas's philosophy. Following Descartes, later thinkers threw Thomas's God-filled world out the window – they couldn't find the *essence* of anything anywhere. The result was that modern philosophy was no longer God-centred. In particular, David Hume, the eighteenth-century British philosopher, and Immanuel Kant destroyed Thomas's metaphysical philosophy, based on their insight into an individual's capacity to understand a world owing its existence to God and even to understand the world in itself.

Knowledge of the world around us became dependent on experience. Thus there was no room left to discover the truth about issues relating to God or the immortality of the soul. According to Kant, 'any metaphysical conclusions concerning the nature of the universe that went beyond his experience were unfounded'. Faith and reason were thereafter divided. Thomism was split asunder. In the division, religion gained faith and philosophy and science gained reason.

But Kant's scepticism went further. While he insisted that humans had access to a certain form of knowledge – namely scientific knowledge – this came at a cost. Humans could never know nature in itself, which was a feature of Thomism. Thomas taught that God had ordered the natural world. But Kant tipped that idea on its head – human beings, he argued, ordered the world. Understanding the world for Kant came from within the mind, which was structured in such a way as to gain certain knowledge.

Philosophy and science were thus ignoring the Church, which had not moved since the Council of Trent in 1563. All of this was extremely disturbing for the papacy, the upholders of the truth, and in particular the Thomistic truth that stated there was a certain correspondence between mind and world.

In response to the challenge, the Church and the modern world faced off and, incredibly, Thomas from the thirteenth century was wheeled in to save the modern Church, not merely from modern errors, but to save the Church at a profoundly fundamental level. It was an extraordinary retreat into the past. But was it the real Thomas? Or was it the Vatican's view of Thomas?

Descartes had begun the process of separating faith and reason. The popes from the time of Descartes watched on as the philosophical thinking of the Church slipped into oblivion. Pope Leo XIII took up the good fight on behalf of reason, not because the Church valued reason per se, but because reason could lead people to God through argument and observation. Philosophy was, therefore, important to the Church, not because of any inherent value it possessed, but because of its importance for theology.

In his encyclical, *Aeterni Patris*, Leo taught that philosophy 'tends to smooth and fortify the road to faith'. The purpose of philosophy was to protect Catholics from error, from 'false conclusions and false opinions'. Leo urged

Catholics to take up that study of philosophy, 'which shall respond most fitly to the excellence of faith, and at the same time be consonant with the dignity of human science'.[129]

None of this reached down to Saint Thomas's parish in Terang where we stuck rigidly to the basics as outlined in the catechism with its question and answer form. I don't have a copy of the catechism in front of me, but from memory it went something like this:

> Question: Who made the world?
> *Answer:* God made the world.
> Question: Why did God make the world?
> *Answer:* *God made the world so that we could know Him, love Him and serve Him, here on earth and be happy with Him for ever in Heaven.*

Much of Pope Leo's *Aeterni Patris* celebrated that 'precious fountainhead', that 'chief and master of all', that Angelic Doctor, Saint Thomas Aquinas himself. Leo called on the Church to spread far and wide the principles of Thomas and in particular he called for select teachers to implant the doctrines of Thomas into the minds of all students. This leads us to the Blue Mountains in 1964 and the little rule book we were instructed to follow:

> The philosophy course will comprise: Logic, Metaphysics, Ethics and the History of Philosophy: at least the principles and elements of the physical sciences shall also be studied, so that the future clerics will be prepared to detect the pernicious errors that are commonly mixed with these sciences. [Rule (26) b]

> Studies in rational philosophy and theology and the student's formation therein shall follow the method, doctrine and principles of the Angelic Doctor, to which the Professors must religiously adhere. [Rule (28) a][130]

Here is the great irony. As students of Thomas at Springwood, we were not simply hiding from the world, we were led to believe that the world and everything in it was a threat to our vocation and our holiness. Our very isolation was to protect us from the world. But Thomas gave to humans and to the natural world a value. Man was not simply filling in time looking

82 Trapped in a closed world

towards his future home in Heaven. There was value in the here and now:

> For Aquinas, the natural world was not just an opaque material stage upon which man briefly resided as a foreigner to work out his spiritual destiny. Nor was nature governed by principles alien to spiritual concerns. Rather, nature and spirit were intimately bound up with each other, and the history of one touched the history of the other.[131]

In his studies, Thomas had explored the writings of pagans and heretics. Thomas gave medieval Christendom a rational and coherent world view. Nothing would have changed if he had reappeared miraculously in the twentieth century.

At Springwood, I am taught the Vatican view of Thomas. It is not the real Thomas, but at the time I had no idea that was the case. What we had was more ideology than philosophy. In 1919, Etienne Gilson, French philosopher and expert on Thomism, travelled to Russia after the Bolshevik revolution. This is what he wrote:

> When I went to Russia in 1919, the St. Thomas of the place was called Karl Marx ... I am sometimes frightened to think that certain people think that the situation of Thomism in the Church is analogous to that of Marxism in communist countries. If this were so, it would be really terrible and intolerable to me; but isn't it really so?[132]

Marie-Dominique Chenu (d.1990), Dominican priest, Professor of History at Le Saulchoir, Belgium, and teacher of two of the greatest Catholic theologians of the twentieth century, Yves Congar and Edward Schillebeeckx, was a critic of the Vatican's version of Thomas. In the 1930s, Chenu researched Thomas within his thirteenth-century setting – historical, social, political, cultural and religious. Chenu learnt that Thomas's achievements were a development of the twelfth-century renaissance. Thomas engaged 'seriously and critically' with the newly-translated works of Aristotle. He drew on the spiritual strength and inspiration from grass-root developments in the life of the Church, in particular the evangelical movements of the new Mendicant Orders. Chenu extolled Thomas's courage in addressing the intellectual challenges of his day and the respect he had for the autonomy of the other sciences.

What Chenu found in the Vatican's twentieth-century version of Thomas was the opposite. The 'vital creativity' of Thomas was lost: 'What was passing for Thomist philosophy and theology had very little in common with the method, inspiration, and thought of Aquinas himself.'[133]

In 1937, the bureaucrats in the Vatican come after Chenu. In 1914, Vatican bureaucrats had reduced Aquinas's writings to twenty-four theses.[134] Pope Benedict XV in his new *Code of Canon Law*, promulgated in 1917, included the philosophy of Thomas in the code. Thus, by a law inscribed in the very Code of the decrees of the Church, teachers in Catholic institutions were ordered:

> ... to treat in every particular the studies of rational philosophy and theology, and the formation of students in these sciences, according to the method, the doctrine, and the principles of the Angelic Doctor, and to adhere religiously to them.[135]

The Curia have the law on their side. They fear the world, fear freedom of choice and fear deviation from their truth. They don't go for their deviants with ice-picks, like the sort that killed Trotsky, but they have ways and means.

The bureaucrats in the Vatican deny Thomas his greatest achievement – his unification of reason and faith, i.e. of Aristotelian philosophy and Christian theology. The Curia do not understand that reason works in an ever-evolving world. That it builds on knowledge that builds on previous knowledge. They replace reason with authority, laws and sanctions. They have the power to destroy people and careers. Chenu has broken ranks and must recant. He is called to Rome to answer their questions.

The Vatican has its once-and-for-all theology and philosophy. It is written in Roman concrete. Thomism has been atrophied. But not Chenu. He wrote that:

> [a] theology that believes it possible to present the word of God in unhistorical and authoritarian formulae is a theology that has forgotten the transcendence of God's word.

Chenu argued that 'being present to revelation in the life of the Church today and in the current experience of Christianity' is the future for the Church. The dear man explained to the bureaucrats the notion of 'holy curiosity', the importance of popular culture and cultural pluralism. He told his inquisitors that theology is an expression of a spirituality, a way of life, and that life is dynamic and any theology, even Thomism, fails when it becomes an orthodoxy.[136] But the Vatican officials are dismayed. They are guardians of the depository of faith. They hold the truth. There can be no such flexibility. To change would imply a previous error. Chenu's prophetic message was lost on them.

Dostoevsky has a relevant tale in *The Brothers Karamazov*. Chenu, like Christ, believed in man's freedom to think and choose. Dostoevsky, too, believed in freedom, for without freedom there can be no love. Dostoevsky says that Christ had a simple and profound message to make man free. Christ wanted people to choose to love him. But the Church won't have it. Humans cannot cope with such freedom. The Church must correct Christ's mistake. The Church gives security and certainty. Sinful men, incapable of following Jesus, prefer the Church with its miracles, mysteries and authority.

Dostoevsky's Grand Inquisitor tells the imprisoned Jesus that his message of love and freedom cannot work:

> You desired the free love of man, that he should follow you fully, seduced and captivated by you. Instead of the firm ancient law, man had henceforth to decide for himself, with a free heart, what is good and evil, having only your image before him as a guide – but did it not occur to you that he would eventually reject and dispute even your image and your truth if he was oppressed by so terrible a burden as freedom of choice.[137]

The Vatican inquisitors listen to Chenu and then present him with a handwritten text of ten propositions. The paper has no heading and no signature. Chenu is asked to sign his agreement. It is repeated here in full for it is not widely publicised and it demonstrates clearly the thinking of the Church I grew up in.

The propositions are:

Dogmatic formulas state absolute and immutable truth.

True and certain propositions, whether in philosophy or in theology, are firm and not at all fragile.

Sacred tradition does not create new truths; one must instead maintain that the deposit of revelation that is, the complex of divinely revealed truths, was closed at the death of the last apostle.

Sacred theology is not some spirituality which has found instruments adequate to its religious experience; it is rather a true science, by God's blessing acquired through study, whose principles are the articles of faith as well as all the revealed truths to which the theologian adheres by at least unformed divine faith.

The various theological systems are not simultaneously true, at least with regard to points on which they disagree.

It is a glorious thing that the Church considers the system of St. Thomas to be quite orthodox, that is, quite in conformity with the truths of the faith.

It is necessary to demonstrate theological truths by Sacred Scripture and Tradition and to explain their nature and intimate meaning by the principles and doctrine of St. Thomas.

Although properly a theologian, St. Thomas was also properly a philosopher; for that reason his philosophy does not depend for its intelligibility and truth on his theology, and it states truths that are absolute and not merely relative.

It is quite necessary for a theologian in his scientific work to make use of the metaphysics of St. Thomas and diligently to follow the rules of dialectics.

In speaking about other writers and doctors one should use respectful moderation in one's style of speech and writing, even when they are found to be defective on some matters.[138]

86 Trapped in a closed world

Only the last is acceptable, but Chenu, broken, unable to kiss his inquisitor on the lips, as Jesus did in the Dostoevsky story, and walk free, signs his agreement to all the above. His book is placed on the index in 1942. His Dominican Order finds him an embarrassment. They banish him to Rouen in 1954, where he lives in a convent and his licence to teach is suspended.[139] He is allowed to visit Paris – once a year, to meet his friends.

Chenu's trial before the Vatican inquisitors explains what happens to troublemakers when they take on the Church. It helps to explains how both staff and students at Springwood are locked into such a repressive system prior to the Second Vatican Council.

But the Curia's success is short-lived. Thomism is on the way out. The Second Vatican Council will seriously challenge the hegemony of Thomas. While we are locked away safely in the Australian bush, unbeknown to us there are serious arguments going on at the Second Vatican Council in Rome about Thomas and the sort of training we should be receiving. The bureaucrats in the Roman Curia write their preparatory documents for the Council as if Leo XIII were still pope and they were still in control.

Unfortunately for the Curia, the members of the Central Commission, a superior body appointed to oversee the production of documents for the Council, do not like what they read. There are criticisms that Thomas's great work, which became Thomism, and then Neo-Thomism, had fragmented. Which Thomism was the document referring to? And why was Thomas favoured over other great doctors and theologians? And how would this document be received by oriental Catholics, the Orthodox, Protestants, Africans and Asians?

A rewrite is required but even then, once proceedings officially start, the Fathers take umbrage from the floor of the Council. Thomas's philosophy, or more rightly, the Vatican version of Thomas, which Leo and the popes in the first half of the twentieth century thought would save the Church, takes a battering, so much so that one commentator writing some years later will conclude that 'the history of the modern Neo-Thomist movement, whose *magna charta* was *Aeterni Patris,* reached its end at the Second Vatican Council'.[140]

In our ground-floor classroom looking out into the cloisters, Walshy takes us through Aquinas's five proofs for the existence of God. I am left dumbfounded. My religion is as natural to me as the air I breathe. The attempt to intellectualise the existence of God appears to have nothing to do with faith. I can't make head or tail of them. Even Walshy seems coolly detached. God has nothing to do with proofs. I am drawn to Thomas, but there wouldn't be a believer left in Terang if the locals were depending on him for their faith. My God is not this scholastic *First Cause*; he's a fellow called Jesus who lived in Nazareth, Palestine, two thousand years ago. I talk to him all the time and we get along well, although my presence here is a problem, but I'm hopeful he'll rescue me. Domine Donnelly tells anyone who listens that you can't prove the existence of God and I'm happy with that.

At some time in the second half of my first year I forget to mark off each day on the calendar. I go for a week and then mark off seven. My clothes begin to fit. The collar keeps me warm. I argue with myself: Will I go? Will I stay? I stay because it seems the right thing to do. If I stay long enough I will grow into the idea of priesthood. If I keep thinking about it I will leave. If I stop thinking about it I will stay. It appears I'm staying. I'm adaptable.

Chapter 6

Teaching and learning

Saint Columba's seminary was a philosophical college in name only. Philosophy, as a search for open-ended truth, was not taken seriously. We had the truth. The purpose of our philosophical studies was to demonstrate how reason can give a rational basis for our faith, and at the same time demonstrate how all other philosophies, while containing some truths, were essentially wrong. Thomism, as interpreted by our lecturers, was the handmaiden of Catholic theology. We were groomed to be gentlemen with a smattering of knowledge as thin as the butter we spread on our stale bread.

In the second half of the year, our history of philosophy teacher is Father Frank Mecham, STL, MA. Frank has arrived from our senior college at Manly. He demonstrates the relative importance of philosophy by combining his philosophy classes with the teaching of Latin. Each class begins with a *repetitio*, which means we repeat the essential points of the previous class in Latin. This is how it works. Frank nominates a student, 'Domine Peoples', who struggles to his feet with pounding heart to carry on a conversation with Frank in a foreign language. We will discuss last week's lesson. Frank is kind to me. He knows I struggle. When the conversation falters, Frank will direct questions more widely. 'Domine Donnelly' saves me from further embarrassment. My Latin is poor and I dread these classes. Frank is slim, serious and I fancy, erudite; a man of steel with steel grey hair and steel rimless classes. I am anxious as is every student in the class. Who will Frank ask? Every night I spend most of my study time going over notes from Frank's previous class and transposing them into Latin. Half the class is *repetitio* time and the other half is Frank introducing us to a different philosopher every week.

Thank God, the second half of the class is in English, but because most of us have no background in philosophy there is no context that might lead to understanding. I am unable to even imagine a question because I am lost in a strange world of concepts that I cannot ground and make mine.

Frank Mecham was a serious lecturer and well prepared. I always thought of him as scholarly in the classical sense. Frank replaced Father John Walsh, also a scholarly and well prepared lecturer, who introduced me to the Presocratic philosophers in my first weeks in the seminary. I remember Frank telling us once that on one of his holidays in Greece he tried out his classical Greek with a waiter in a restaurant. To his dismay the young Greek man had no idea what Frank was saying.

Veechy was a unique lecturer. The vast majority of our lecturers were sane, but Veechy was one of three eccentrics on the staff. His idiosyncratic teaching method was to tell stories. He wasn't the first to do that, and the Gospels are filled with parables. Of all my lecturers, it was Veechy who accompanied me when I left in 1966, and the one who taught me more about teaching history than anyone else. I cannot write about him without dramatising the scene.

He bursts into our classroom, as if running late to catch a train. Black soutane flying, grey hair immaculate, face red, he heads for the security of the podium. No book or paper in sight. Purposeful and serious; he looks through us, gives himself a wriggle and becomes someone else – Pavarotti – except he doesn't sing. Then he relaxes and seems to smile at someone away in the distance. At first he says nothing. I wait for him to speak. Huffing and puffing he builds up steam and suddenly the quiet, uncertain voice stutters into being. We're away. This is the highlight of my week.

Last week he paraded two Russian poets – Pushkin and Lermontov. One day, when I am back in the world, I will read *Eugene Onegin* and *A hero of our time*. Hopefully today he will tell us two stories. He dispenses with background, dates and other incidentals. He brings alive real people, who sit beside him and discuss what it is to be human.

But what will it be today? From my little knowledge of Russian history gained at Chevalier College and Veechy's cultural history over the past few weeks, I am overwhelmed by the poverty, sadness and tragedy of the Russian people. Anything is better than the House of Romanov.

He purses his lips, then with a shake: 'Ah Gentlemen. Dostoevsky. Fyodor Dostoevsky'. Dostoevsky has been arrested. He has joined a group of intellectuals, mainly utopian socialists, democrats and republicans. They meet on Friday nights and discuss, not revolution, but visions for a better Russia free of serfdom, censorship and autocracy.

Dostoevsky then spends months in solitary confinement. He is twenty-eight years old. Some of my class mates know this story, but not me. Veechy, the old actor, knows every line, every word. As usual, I am captivated.

After eight months, the prisoners are taken out of solitary and placed in horse-drawn carriages. It is snowing. The celebration of the Christ child's birth is three days away. The men have no idea what is going on. No charges have been laid and no sentences given. No one suspects they are about to be shot. On meeting each other, the men hug. Dostoevsky, looking to the sky, gives praise to the rising sun. It is early morning and soldiers surround the fifteen men and the carriages.

After thirty minutes, they arrive at the city square where there is a tall platform and next to the platform are three stakes in the ground. The men mount the platform where they are met by a priest holding up a crucifix. Dostoevsky is excited, edgy, unable to understand what is happening. In the distance he sees groups of early morning risers standing in the snow, watching, waiting. Up on the platform, an official comes along the line of men reading from a page. Standing before each one, he reads out their sentence: 'The Court has found you guilty and condemns you to death by firing squad.' Jesus, Mary and Joseph.

Another official comes along the line handing out white shrouds and nightcaps. The priest then, holding up the cross, calls out to the men: 'Brothers, before dying you must repent … the Saviour forgives those who repent. I call on you to repent.' The priest waits for a confession. Silence. The priest then moves along the men holding up the cross to their lips. Even those who are atheists kiss it. Dostoevsky says to one of the atheists: 'We shall be with Christ.' His comrade replies bitterly, 'A bit of dust.'

The first three men are bound and taken to the stakes. Their nightcaps cover their heads, but their leader, one Petrashevsky, rejects it and stares at the soldiers lined in front with rifles ready. Dostoevsky is one of the next three. The men wait for the direction to fire. They wait a minute. Nothing.

Then there is the roll of drums and the soldiers retreat. The three men are released from the stake. One man is distraught, broken, and is never the same again. One of the Tsar's men has arrived galloping on a horse, with a message from Nicholas I. The Tsar has mercifully saved their lives. God bless the Tsar. The whole was deliberately staged by the Tsar as a warning. Dostoevsky is sent to Siberia for four years. After that he will join the army for an extended time to be determined. He, too, will never be the same.[141] And neither will I.

Veechy's second story today is about a Russian author named Lev Tolstoy. The atmosphere changes. He shakes his head as if some great tragedy is about to be revealed. He looks down at the floor. Everything stops. He says nothing for a minute. We are spellbound. Has he forgotten his lines? Is he having one of his fits? Then suddenly, 'Ah, Gentlemen, Tolstoy.'

Yasnaya Polyana is the birth place and ancestral home of Tolstoy. I have never forgotten that name and whenever I think of Tolstoy or someone says his name, inside my head roll the beautiful sounds and rhythms of *Yasnaya Polyana*.

And I remember Veechy and a cranky old man who appears to have lost his mind leaving home in the early hours of the morning with his doctor and falling ill at a railway station and the station master taking him in and a miracle happening and people coming from the surrounding district and kneeling outside the door and muttering their prayers and singing their songs and Sonya, she who bore the cranky old genius thirteen children, hammering at the door and being refused entry and when she finally enters he is unconscious and can't speak.

And then there is another wonderful word, *Astopovo*. I had never heard such beautiful sounding words. *Astopovo*. The railway station. And when the mad saint dies in the stationmaster's bed, a train takes the coffin back to near *Yasnaya Polyana* where huge crowds of students and secret police and members of the Orthodox Church, they who have excommunicated the saint, gather with the family and peasants. And then Tolstoy's sons give the coffin to the peasants from *Yasnaya Polyana* and they carry it on their shoulders for three hours to Tolstoy's chosen resting place at *Yasnaya Polyana* and with the exception of the police, the entire crowd sing softly the Orthodox funeral hymn, *Eternal memory*.

And Veechy ends his story and leaves his podium, and *Yasnaya Polyana* and Tolstoy's death are burnt into my brain.

There was another side to Monsignor Veech. Veechy liked to invite students to his office in the evening. The purpose was, I suppose, to check on their progress. Peter D. entered Springwood straight from school and joined the Pre-Philosophy class in 1963. Pre-Philosophy students concentrated on improving their Latin. Veechy asked Peter some esoteric questions about history of which the seventeen-year-old knew nothing. Veechy dismissed him but not before referring to his 'dismal ignorance'. Some years later, Peter left Propaganda Fide College in Rome one year before his ordination. He was extremely intelligent, an outstanding theological student and had an illustrious career in publishing, becoming Managing Director of a multinational publishing company.[142] He still remembers Veechy's comment. Peter did not enjoy his time at Springwood. It was, 'the worst experience of my life', he said, when I met him recently after forty-four years.

Paul Crittenden knew Veechy reasonably well; much better than I did. Crittenden met him first as a student at Manly College in 1955, when Veech was the Vice President of the College; and in 1961, when Veech was the Director of Graduate House, they lived together in a small community for eighteen months. By that time, Crittenden was ordained.

According to Geraghty, 'Tommy [i.e. Veech] often tumbled over the edge of sanity'.[143] Crittenden has much to say about Veech, but makes no mention of Veech's state of mind. He refers to his 'nervous twitches', but not to his psychological state. He found Veech a difficult man to get to know, but 'intriguing and interesting', a man with an 'obsessive concern for privacy'. Veech, he writes, was 'withdrawn, cautious, conservative' and, 'suffused with a certain spirit of European – essentially French – culture'. He was a man who stood apart from the world and observed it, 'from an oblique angle, slipping away unnoticed'. Crittenden believes that Veech:

> may have been unhappy in some deep sense, and was certainly anxious most of the time; but he made a special effort, it seemed to me, as head of our small community.

On the other hand, Geraghty's relationship with Veech was tempestuous. The two men didn't get on. Perhaps Veech, buried somewhere in eighteenth-century France, felt threatened by the intelligent younger man hungry for a new, modern Church.

Crittenden is more to Veech's liking. Reading his excellent autobiography, I gain the impression Crittenden is a man who plays a very straight bat; a man who hides his deeper self behind a rigorous adherence to objectivity. He is cautious and possibly a private person himself and careful with his judgements of others; whereas a more passionate Geraghty wants to plunder the bowling and hit each ball for six.

Before leaving for overseas in 1964, Crittenden paid a visit to Springwood to say goodbye to Veech. After lunch the two men walked around the grounds. They talked about, 'many things, people and times past, and what might be ahead'. Geraghty could never have had such a walk.[144] I was there at the time. Did I perhaps see them?

Despite his eccentricities and his capacity to hurt others, I find Veechy mesmeric. He enters from stage right, purposefully, shy smile, huffing and puffing. As usual he takes his seat but appears not to see us. Today he is not Monsignor Veech, rector, but someone called 'Don Ton [sic]'. I take notes. There is no text book. I know nothing. 'How do you spell Don Ton, Monsignor?' Maximilien Robespierre and 'Day Muloon [sic]' with the help of Don are staging the French Revolution. This is less history than drama. People move on and off the stage, but the huge figure of Don Ton dominates. He sits up high in a Convention Hall at a place called 'The Mountain'. When the Don speaks everyone listens. I stop writing and watch. Veechy comes alive in his characters. I am drawn into the excitement with wonder. This is a history I will learn, but not today.

In 1998 I am in Paris. We are led by a French tour guide who takes us around the city. She is fascinated by Napoleon Bonaparte. She tells us about the French Revolution, but it turns out to be another story about Napoleon. Getting off the bus I ask her, 'Where are the monuments to the people who made the revolution?' She looks puzzled and questions me. 'To whom are you referring?' I reply, 'Danton, Robespierre and Desmoulins.' She tells me they are honoured out in some suburbs. Not in the city. She smiles, 'There may be a relief of Danton at some Met railway station.' She senses my disappointment and explains why she does not talk about them. 'It's the Terror,' she says, shrugging her shoulders, 'too many deaths. The guillotine, you know. It's a history we like to forget.' I tell her that Napoleon lost more men in one day's walk from Moscow. She looks at me hard and wonders at my accent. Most of the tourists on our bus are Americans. I remember Veechy and Don Ton and I remember parts of our own history we like to forget.

My second eccentric is Doctor George Joiner. George is a brilliant man and from memory the only lecturer with a background in science. George is an unhappy member of staff and probably dislikes the seminary more than I do. To my knowledge no-one on the staff has any teacher training. Staff members appear to be chosen as seminary professors because of their academic achievements. Most of them will have studied overseas.

George organises work parties in the afternoons, and lectures us in Cosmology and Psychology. He carries in copious notes and journals. He regularly refers to something he read recently in the *New Scientist*. He has a booming voice and moves his huge frame backwards and forwards in the podium as he dictates his notes to us. We take notes and learn them off for examination purposes. No references or reading material of any sort are necessary, although some of the more scientifically minded students will obtain copies of journals from George. My task is to memorise George's notes. We are spoon-fed this information and no questions are asked. Learning and understanding are irrelevant. Memory is all. With no science background I have no understanding of what George is dictating. Luckily, there are two post-graduate science students in our class, and Terry Blake and Bob Donnelly help answer my basic questions. During breaks between classes, we walk in threes and I question them about the biology of a cell. In thirty minutes I have an image of something resembling a cell with acids and proteins flying around in my brain. I cannot even spell chromosome!

A clever young man in my class, named Greg Williamson, asks me if I believe in evolution. I am uncertain. He points out to me how horses have evolved. I believe in angels, archangels, guardian angels, the Immaculate Conception, the Assumption and original sin, but on the evolution of horses I am uncertain. Later in the year, on the feast of All Souls I follow the traditional practice of making a short visit to the chapel, then out and back in again, ad infinitum, to pray for the souls in purgatory, so that with every visit I gain a plenary indulgence for some poor suffering soul. Donnelly is aghast. He says it's all nonsense. Is Donnelly a Catholic? My brain is filled with hocus pocus.

I once asked my friend John Molony about George. John studied at Propaganda Fide College in Rome and was ordained a priest in 1950. When George, an older man than John, came to visit the Australian students at *Prop*, as it was called by students, he brought loads of gifts and other contraband. John said that if George was now somewhat less than sane, the seminary had made him so, for in his younger days he was a cheerful and kind man.

George is a big, bluff, no-nonsense man's-man, who invites imitation and critique. We call him 'Anyway' as did hundreds of students before and after us, because of his extraordinary habit of saying 'Anyway,' mostly prefaced with 'Right!' throughout his sentences.

Domine Geraghty once found a book in the library that he thought unsuitable and warranted a report to George, who held the pretentious title of 'librarian'. On hearing the details, George demanded to know where the book was now. 'In the library, Doctor,' said Geraghty. 'Right anyway, we had better deal with this straight away.' George with Geraghty in tow 'thundered' to the library and Geraghty handed the book to George. After a cursory examination George began to rip the book to pieces.[145]

George is happiest working with students outside the classroom. Some of the students, but not me, warm to this George. Dressed in his old clothes, George resembles the farmers I met out in the paddocks when I was working for the National Catholic Rural Movement. Most afternoons he drives an old utility truck on work-parties. Students throw shovels, spades and picks in the back before jumping in themselves. George roars, 'Right anyway, everybody in,' before racing off into the bush, a group of big boys going off on an adventure with the biggest boy of all driving. If Molony was right, then Cardinal Norman Gilroy had much to answer for in keeping George trapped in the seminary.

George goes out of his way to provide amenities for us, including in my time, the making of a swimming pool. George's classes begin with a reading of the front page of the *Sydney Morning Herald* and if students want to know if their favourite football team won on the weekend they only have to ask George. Radios and newspapers are forbidden. We have no access to telephones. Ours is a closed society. At the end of his class, George pins the front page of the paper on the notice board on the verandah of our recreation hall. Over time, I accept the problems this causes and stop whinging when a front page article has a note at the bottom, 'continued on page 5'. The front page is better than nothing. George is the only lecturer who lets a little free air from the outside world into our hermetically sealed bush home.

As I think about George now it is difficult for me to know if George was madder than Veechy. That they were both eccentric is beyond doubt. Madness is too hard a judgement and requires definition. I don't like the word and prefer the slang word, 'wacky', but the truth is that the rest of us were probably a bit wacky after one year in the place. The seminary system, I suspect, drove George wacky. On the other hand, Veechy was, possibly, always a bit wacky.

When George eventually retired as a parish priest, he, surprisingly, made his way back to live out his final days with his ghosts at Springwood. Some of his ex-students found him there one day. He asked them what years they were there. With tears in his eyes, he apologised for his behaviour and any pain he may have caused them. He told them he was unhappy at Springwood and had tried on numerous occasions to escape. He explained to them that, 'at the time, the man-in-charge had been completely mad'. Veech was the man.[146]

In his retirement, George lived in the presbytery near the front of the old seminary building. Previously, the presbytery was the convent. George's body lay inside for a number of days before someone thought to ask, 'Anyone seen Doc?'.

George has a problem with bell-ringing in his private Masses. Most students are warned by the sacristan not to ring the small bell, either the warning bell that rings out before the Consecration, or the bell that the server rings during the elevation of the host, when George is the celebrant. But sometimes, for reasons best known to a recalcitrant sacristan, a poor unfortunate student rings the bell. George immediately stops his Mass, grabs the bell from the student, goes over to the window, opens it and throws the bell outside.

At some stage, probably not my first year, some of us decide to take on George. All the priests take it in turns to offer the Mass in the main chapel for the whole community. With George this is a communal disaster. His back is to us. These are the days before the priest said Mass facing the people. George says his Mass as if we are not present. When we all stand to recite the Nicene Creed with him, George continues at such a pace that he is finished before we are halfway through. He then moves into the Offertory with the washing of his hands and by this time the student body is forced to give up on the Creed and kneel down.

We arrange that some of us will continue with the Creed as if George is not present. So we continue, in solidarity, slowly reciting the Creed, but with the Consecration looming we are defeated. George races along with his Mass, oblivious of our presence.

George also has a problem with students getting their hands too close to his at the washing of the hands during his Mass. We are warned to tip the water on his hands from a height that doesn't embarrass him. Some of us are cruel and tip the water from such a height that water splashes on George and the floor. We are all victims here.

I now know there are at least two fundamental principles which must be observed if learning is to occur: the learning must begin where people are at and it must be experiential and personal, i.e. involving a subjective encounter by the learner with the material. No two people will be at exactly the same level and this is what makes teaching difficult. But if the learner fails to make learning their *own* then nothing changes. The problem for me in the seminary was that too many of the ideas I encountered I was hearing for the first time. They were essentially meaningless, because I was hearing answers before I heard the questions or even before I knew there was a problem.

We were thus instructed, not educated. I had the distinct impression the real work of becoming a priest would begin at Manly when I graduated to the study of theology. At Springwood, the system was sorting out the serious contenders. We had no textbook, apart from a book we had all purchased on Scholasticism and Aquinas, which was in Latin. I bought small English paperbacks by Father Frederick Copleston, SJ, an expert on Aquinas, and author of a history of philosophy. These paperbacks we bought cheaply from students who cashed them in when leaving. Who reads Copleston on the other side of the sandstone heritage gates one mile down the track? Yet when I left in 1966, I brought home all my Copleston paperbacks. I still have them. In nearly three years of study, I have no recollection of any philosophy lecturer attempting to engage me personally in any process of learning. The lecturing mode did not lend itself to learning. We desperately needed some form of tutorial discussion group such as I experienced at the University of Melbourne in 1967. At Springwood, I was never set a problem to solve, never given a reading list, never directed to the library to do research, never asked to write an essay. Examinations, either written or oral, meant regurgitating our notes from class.

At the time, educational practice at Springwood was probably an *extreme* case of generally poor practice in formal education institutions throughout Australia. Education was a top-down process where empty vessels called students were filled to the brim with known facts. Learning was directly related to passing examinations and facts were presented with little or no attempt at critical understanding. According to John Burnheim, ex-priest, lecturer at Springwood and later head of the General Philosophy Department at Sydney University, the radical philosopher, John Anderson, dictated his lectures to students who were expected to take them down and regurgitate them in the examinations.[147] Doctor George Joiner was in good company.

My ideas about learning, however, came not from any formal educational institutions. What I learnt in my Diploma of Education at the University of Melbourne in 1970 was a mere gloss on what I had learnt in the YCW. I had developed an action-learning model through following Joseph Cardijn's method of changing the world through his See, Judge and Act formula. The YCW presented me with problems that required answers that only I could solve. I learnt to think because I was required to act.

In 1965, Cardijn became a cardinal. The Second Vatican Council had six months to go. Cardijn wrote to Yves Congar, the Dominican scholar and theologian, to arrange a meeting. Some few months later Congar met him at the airport in Rome and they spoke in the taxi. This is what Congar wrote in his diary:

> We talked about religious freedom, about schema XIII, the Lay Apostolate, Missions, Priests. Cardijn had prepared reflections on these texts; he is counting on me, on us, to test them and put them into the form of conciliar interventions. Basically Cardijn has only one idea. But it is consubstantial with himself; he is as absolutely faithful to it as he is to himself. It lights up everything. His great idea is to start from the real, the concrete. People must be taken as they are.[148]

Cardijn's one great idea hitchhiked from Ballarat to Terang circa 1956. It came in the form of the full-time organiser of the YCW, Jim Ross, who had Cardijn's great idea emblazoned on his heart. If he hadn't come I wouldn't be writing this.

My third eccentric is Father Noel Carroll. Well into the year, the first philosophy class discovered, that it was indeed our novitiate year. Our novice master was Father Noel Carroll, known as 'Say', because most of his sentences began with the word, 'Say'.

One identifying activity that separated the novices from the rest of the College was afternoons with Say. We divided into work parties and Say had us moving rocks from one place to another and then moving them back again. He was teaching us obedience. Most of us entered into this *spiritual* exercise in good faith, especially those who liked to keep fit. At other times we dug holes and filled them in. After some time, Say decided to give me a serious job painting the railings along an overhead path that linked the private quarters of the building (where Veechy lived along with some other priests) and the chapel.

Say could not be taken seriously. He had a lyrical sing-song voice that sounded part Irish and part American. Noel had picked up his Irish brogue at All Hallows seminary, Dublin, where he was ordained. Some of the students thought he picked up the American drawl when his plane stopped over for an hour in Chicago.[149] Wherever it came from it was phoney and did nothing for his reputation with most students. He 'taught' us Ancient History beginning with the development of human civilisation in the Fertile Crescent between the two mighty rivers of the Tigris and the Euphrates. The impression gained from his classes was he was one page ahead of us, which presumed we had a text, which we didn't, and presumed he had a plan, which he didn't. Not surprisingly, he told us that it wasn't so much the historical details that were important, but rather his words of wisdom filling in between the facts – 'the in-between bits', he'd say. He could meander for an hour, like a lazy river, telling stories, offering advice and filling in time. He was frequently late for his class. The authorities had appointed Ray Liggett as our leader. Ray had done brilliantly in his final secondary year at school, which earned him the respect of those in charge. Ray was a wonderful young man, who would stand outside our classroom waiting to greet Say when he eventually turned up. Ray would see him gliding along and warn us, 'He's coming.' Of all our teachers, Say was by far the worst, but thinking of him now, I wonder if he was profoundly unhappy and deserving of my understanding and empathy.

I cannot make him out. He has bulging eyes like a hare caught on the road in the headlights of a car. He often appears distracted, as if he is somewhere else, as if there is a mystery about him that he is hiding. Mark Twain has a wonderful scene featuring an undertaker in *Huckleberry Finn* who 'slid around in his black gloves with his softly soothering ways … making no more noise than a cat'. He was, said Twain, 'the softest, glidingest, stealthiest man I ever saw; and there warn't no more smile to him than there is to a ham'.[150] Carroll glides along corridors, smooth-looking, self-consciously aware and flipping back his shoulder cape above his soutane. His manner and voice seem to say, 'Look at me', and we do. Chaucer would have found him extremely interesting; he may have found him a place riding with the Pardoner.

Chapter 7

Mister In-Between

Before we leave for home in December, I bounce around in the back of the bursar's utility with some of the students aged over twenty-one. Father Lenny Wholohan is the bursar and Robert Menzies is the Prime Minister. Sir Robert, sensing an advantage in 1963, calls a premature federal election as Arthur Calwell, Leader of the Australian Labor Party (ALP) and Gough Whitlam, Deputy Leader, collide, and Menzies has ammunition to play on his old theme of the so-called 'faceless men' who make decisions on behalf of the parliamentary wing of the ALP. Menzies' early election in 1963 split the vote for the Senate from the House of Representatives and on 5 December 1964, Lenny Wholohan drove us to a small country polling booth to vote in a half-Senate election.

I was highly political. Caught up in the Labor split in Victoria in 1955, I handed out how-to-vote tickets for the anti-communist party, which would later become the Democratic Labor Party (DLP). And all this before I was eligible to vote. My time working for Santamaria's Rural Movement (1959–61) brought me even closer to the DLP, although I never became a member. This is what I was like in 1964.

One of the people on the back of Lenny's utility with me is a friend, Maurie O'Sullivan (not his real name). Maurie is a late vocation, about my age; he had a senior management position in the public service before coming to Springwood. I sense his ambition and that he will make a career in the Church. He is quietly spoken and reflective. Earlier in the year he received a letter from a young woman who told him she was pregnant and without naming him as the father hinted it was a possibility. Maurie was devastated. He acknowledged the possibility to me and a few other friends, but unlike me, Maurie wanted to be a priest and this setback would not stop him. In the short term, he decided to lie low and not reply. No second letter arrived and Maurie continued on with his priestly studies.

Maurie has contacts in the Catholic Right who run the New South Wales Labor Party. He names people as friends that I regard as the enemy. Maurie sets the tone on the back of Lenny's ute. We argue calmly, all the way to the polling booth. I've lost some of my zeal and I'm three years away from the action. My politics are stuck in 1961. In late 1964, Menzies and the Liberals fear Indonesia and are courting American support. That means helping the Americans in Vietnam. A month before we go to vote, Menzies introduces conscription for twenty-year-olds. Four thousand young Australians aged twenty will have their names drawn out of a barrel. Calwell calls it, 'the lottery of death'. Maurie and I know nothing of this. He is as anti-communist as I am, but he supports the New South Wales policy of *stay-in-and-fight* favoured by Cardinal Norman Gilroy and Archbishop James Carroll. I argue that Catholics in Victoria did not have the luxury of staying in as they were expelled from the party. The argument is a nil all draw by the time we reach the polling booth. Labor's dramatic slide from favour with the voters is in full swing and it will be 1972 before Whitlam wins government. By that time I am an executive member of the Bendigo branch of the ALP and Maurie is making a career for himself within the Church.

In 1980 I will meet Maurie again. He's a big shot – Vicar General of a diocese, a Monsignor and, barring accidents, on the way to becoming a bishop. I'm applying for a position as a Deputy Principal in a Catholic School. Maurie meets me before the interview, calmly and quietly. It's as if fourteen years haven't passed – as if we had just jumped off the back of Lenny's ute to go in and vote. He asks me nothing about myself and I am silenced by the coolness. His priestly office has eaten away part of his soul. He then tells me I am being interviewed for the Principal's position. I find that hard to believe, but I've driven since early morning and expect a cup of tea, but no offer is made. Maurie shows me to a room and I sit and wait for him to reappear. I look around for water. This is not the first interview for a job I've had over the last few weeks. At two previous interviews at Technical and Further Education

Colleges (TAFE) someone was appointed to show me around, introduce me to staff and share a tea or coffee with me.

The interview was extraordinary. Twelve people sitting around me in a semi-circle ask me questions. I sit on an electric chair in the middle. The atmosphere, for some reason unknown to me, is toxic. Some of the questions relate to my interest in politics. 'Are you a member of a political party? Are you likely to become involved in politics?' And then, 'Would you be prepared to work under the guidance of the parish priest?' The parish priest, one of the twelve, waits my answer. I reply, 'No.' No one seems interested in education. Maurie sits with the twelve and says nothing. When I realise this is a job I don't want, I answer their questions with hand grenades. I'm thinking of asking Maurie a question of my own. One dating back many years.

After the interview, Maurie escorts me to the front door. I'm thinking he is going to invite me for coffee or lunch. We talk amiably enough in the sun and he apologises for the interview. He tells me that the previous Principal had been robbing the parish funds for years. This, in part, explains the aggressive nature of the interview. The other eleven apostles toddle out in the sun and advise Maurie they will meet him over at the usual restaurant. Maurie shakes my hand and wishes me well. His final words are, 'You'll hear from us.' I never did. Maurie died before becoming a bishop. Rest in peace, Maurie.

An oral examination with Veechy! How can I prepare? I have no notes. I've read nothing. There is no text. His stories might have cut into my heart, but it's possible I'll make a fool of myself. The orals are conducted in his office at night. A few of us line up outside his door on the second-storey verandah. In the distance the lights of Sydney are blinking. We whisper about the possibilities. What's he asking? Dreyfus! It's Dreyfus. Jesus, Mary and Joseph! I think of Emile Zola, *J'accuse*, Devil's Island, Anti-Semitism, the Church, Anatole France. I'll be right.

Inside he is gracious. 'Ah, it's you,' he says, beckoning me to sit. His face is redder than ever, clashing with his white hair. His table is covered in papers, along with various piles of books. He has no idea what his stories mean to me. I leave the talking to him. When he hesitates and looks at me I take it that is my cue to speak. He leads the dance and I slip and slide around the corners. One actor and one would-be actor discuss the appalling treatment of an innocent man. I'm doing so well I'm looking for scones and tea. He wishes me well and as I move to the door he asks me gently to send in the next student.

The end of the year finally comes and we travel to the Springwood station in buses. Despite the warnings from our superiors to remember who we are, there is a new bounce, a bubble of excitement, a surge of energy and, I suspect, a flow of testosterone. Some of us will be tempted and not return. I am filled with joy at leaving my bush home for eight weeks. We come into Sydney on rail tracks that run past the back doors of small homes. Overnight, I stay with one of my seminary friends in Sydney and the next day a few of us meet to play golf at Randwick. In between rusty golf shots we discuss the problem of God. Where is He? Is He inside this world? Outside this world? Inside our beings? A female God is beyond our comprehension. A clever young man named Marshal announces that he has become a pantheist. God is in all things. But I have other things on my mind.

My friend John Molony will leave Ballarat and his practising priesthood over the summer of 1963–4. I was unaware of the details. His influence on my life and spiritual development has been profound. Because of him I am here in Sydney.

The next day I visit John at Ashfield, a suburb in Sydney where he is renting a house with his mother. She has come from Victoria to care for her son. I think now I should not have visited them as it undoubtedly put added strain on both of them. His other Mother, Holy Mother Church, who has educated and nurtured him at Werribee and Rome, cannot believe any sane person would leave the priesthood. They insist he visit a psychiatrist. Being proved sane once was not sufficient. A second psychiatrist is asked to confirm the decision. Not only does he confirm the first diagnosis but tells John he is one of the most innocent adults he has met.

Mrs Molony welcomes me at the door and points to the back room where John is reading. He is wearing dark glasses and the old Molony is somewhere else. We talk for fifteen minutes and I ask him what he is reading. He picks up a small paperback beside his chair. *A short history of Australia* written by Manning Clark. When he recovers, he would like to teach Australian History. There will be better days than this.

Mrs Molony walks me to the front gate and thanks me for coming. She blames others for her son's predicament. She is his real mother.

Many years later I am at John's home in Canberra. He is the Manning Clark Professor of Australian History at the Australian National University. I look at the books he has written and next to them is a small well-worn paperback entitled, *A short history of Australia,* by Manning Clark. He comes back into the room and I say, 'I remember you reading that book, at Ashfield, in 1964 or 65.' He looks at me, trying to remember what he's been told to forget. He pulls it out fingering the pages. 'It's yours', he says, handing it to me. I still have it with his scratchy faint pencil annotations down the side of the odd page.

I soon discover I am lost, separate, in my own ecclesiastical space designed to keep others at a distance. It is clear that outside the seminary, I have become an outsider. I do not belong in either the real world or the seminary. Half alive in both places. 'Mr In-Between', as Burl Ives's song would have it.

On the train from Melbourne to Terang, I suck in the familiar and relive my youthful days. Cypress trees and hedges provide shade and shelter for the dairy herds from the southerly winds. From the window of the train I watch fences dip and rise, dip and rise. Crossing MacKinnon's Bridge about five miles out of Terang, we slow down over the knotted rails and below I see the water hole in Emu Creek, where Clarrie Carmody, married to one of my many Slattery relations, fished for eels with Alan Marshall, writer and storyteller. Mount Noorat, where the black tribes gathered, sits incongruously on the otherwise flat surface of the land.

But I have changed. Inside my head I sing the words of Wagner's *Tannhauser,* which choir master, Father John Walsh, Dean of Discipline, master of coughing and nose-blowing, has taught us:

Once more dear home
I with rapture behold thee
And greet the fields that
So sweetly enfold thee.

My family has never heard of Wagner. Has anyone in Terang? I now cut bread in small slices – eight bits to a piece and butter only when sliced. Soup spoons out, dessert spoons in. Always start cutlery from the outside. White napkins and silver holders. Never walk with hands in pockets. Never shout or laugh loudly. Never seek attention. 'Prudence, gentlemen, is the greatest virtue.' Veechy. Pronounce the past tense of 'eat' as 'et'; 'it's not Cons-table, gentlemen, but Kunt-stable', when referring to policemen or to the artist who painted a mean cloud. I look down at my desk as Veechy passes on this piece of trivia. I am educated to be a gentleman – one who has a wide knowledge, one who knows nothing in depth, one who can smile knowingly and one who is comfortable in any company: 'If you must use the word "one", gentlemen, remember to stay with it.'

Should I tell my friends I study screaming cicadas and feverish ants in my spare time? What would they make of Thomas McNiven Veech, George Joiner and Say Carroll? Would anyone be interested in Schliemann and Troy and Crete and Agamemnon and the Bull of Minos? What would they make of Plato's Forms and Aristotle's Universals? Perhaps I might interest someone in George Sand, who was in fact a woman and made love with Chopin.

Many of my old friends are married. They have other interests. I do my best, but after a few weeks one of my best mates tells me he can't talk to me anymore. It becomes clear that apart from my immediate family, my wider relationships are either 'rickety-rackety' or non-existent.[151]

And for the locals, I am already half a priest. Expectations are high. It is why I must return. When I left for the seminary in February 1964, the parish sent me off with great fanfare. The local newspaper announced my departure on their front page: *Young Terang Resident Farewelled*. The Gold Tones Orchestra played the dance music before 'a large number of people'. Neville Clark, Lynette Ryan and Betty Shady sang, Laurie Ayres spoke on behalf of the parishioners and Terry Arundell from the YCW wished me well. The Right Reverend J. H. Gleeson, Parish Priest, presented me with an envelope of notes.[152] Jesus, Mary and Joseph!

On Monday afternoons Terang comes alive. It's sale day at Dalgety's and the farmers come into town. Walking up Main Street I see Eddie Conheady making his way towards me. As soon as he spots me, his hand goes into the inside pocket of his suit. It's a tie and coat day. Eddie greets me warmly and I lie to him when he asks how I'm getting on. Eddie has found whatever it was he was looking for inside his coat.

'Kevin, I would like to give you something.' Eddie is the sweetest of men. He owns a dairy farm about six miles out of town.

'Please, Eddie, no.'

'Kevin,' bowing his head reverently in time with his slow delivery and my new status, 'it's the least I can do.'

'Eddie, I can't take it. You must not.'

'Kevin, I will be embarrassed if you don't take it. I insist. You need it more than I do. It's an honour to help you.'

I realise this has little or nothing to do with me. It's the priesthood Eddie is honouring.

Eddie can't see inside my heart. I cannot take it.

'Kevin, I'm going to walk away and if you don't take it, I will drop it on the footpath.'

We are outside the Co-op Stores. People walk around us and smile when they recognise me. It's Kevin. He's going to be a priest. I have Hawthorne's scarlet letter, in this case a 'P', marked deep on my forehead.

Eddie drops a £10 note on the ground and walks away. My father's weekly cheque from the factory is about £15.

I bend down, pick up the note, put it in my pocket and walk home. Wherever I was going, I've changed my mind. I am trapped.

I paint roofs and window frames. Relations and friends give me work. At my cousin Blondie's home I paint his windowsills. I've fallen in love with Barbra Streisand. She knows more about life than Veechy and his mob. She reminds me of something that I am in danger of losing, namely, that deep inside we are all like children needing to be loved by someone special, and when we are then we're the luckiest people in the world.

Blondie's neighbour, Joe, a good friend of Dad's, listens to my singing and worries about my work output. I'm slow he says. He's right of course – it's one reason why I won't 'crack-up'. Joe asks if I'm being paid by the hour. I answer in the affirmative and he's horrified. After a day in the hot sun I call into the Middle pub for a beer – against seminary rules. Despite my casualness, there is an exaggerated respect, a subdued tone as I line up at the bar. Even the demeanour of my non-Catholic friends takes a turn for the worse. They shake my hand and ask how I'm doing. After that they're stuck for words. I wonder if I should mention Veechy? I've left the world behind and joined the priestly caste. I'm no longer part of the mainstream. I don't belong here and I don't belong in the mountains.

During the day, to keep sane and balanced, I sing while I work. I convince myself that sane people sing. If I keep singing all will be well. The working-class lads from Liverpool, John and Paul, George and Ringo, and Gerry and the Pacemakers, help me paint Blondie's windowsills. I cross the Mersey on a ferry with Gerry and his lads and accept their good advice – aches and pains are best kept to the quiet of night. The sun will not catch me crying. I'm leaving Sinatra and the love ballads of the fifties behind and joining the swinging sixties. But some days, painting the hot tin roof of cousin Lorraine, I'm back in the mountains with the other inmates, mad cicadas are screaming for a mate, I'm wearing a long dress in the all black colours of the club, and in the ablutions block next to the jakes I'm knocking out the beat with Peter D. and Foxy while Kev Rowley drums out the rhythm on his bongos.

Terang is a small town, a few thousand people. We are country people. Even though we live in the town we have a horse and two dogs. Dainty is Dad's mare; she is a fine stock horse with a quick walk, which Dad values. Dainty is fed on chaff and oats and has a pick on the grass in front of our home in the long evenings. As a result she is as fit as any racehorse. On Monday afternoons, if Dad is not at his factory job, he shifts cattle after the sale for Dalgety's Stores. He is pleased that I ride Dainty during the week. I have been brought up with horses and I have the same gentleness with them as my father.

I ride Dainty out the Noorat road, then turn left along by the creek on the edge of town, past the abattoirs with black ravens screeching like cicadas and doomed cattle staring, then past Stan Fenton's farm and the entrance to the racecourse and back home along Grey Street past the saleyards. I have been riding this circle since I was a young boy. I like the steady go of Dainty, the quick walk and the swish of the tail, the occasional snort and the jingling bit, the loose rein and the bobbing head, the waving mane and the squeaking saddle. The go and smell of her. Is this where I belong? I think not. But where do I belong? I seem to be congenitally uncertain. Jesus, what am I doing with my life?

Back home I buy sheep heads from the butcher, George Adams, for the two dogs, Nip and Judy. With the axe I split the heads in half on the chopping block and give a half each to the dogs. They lick the inside of the heads looking for the brains. What would Thomas think of this? I like Thomas. I like his sense of the real world that I can see, and touch and feel. And I prefer Aristotle to the other-worldliness of Plato. Not that I was in any sense a realist. My idealism and romantic view of the world meant that I never saw it as it was. I was no philosopher, never would be, but I was interested.

On New Year's Eve I wander up the street to see what's happening. There is a dance on in the Main Hall. I peep through a window into the supper room, but don't go in. On the walk home I meet Mrs Rollo, a poor woman, worse for wear. Her hair is unkempt. She stares at me through dulled eyes. Suddenly she smiles and we exchange the compliments of the season. I love you Mrs Rollo. We are the only two on the street. Lost. Both of us. Where is your husband, Mrs Rollo? I once knew him. Tom. The house-remover. A yard full of trucks, bits of trucks, broken trucks and trailers everywhere. The town clock at the post office strikes midnight. It's 1965.

When I write of Mrs Rollo now, I imagine her as Dulcinea del Toboso, the creation of Miguel de Cervantes in his *The Adventures of Don Quixote*:

Montesinos' Cave

> We met but once my Dulcinea.
> The street was ours that night
> and as we drew closer
> you hesitated
> then reaching down
> you lifted your skirt and
> stepped out of your silken petticoat.
>
> A frisson of delight
> your head regal, hair golden, eyes suns,
> You sought ten pounds in exchange for your slip.
> A trophy for my celibate cave.[153]

During the holidays about half a dozen of my seminary friends come to join me for a week's holiday somewhere between Sorrento and Portsea. At least two have journeyed from northern New South Wales. One of our number fancies himself as a runner. Gerry reckons he's met Betty Cuthbert, a great Australian female sprinter who won gold at the Melbourne Olympic Games in 1956. Gerry wants to meet Percy Cerutty who lives in Portsea and trains some of Australia's best athletes, including champion miler, Herb Elliott, who won a gold medal at the 1960 Rome Olympics. I'm uneasy. I advise against the visit. I don't like Cerutty. My experience of him is limited to his persona on television and in the press. I find him an exhibitionist, a crass and egotistical person, and I sense a degree of madness in him. Nevertheless we go and knock on Percy's door. His wife greets us on a Sunday afternoon and is somewhat interested to find six or seven clean-cut young men looking as if they have just been to Mass and asking to talk to Percy.

Percy comes out in his gear: running shoes, white singlet and shorts. He stares at us trying to work out who and what we are. Percy is not just a coach. He's a whole of life man, who works on bodies and minds. His runners read Plato and poetry. He wants to get inside their minds, to taunt them and make them the best they can possibly be. His system is based on Spartan and Stoic philosophy, which Percy has studied. He likes his athletes to shed all their clothes in the open at least once a day. Gerry is our spokesperson – charming and plausible. Percy ignores the voice while he takes us in. When Gerry finishes, Percy looks at him and says, 'Where's ya wimin?'

Gerry refuses to get involved. He sticks to the running. Percy, I think, smells our religion and our celibacy. He begins telling us of his 'wimin'. What he did with this one and that one and what he is doing at the age of seventy to some of the celebrity 'wimin' who holiday in Portsea. This is much worse than I could have ever imagined. Eventually he takes us out into his back yard where there is a small running track. Percy wants to show us how stupid is Ron Clarke's running style; Clarke is another champion runner, one who ignored Percy. Then he shows us how he taught Elliott to run. While he runs he talks. His energy is extraordinary. Gerry is satisfied and thanks Percy on behalf of us. I can't leave quickly enough.

Just prior to leaving Terang in February, I journey to Ballarat to see my old YCW mates and with them I go to the Ballarat horse races. I'm in luck. With

Burt Bacharach and Dionne Warwick providing background music, I back Belladonna, a local mare owned by the Heffernan family from Dalvui Lane, a few miles out of Terang. The horse is a rank outsider but I take it in a quinella with the favourite and it runs second. I cancel my train ticket and with the winnings I buy a plane ticket for the trip back to Sydney. My mountain range in Springwood waits for me. I don't need a mountain, Lord. All I need is love, sweet love.

PART TWO

1965

Among the many criticisms of the Church during the Royal Commission's hearings has been the way in which the Church culture – in particular, clericalism – has played a role in the original crimes and then been a factor in their cover-up.

Francis Sullivan
CEO of the Truth, Justice and Healing Council
Blackfriars Lecture Series, Australian Catholic University
20 October 2015

Chapter 8

The cultic priesthood takes a hit

Over the summer of 1964, to my dismay, I learnt that many of the locals in Terang thought I had reached some clerical status. In their eyes, God had already chosen me as somehow special amongst men. I could see it in their shy smiles and when they stopped to shake my hand and wish me well. I was embarrassed. I felt such a fraud. Evidently, being a mere seminarian was a sufficient cause for many of the townsfolk to lift me up into the stratosphere where angels and priests flittered together.

But I was virtually nothing. A reluctant seminarian who thought he was doing God's will. Two years back at school and one year in the seminary. I had barely begun. I had not even reached the study of theology. Nevertheless, despite all the good will in the world, apart from my relationships with family and close friends, my dealings with others quickly took on a reverential tone. Evidently, I had put on a new garb, but it was an ill fit. I was not descended from the priestly tribe of Aaron, but it seemed I had joined the ranks of that mysterious and shadowy figure called Melchizedek, king and eternal priest, who rated just two fleeting mentions in the Hebrew Bible. But as far as the locals were concerned, I was up there with the angels and Melchizedek.

This new exaggerated esteem, which the locals gratuitously gave me, was due to the respect, even veneration, which the Catholic laity had for their priests. The Church had cultivated the myth for centuries. In the 1960s, the Catholic priesthood was still cultic. The notion of a cultic priesthood is based on a distinction between the profane and the sacred. Profane refers to the ordinary, day-to-day matters of real life, e.g. eating, sleeping, working. Sacred refers to other realities that are in some way shot through or penetrated by God's presence. In this sense they become sacred, i.e. presumed holy. Therefore, we have sacred times (the Sabbath), sacred places (churches), sacred objects (vessels used in worship) and, importantly, sacred persons (priests). In this cultic priesthood, priests are consecrated by God and thus endowed with holiness.[154]

This cultic form of clericalism places great power in the hands of clerics and is directly linked to the sexual abuse scandal, according to the Australian Church's own *Activity document in response to the Royal Commission into Institutional Responses to Child Sexual Abuse*:

> There has also been much discussion about the impact of 'clericalism', which can be understood as referring to approaches or practices involving ordained ministry geared to power over others, not service to others. Clericalism has been seen as a contributing factor in the way in which the Church has responded to abuse claims and engaged with survivors.[155]

Clericalism is a central feature of Catholic culture. It was a necessary contributing factor in influencing the decisions of Catholic bishops around the world to give their primary loyalty to their priests, in preference to innocent victims whom those same priests had sexually abused. Clericalism is also a necessary cause in explaining why individual clerics offended. It is important to note that the Australian Royal Commission is concerned with an analysis of institutional *responses* to sexual abuse. That is its brief. Initially, I thought the Commission may well ignore causal factors but I was wrong. The final report will certainly address causal factors directly related to the failure of the institution. It will be less concerned with providing a causal analysis as to why individual clerics sexually abused children. I am interested in both, but in particular the reasons why individual clerics offended.

It is no easy matter to keep these two separate. We see this in the Church's *Activity document*. While essentially concerning itself, rightly, with the institutional response to the sexual abuse scandal, the document easily drifts into an analysis of why individual priests offended. This can be confusing. When the *Activity document* lists the following contributing factors relating to the institution's response, namely, its clericalism and obligatory celibacy, its manner of recruiting candidates for the priesthood, its emphasis on obedience and its closed religious environments, it appears that many of these apply equally as well to the crimes of individual sexual offenders.

Clericalism and power are synonymous. We see this in the response of the Catholic laity to the sexual abuse scandal in Australia, the United States and Ireland. In Australia, the *Activity document* recognises that Catholic parents were reluctant to believe their children when they accused Father of violating their innocence. This is not surprising. That many parents were slow to confront Church leaders about sexually abusing priests was due to the deeply felt veneration that Catholic lay people had for their priests. In the eyes of the laity, their priests belonged in a separate sphere, a sacred place; they were a different order of being.[156] The unwarranted esteem, which I experienced in my home town, was repeated around the world.

In the United States there was a twist to the argument about reluctant parents reporting offences to their bishops. But the end result was the same. Parents wanted to protect their children, but they also wanted to protect their priests. Before 1985, when parents learnt that their children had been sexually abused, more than 80% of them went, within a year, directly to their diocese to report the incidents. Note well: to report the incident, not report the offending priest. On reporting the incident, the most common request by the families was that help be provided for the priest-offender. Father was still supreme. Often, the families did not want publicity nor did they wish to confront the priest. It was not only bishops who wanted to protect the Church. In other cases, families were pressured by Church leaders to keep the incident confidential.[157]

The Catholic laity have been betrayed by their bishops and their abusing clergy. And when the small children expressed anxiety to their mothers about their all-powerful sacred priests they were told to cooperate with *Father* and not to be silly. *Father* had been consecrated by God. *Father* was our mediator with God. *Father* could work miracles. *Father* could forgive sins and change bread into the body of Christ. *Father* was a kind, good man. If *Father*

sacrificed his time in a busy life serving the parish to take you camping, or picnicking or swimming, then, dear children, you should go with him. So the children went and later they could not tell their parents. And when they did they were not believed. And it wasn't only mothers. There were others. With a wink and a nod, the police assured *Father* not to worry: 'We'll look after this, *Father*.' And the Catholic lawyers snuck out to see the bishop after hours and agreed to work quietly behind the scenes and keep the whole unfortunate matter a secret. *No worries, My Lord.* And the journalists read the stories and put them away in the bottom drawers where no one could see them. *Father* was above the law. He was trusted because he was special. The parents of one young girl in the United States invited their priest friend to dinner each week. Each week they allowed *Father* to tuck their daughter into bed. *Father* took the opportunity to sexually abuse her.[158]

Not surprisingly, the cultic priesthood reigned supreme in Catholic Ireland, but it was to take a big hit before the turn of the century. Initially at least, the same exaggerated esteem, empathy and support for priests accused of sexual abuse followed the pattern in the United States. In Ireland the Church and her priests held privileged status. The 'close alliance of Church and State has been a distinctive feature of Irish polity and society'. This had led to such a deference towards the Church by governments that individual clergy, and state-funded institutions managed by the Church, have been 'somewhat beyond the reach of state police and inspection'.[159] Of the 3200 primary schools in Ireland, 3000 are still managed by Catholic priests.[160] Republican governments over the second half of the twentieth century had failed to act despite overwhelming evidence of the brutal treatment of children in state-funded institutions. Bureaucrats within the Department of Education and the police, taking their cue from their political masters, were less than anxious to provide any form of leadership.

When change came early in the twenty-first century, it was the victims and journalists, in particular documentary film-makers, who made it happen. The Catholic Irish laity as a body were slow to take sides. But over time, with the evidence coming into their homes via their television screens, lay support for the clergy began to wear thin. The cultic priesthood in Ireland was about to crumble.

In certain dioceses in Ireland, the figure for Catholic clerical abuse would seem to be higher than in the United States. Many of the cases litigated in the United States in the 1980s involved priests brought up in Ireland.[161] Research by Professor Gerry Kearns at the National University of Ireland, Maynooth, revealed that spikes of sexual abuse by priests reached a peak of 10%, 'some three times higher than the calculated average percentage of paedophiles in Western countries'.[162] Sadly, Australia now leads the world with a number of its dioceses higher than 10%.[163]

The report by the Commission of Investigation into the Catholic Archdiocese of Dublin (2009) found that one priest admitted to sexually abusing over 100 children while another accepted that he had abused on a fortnightly basis 'during the currency of his ministry which lasted over 25 years'.[164] The bishops claimed ignorance of all such matters, telling the Commission they were on 'a learning curve'. One Church source claimed that sexual abuse in Ireland came on as a 'tsunami: an earthquake deep beneath the surface [hidden] from view'. The implication, as noted by the Commission, is that Church authorities were somehow taken by surprise. The Commission dismissed such claims and assertions:

> The Dublin Archdiocese's pre-occupation in dealing with cases of child sexual abuse, at least until the mid-1990s, were the maintenance of secrecy, the avoidance of scandal, the protection of the reputation of the Church, and the preservation of its assets. All other considerations, including the welfare of children and justice for victims were subordinated to these priorities. The Archdiocese did not implement its own canon law rules and did its best to avoid any application of the law of the State.[165]

Apart from the Irish bishops' dissimulation about knowledge of the events, their response was the same as it was in Australia and the United States. Sexual abuse in the Church did not start in the twentieth century. It had been a delict and a sin under Canon Law, and a crime in the law of the state. Child abuse in the Catholic Church has been a deplorable feature of some of its clergy since the early centuries. In practically every century since the Church began, 'the problem of clerical abuse of minors was not just lurking in the shadows but so open at times that extraordinary means had to be taken to quell it'.[166]

In 1990, Father James Doyle pleaded guilty to charges of indecent assault and common assault on a young man and was given a three months' suspended sentence. Doyle's suspended sentence was in part due to his promise that he would leave Ireland. Church authorities were warned about Doyle before he was ordained and they did nothing. Soon after his trial, Doyle left for England. His was the first prosecution in the courts of a priest from the Diocese of Ferns, which embraces County Wexford and parts of County Wicklow. Colm Tóibín, one of Ireland's finest modern writers, knew Doyle as a teenager and liked him. Tóibín was a student at Saint Peter's secondary school in the early 1970s and Doyle was a seminarian at the same campus. Tóibín writes about the reaction by some Irish Catholics:

> It is not hard to imagine how much the people of the diocese could have hated James Doyle. Surely he would have been pelted with turnips, which grew plentifully in the area, as he left the court? Instead, people blamed the local newspapers for printing the story, provoking, the *Ferns Report* says, 'a considerable backlash' against one local paper in the Wexford area 'as it was felt that Father Doyle had been badly treated by the publicity his case had attracted. As the media had already given enough information to disclose the identity of the complainant, this backlash was also directed towards him and his family.'[167]

I make no apology for detailing the following. The term sexual abuse now rolls too readily off the tongue. In some ears it has become insipid, devoid of content. We need to know what we are talking about. Catholic lay people around the world found it difficult to believe that their priests would sexually abuse their children. But in Ireland the early support for the clergy would weaken, and eventually Ireland wanted to rid herself of these predatory priests from Wexford. Fathers Doyle, Collins, Grennan, Clancy and the notorious Sean Fortune became the ugly face of the Catholic Church in Ireland. Grennan abused young girls in the confessional. He died in 1994. One of his alleged victims committed suicide in 2002. In 1966, Father Donal Collins, it was alleged, inspected and measured the penises of up to twenty boys in

Saint Peter's school dormitory on the pretext of checking their development. His bishop sent him to England for two years as penance after which he returned to Saint Peter's and continued his teaching. He was later to become principal of Saint Peter's school from 1988 to 1991. Accusations of sexual abuse continued against Collins up to 1993. In 1998 he pleaded guilty to four charges of gross indecency and one of indecent assault against students at Saint Peter's College. He was sentenced to four years imprisonment and served one.

Sean Fortune was deranged and should never have been ordained. He entered Saint Peter's seminary without the support of a bishop and without any screening. He found the unfortunate Wexford bishop, Donal Herlihy, willing to accept him into his diocese. Herlihy, it turned out, knew more about the Roman poets, Catullus and Horace, than he did about Fortune, who was granted an exemption to enter the seminary, as he had previously been in a Brother's Juniorate.

Fortune was a liar, manipulator and blackmailer who went from one psychiatrist to another. He violently raped young boys including Colm O'Gorman who vividly recounts his own rape and Fortune's devious nature in his book *Beyond belief*. I read O'Gorman's book on a beautiful sunny autumn afternoon in Canberra at the National Library. The events of the rape are shocking. The aftermath is nearly as bad. When Fortune was driving the young boy, aged twelve, back to his parents, he informed the boy that he would have to speak to his father. 'What do you mean?' asked the boy. 'That you have a problem,' replied Fortune. And after that not a word was said to anyone and the rapes continued. The autumn sun stopped shining for me that afternoon. I left the library soon after, and for the first time that I can remember, I failed to write down the details or take a page reference.

One of Fortune's victims committed suicide in the 1980s. Fortune told different stories to each new psychiatrist and no one seemed to know what he had previously invented. His bishop failed to provide health officials with the litany of his evil deeds. Fortune was abusing young boys before he was ordained. He seemed incapable of realising what harm he was doing; to one health official who asked him why he did these things, he shrugged it off as 'just messing'.[168] When one of his young victims approached another priest to report that Fortune had abused him, the priest asked the young man to demonstrate what Fortune had done. This included touching his penis, thus beginning the abuse all over again.[169]

Canon Clancy developed a relationship with Ciara aged 11. Ciara later became pregnant aged 14 and had her baby in England. She told no one who the father was. At 17, Clancy threatened to have the baby taken from her if she revealed the father's name. When he died in 1993, Clancy left Ciara three thousand pounds in his will to be used for her future 'musical education'.[170]

Doyle's court case in 1990 was early days. Ireland was never the same after the showing of *Suing the Pope*, the BBC television documentary in March 2002, which presented a series of testimonies from young men who had been abused as children in County Wexford. This led to the Irish government establishing the Ferns Inquiry in 2003 under the chairmanship of Francis D. Murphy, formerly of the Supreme Court. The Ferns Inquiry was just one of four other inquiries in the first decade of the new century. *Suing the Pope* shocked the nation. By the time Father Sean Fortune had committed suicide in 1999 with rosary beads clasped in his hands, and sixty-six charges of child sexual abuse against his name, support for the clergy had dissipated. With the release of the *Ferns report* in 2005, the all-powerful priestly caste in Ireland had fallen from its pedestal. Tóibín sums it up: 'No-one is afraid of the priests any-more.'[171]

It is hardly surprising the Irish Church now struggles. Nuns are spat on in the streets. Young men can no longer be enticed to study for the priesthood. The Co-Founder of the Association of Catholic Priests calls it a crisis. Nineteen of Ireland's 26 counties did not attract any candidates for the priesthood in 2014. In 2012, just twelve men began studies for the priesthood – the lowest number on record. On average, 50% of seminarians drop out before ordination. On projected trends, Ireland's priests will shrink by 75% in the next thirty years.[172]

Chapter 9

Curtains

Late February, 1965. One year behind me, and like Sisyphus I return to climb my mountain – my wild and scraggy mountain range oblivious of my presence.

I wave goodbye to the women in my family who gather along the railway tracks, in vegetable gardens and on roads with their white handkerchiefs waving above their heads. In my bags I have a new Maxply tennis racquet from cousin Evelyn, white curtains from Maureen and my new golden guitar in a strong black case purchased from Murnane's Electrical Store in High Street. The Rhinestone Cowboy, skating on life, living on handouts, educated by the Church, returns to the seminary for another year. I'm still at a loss about my future, but feeling a little more comfortable. I know what to expect. Life is taking shape even if it's the wrong shape. One thing has become clear. My future is not in Terang.

The Spiritual Director at Springwood, Father Ted Shepherd, is someone I can talk to and I think he would be reasonably pleased with my efforts over the long holidays. Before we had left Springwood for the summer break, Ted gave the following instructions: morning Mass and communion, regular prayers, daily rosary, weekly confession, spiritual reading and daily meditation. There were some don'ts: no drinking in hotels, no reading of tabloid newspapers, no associations with young females, no parties or dancing. I am not the most conscientious seminarian, but when I get back and Ted asks me how I managed I'll report, 'Not too bad, Father.'

I'll tell Ted that I travelled to Wagga in January to report to my bishop, Francis Henschke, and while there I met with the other Wagga students. There is a fine camaraderie amongst the priests in Wagga, and I'm made to feel welcome. The bishop is paying all my expenses and I owe it to him to give this another year. I never at any stage misled him about the strength of my vocation. He knew I struggled and we had talked about sending me to Beda College in Rome to hasten the process. Beda ran a shortened theology course for older men. I rejected these offers, which he had first mentioned when he sent me to Chevalier College.[173] It would be hard enough leaving from Springwood, let alone Rome.

Back in New South Wales, to my dismay, I find myself alone at Sydney Central Station – the one seminarian to catch the train to Springwood. Something is terribly wrong. Where are the boys? I realise I have the wrong date. Am I early or am I late? I'm late. Two days late. This is a serious error on my part and I front Veechy in his office that night. I am generally happy to go to his office at night because in the distance I can see the glittering lights of Sydney, but this night is different.

Veechy is agitated and finds it hard to contain himself. It is the only time he shows impatience with me. He informs me he has spoken with my bishop to check if I was indeed coming back. The whole matter is a great embarrassment and I have let everyone down. I apologise for my carelessness but offer no reason. I fail to mention that I love Barbra Streisand or that I had a win at the Ballarat races.

We are not immune from life in the world outside. I learn that one of our number is dead. A young man from our Pre-Philosophy class in 1964 has been accidentally killed, one week before returning. With four or five other students I travel back to Sydney with our bursar, Father Lenny Wholohan. We form a guard of honour outside the door of the church in Hunters Hill.

At least this death was recognised. It was not always the case. Peter D. has music in his fingers. He is one of the musical leaders of our small group who feels the rhythm of the 1960s. We gather to knock out the Mersey beat in the ablution block next to lockers and showers for the fifteen minutes available to us after the evening meal and the customary visit to the chapel before we go to our rooms for study. In 1965, Peter's younger brother, aged thirteen, is killed riding his bike home from school in Broken Hill. Peter goes home for a week. I see him now on his return, catching my eye and genuflecting before taking his place near me in the chapel for morning prayers. This terrible loss is never named. There is no communal acknowledgement. There is no Mass. Yet we have regular Masses for unknown clerics who die and who at one time graced this place. We will become important on ordination.

I settle back in Springwood with a new room on the second floor – one to go to the top – facing away from the mountains. But there are changes. Father Bede Heather has returned from overseas study and resumes his teaching. Most surprising of all, the authorities have made me a prefect. They trust me as one of their own. This is a worry and expectations mount.

The first thing I do on returning is hang Maureen's white curtains in my new room on the second floor. The window faces the main building and my room is visible from the study hall where classes are held. Maureen Bourke had offered to make me the curtains when I described to her the barren cave I lived in. Curtains are symbolically important. For me they represent civilisation, they offer a sense of privacy and psychological security. They soften hard edges and suggest stability and permanence. As a teenager I complained to my mother when she took down the kitchen curtains to wash every spring. Curtains go up when one intends to stay.

Sitting in class I see my curtains fluttering in the breeze. I am suddenly aware they are dancing in ways I had not anticipated – three floors of barren windows except this one hussy of a window, flaunting her femininity in the face of radical maleness. Jesus, Mary and Joseph, what have I done? If they had been French lingerie, they could not have caused more excitement. When the students realise they are mine they are puzzled. In their eyes this behaviour is out of character. I am an older man, reasonably sane, a prefect, a rugby footballer, a country bloke and not obviously gay.

I wait for one of the deans to visit me and tell me to take them down. But the first night nothing happens and Maureen's curtains sail through the next day as brazenly as they had the day before. The second night I hear a knock on my Plato's cave. It is Peter H., one of the prefects in third year. Peter is a good bloke and a mate. He excels in all sports and played A Grade cricket for Glebe in Sydney before entering the seminary. He says the senior prefects have held a meeting and decided the curtains must come down. I protest strongly. Peter is embarrassed. I ask him for a reason. 'You know why they must come down,' he agonises. I wait for him to say they are 'girly' or 'sissy'. I am twenty-eight, he is, I guess, nineteen or twenty. I ask him if he has curtains in his home. 'That's not the point,' he argues, 'this is not home.' I knew I could not win and I admire Peter for volunteering to tell me. He is not the Head Prefect, who should have delivered the decision.

I am surprised the move against the curtains comes from the prefects. I remember asking Peter if he was doing the work of one of the deans, but he denied any priestly involvement. The prefects are the eyes of Veechy and the Deans of Discipline. Surveillance officers, they go where the authorities cannot. The curtains are an embarrassment for all. That night I take them down and to my surprise, the next morning an Irish-born student by the name of John Smith (his real name) asks me if he can have them. John explains that his window faces the mountains and if he keeps his window shut they will go unnoticed. And so they did. He thanked me and offered me in exchange some contraband fruit cake which his mother had hidden in his *portmanteau* – the New South Wales word for 'case'. We all have mothers, we all have homes, we all have curtains in our homes, but the femininity and domesticity represented by the curtains was a veiled threat to everything for which the seminary stood.

Many years later, I am invited to a barbeque with friends, most of them ex-priests. I wear a T-shirt with the message, *Free Mandela*. One of the ex-priests says to me, 'Why do you always have to make a statement?' I didn't realise I did, but at the time it made me think about how I conduct myself. I suspect my friend thought Mandela was a communist undeserving of my support. It seems clear to me now, however, that with the curtains I was intent on making a statement. If I had kept my window shut, they would not have attracted attention. I think I am inclined to the grand gesture, a certain hankering for martyrdom. Despite grand gestures, the curtains were indicative of something alien to the Catholic priesthood. They symbolised families, home and mothers. The authorities should have sent me home immediately.

Most of our meals in the refectory are eaten in silence. For company we listen to our mates read. But on special feast days, e.g. Saint Columba or Saints Peter and Paul, or when important visitors sit at the top table, Veechy tinkles a tiny bell signalling we can talk and a cacophonous roar explodes. Joy fills the refectory. A student at one end of the table of eight cuts the stale bread and someone at the other end cuts the strange slabs of unrecognisable meat: 'Where does Lenny [the bursar] get this meat?' One of the sisters from the kitchen wheels past the first course to the priests at the top table. Delicate white linen hides the food from our eyes, but we devour the odours.

These are some of the best of times. At my table is Dave Ryan. Dave is in my year. He arrived at Springwood straight from secondary school so is ten years my junior. He has an older brother who is also a student. Christmas holidays are still on our minds and so are the new popular hit songs. Dave is at one end of the table and I'm down the other. After our meal we wait for the priests at the top table to finish. I begin singing softly *Downtown*, Petula Clark's latest hit. Sane people sing. There's a line somewhere about troubles disappearing if only we all went downtown.

Dave gives a smile and joins in. Hands and fingers hit the table. We're swinging. In rhythm. We won't be broken. The singers will survive. Veechy rings the bell and we stand for grace and march in pairs downtown to the chapel. I'm accompanied by Ms Petula Clark. Like Viktor Frankl, Holocaust survivor and author of *Man's search for meaning*, I have a world inside my head, which no one can see or even guess at – and certainly not control. I'm no Frankl and my situation here at Springwood is a luxury holiday resort in comparison. I am here of my own volition. I can walk out through the sandstone heritage gates one mile down the track tomorrow. But I can't go yet and while I'm here I must bend and adapt. I live in any number of worlds. On the way to the chapel Petula and I walk in step. Neon lights and cars flash by. *Downtown and a Happy New Year to you Mrs Rollo and remember Jesus loves you.* All is not lost. Hope is innate. My dreams of another life, of a life already lived, cannot be destroyed. When I stop hoping and dreaming, I'm done. I tip my fingers into the Holy Water font and move my arm to touch the fingers of another, but Donnelly, holding his red head high in the air, ignores my medieval touch and swings in through the chapel door.

And who is Sisyphus? He is a figure of Greek mythology who defied the Greek gods and put Death in chains. But when Death was liberated and Sisyphus came to die, he went to the underworld. He managed to escape, but in vain. The gods captured him, returned him to the underworld and as punishment Sisyphus was destined for all eternity to push a rock up a mountain to the top from whence it fell down and he pushed it up again, and again, and again ... Albert Camus, Algerian born, Nobel Prize winning author and philosopher, taught me about Sisyphus.

At the top of his mountain, Sisyphus watches as his rock rolls back down the mountain. Turning slowly, he begins to follow it down. Sisyphus is modern man, caught in useless work, in a futile existence. Yet there is no tragedy until Sisyphus becomes aware of his predicament. When he becomes conscious of his situation, he becomes Camus' absurd hero.

Sisyphus has one hour on his way down the mountain, and in this breathing-space he finds it possible to consider his situation. It is up to him alone, this individual, this conscious man, to decide, within the limits of his freedom, what is his relationship to his fate.

There is no escape for Sisyphus. He accepts his fate, stares down his gods and in so doing becomes superior to his fate. Sisyphus thus becomes stronger than his rock. He pokes scorn at his tormentors. In the silence of his mind he gives a *Yes* to his predicament. Yet there are moments. Other moments. At these times he gives in to melancholy as he recalls the joys and passions of his past life. But he realises there is no future there. At such moments his rock is stronger than him. He rejects that path.

Sisyphus, despite his entrapment and pain, is able to find a certain peace, even happiness, pushing his rock up a mountain. As Camus tells us:

> I leave Sisyphus at the foot of the mountain! One always finds one's burden again. But Sisyphus teaches the higher fidelity that negates the gods and raises rocks. He too concludes that all is well. This universe henceforth without a master seems to him neither sterile nor futile. Each atom of that stone, each mineral flake of that night-filled mountain, in itself forms a world. The struggle itself toward the height is enough to fill a man's heart. One must imagine Sisyphus happy.[174]

I am happy enough. I am part of the place. I am doing what I believe I must do. In 1965, I had never heard of Camus, who turned out to be as heroic in his life as Sisyphus was in his. As if to prove his philosophical argument of the absurd, Camus died, tragically, in a car accident in 1960, aged forty-seven. I see now I had much in common with Sisyphus. I had a mountain to climb, a rock to push. My entrapment was my own doing, but absurdly, after I made that decision, my head and my heart were at odds with my apparent vocation. Unlike Sisyphus my situation was not desperate. Sisyphus was bound to his rock for eternity. I was free to walk out of the seminary at any time. Like Sisyphus I too had to come to terms with my mountain. I had to stare it down and learn to live with my indifferent mountain. And I think I did.

Inside my head I recall another world: my wonderful family, my women with their handkerchiefs and tears, good times, bad times and missed opportunities. I lead multiple lives inside my head where I plan for the future. The seminary authorities, despite their almost total control, cannot touch my consciousness. A part of me is free and in this I rejoice. The trick for me will be to match my freedom of mind with a reality that matches my dreams. At the moment that is not possible. Half measures must be put in place. I have obligations, which override dreams. The situation will resolve itself, but in the meantime I will continue to push my rock up the mountain. In 1965, I am not marking off each day on my calendar. In 1965, like Sisyphus, I have found a meaning of sorts.

Take note, Church. Viktor Frankl is special. Frankl is human. He understands what love is because of the love he gave to his wife and the love she gave to him. The more fully human we become, the closer we get to God. Frankl is closer to the truth than Augustine. His words reflect those that John gave to Jesus in the fourth Gospel:

> A new command I give you: Love one another. As I have loved you, so you must love one another. By this all men will know that you are my disciples if you love one another. (John 13:34–5)

Frankl stumbles along in the darkness surrounded by broken men. One whispers to him: 'If our wives could see us now.'

> That brought thoughts of my own wife to mind. And as we stumbled on for miles, slipping on icy spots, supporting each other time and time again, dragging one another on and upward, nothing was said, but we both knew each of us was thinking of his wife. Occasionally I looked at the sky, where the stars were fading

and the pink light of the morning was beginning to spread behind a dark bank of clouds. But my mind clung to my wife's image, imagining it with an uncanny acuteness. I heard her answering me, saw her smile, her frank and encouraging look. Real or not, her look then was more luminous than the sun which was beginning to rise.[175]

What is love, Church? Who is special, Church?

Frankl and Camus are in some ways alike. Both men are advocating an accommodation with reality, whatever that reality happens to be. Frankl believes that in any situation it is possible to find meaning. For Frankl, it is a question of attitude. In Auschwitz, the strong of mind survive longer than others, but at any moment, even the strong can lose everything. Death is a moment away. But that's the point. The strong know that and yet they persist. For the strong, false hope and false consolation are disdained. The strong continue to search for meaning and continue to hope. The alternative is madness and death. Frankl says that when we are no longer able to change a situation, we are challenged to change ourselves. Frankl names it attitude, Camus names it acceptance.

Chapter 10

Seminaries for young boys

I joined the seminary at the peak period of vocations. What I didn't know and what the authorities didn't know was that Saint Columba's was living on borrowed time. The system was about to collapse. When the seminary opened in 1910, 26 students arrived. When 60 students arrived in 1923, a new wing with additional classrooms and dormitories was added. Economic depressions generally led to an increase of vocations and in 1931 there were 100 students. The 1950s and 1960s were boom time. The 1950s averaged around 150 and in 1964, my first year, numbers peaked at 173. A new three-storey accommodation block was built in 1958 and a new chapel in 1960. But in 1967–8, the numbers of students fell to 131; by 1974 they were 76 and by 1977 the numbers were 40. At that point, the seminary was closed. It was a spectacular crash. The 40 students transferred to Manly.[176]

Patrick Francis Moran (1830–1911), Cardinal Archbishop of Sydney, had attempted to break the Irish mould in 1889 when he opened Saint Patrick's College for the training of Australian priests overlooking the beach at Manly. The seminary was built and fully equipped at the sole expense of the Archdiocese of Sydney. Wishing to be remembered, the Cardinal had his personal coat of arms and his initials cut into the stone and the iron lacework.[177]

A small, but prophetic number of 12 students arrived to begin their training, one as young as 12. Moran had been the Bishop of Ossory in Ireland and arrived in Sydney in September 1884. He wanted Manly to be a national seminary with Australian priests trained in Australia, but his Irish countrymen, exercising authority in their dioceses, would have none of it. Moran struggled and by 1900, 87% of priests in Sydney were still Irish born. Not to be deterred, in 1908 Moran bought land nearly ten kilometres out of Springwood, a small town approximately eighty kilometres from Sydney, for a junior seminary to complement Manly. Students for the priesthood would study philosophy at Springwood and theology at Manly.[178]

My decision to join the Wagga diocese as a student priest had important repercussions, the most important being that at Springwood I came under the overly protective wing of the grand ringmaster of the circus, Cardinal Archbishop of Sydney, Norman Gilroy. Norman was a ready-made candidate for Alexander Pope's wit in his great satirical poem *The Dunciad:*

So sweetly mawkish, and so smoothly dull ...[179]

Norman was something of a quasi-military man; on Anzac Day 1915, he was a 19-year-old junior naval wireless operator on the transport ship *Hessen*, off the coast of Turkey. He was an unpretentious, simple person drawn to piety, and lacking in vision and imagination. With his set smile and red socks, he ran a tight clerical ship. The laity under his wings were expected to follow their pastors, who were in turn expected to follow Norman. Not only were the lay people expected to turn up for weekly Mass on Sunday, but also to play housie one night a week. If I had studied in Victoria, the Jesuits at Corpus Christi College, Werribee, might well have provided me with a more rounded and cosmopolitan education.

Corpus Christi College opened its educational doors in 1923.[180] Having failed to come to an arrangement with the Sydney archdiocese, Archbishop Daniel Mannix invited the Irish Jesuits to Victoria. Mannix wanted some say in the training of his priests in New South Wales and when rebuffed he turned to the Jesuits. According to John Molony, Mannix probably had misgivings also of the suitability of diocesan priests to conduct clerical training.

Although the Victorian seminary was isolated some miles out of Melbourne, the Jesuits, in particular Father Charlie Mayne, Dean of Discipline, were aware of the negative aspects of isolation. The opposite was the case at Springwood. Isolation was the deliberate policy. Charlie Mayne, however, invited visiting speakers, including women, to address the Victorian seminary students. Debates were held and adjudicators from the world outside awarded the points. Students had access to a telephone and went home for one week in the winter as well as enjoying the long summer break. Unlike Springwood, students were encouraged to take an interest in Catholic Action. Under the laissez-faire policy of Daniel Mannix, various lay bodies flourished and their leaders were welcomed at Werribee. Corpus Christi, even before 1950, had an intellectual vitality that Springwood never had in the 1960s. Students could listen to classical music and had access to a 'rich library of 20,000 volumes'.[181]

Reading John Molony's autobiography I sense that relationships between staff and students at the Jesuit seminary in Werribee may have been more civilised than at Springwood, although I cannot be certain. Clearly, there was much in common – obedience and authority were paramount in both – but in 1945, his first year at Werribee, John, along with other first year students, was asked to read to one of the older Jesuits who had failing health and poor eyesight. Father George O'Neill, SJ, was a language and literature scholar. He had studied in Ireland, Prague and Paris, had mastered six languages and in 1910 had become the first professor of English at University College, Dublin. James Joyce was one of his pupils. I cannot imagine any of us being asked to read to our staff members.[182]

But these positives may give a wrong impression. They require balance. Cardinal Joseph Cardijn visited Australia and spoke to the students at Corpus Christi. The year was 1965 and recently I met with one of the seminarians (now a parish priest) who met him on that day. Following Cardijn's address, staff and students assembled for tea and coffee. Mike, aged 27, had worked fulltime for the YCW as Melbourne Secretary of the movement before entering the seminary. Cardijn was his hero. Mike noticed him, aged 82, sitting alone in a corner of the room and he went over and spoke to him. Cardijn welcomed him and invited him to sit. Mike placed his arm behind Cardijn, resting it on the back of his chair. A week later the students were gathered together and addressed by one of the senior Jesuit priests. The priest drew attention to the 'inappropriate behaviour' of one of their number. It seems Mike had displayed an over-familiarity with 'a prince of the Church' by placing his arm on the back of Cardijn's chair.[183]

Initially, seminary training for the priesthood began with young boys, not young men. It was one of the Church's responses to the Protestant reformation of the sixteenth century. The Church turned to the young with a view of moulding them in her image. The Fathers at the Council of Trent (1563) thought that by educating the young in its new seminaries it would assist them in improving the image of a poorly-educated diocesan clergy, as well as improving the observance of celibacy. Ironically, their efforts failed to impress the Protestant reformers, who quickly rid their churches of celibacy. In particular, however, the Council Fathers were keen to arrest the ongoing sexual abuse of minors and the solicitation of women in the Sacrament of Penance.

The Decree on Reformation resulted in setting up Cathedral Colleges for the training of boys of 'a tender age' (i.e. at least 12 years old) to protect them from the 'pleasures of the world'. The Catholic Church for centuries had a jaundiced view of 'pleasures of the world', its way of speaking about women and sex. Believing we are all 'born-bad' due to original sin, the Council decided that early discipline would capture young boys, 'before habits of vice have taken possession of the whole man' – the Fathers' euphemistic way of referring to girls, sex and impure thoughts. These boys were to begin their formation as future priests under the strict control of Holy Mother Church. The world was a contaminating influence, and the same principle operated at Springwood four hundred years on. In particular, the Council Fathers were keen to capture and protect the 'children of the poor' who would progress with their schooling under the necessary 'ecclesiastical discipline'.[184]

New seminaries were seen as a way of complementing Church law relating to celibacy. Dating back centuries, all previous Church legislation had failed to convince many of its clerics to remain celibate. The Trent legislation followed the same pattern of failure. While seminary training may have helped greater observance of celibacy, 'at least for a time', sexual abuse continued with violations of women, men and young boys. In the first year of his pontificate, Pope Pius V (1566) found it necessary to publicly denounce clerical sodomy.[185]

But the new seminaries brought subtle downsides. Until ordination, young men were isolated from families, women and the world. They were to live in all-male environments and encouraged to think of themselves as specially chosen. They were taught that the power conferred on them as priests was unequalled in human understanding or reason. Separation, and the idealisation of the priesthood, led to clerical notions of superiority, in particular over those in the Church whom they were called to serve. Moreover, a high priority for the new seminaries was to convince young boys that the spiritual benefits flowing from celibacy far outweighed anything the marriage state could offer. Celibacy presented a path to spiritual superiority, which in turn supported the mystique that clerics were able to withstand the urges of the flesh and devote themselves totally to God. This 'mystique further isolated clerics and fortified the clerical caste as a social and religious elite'.[186]

Being celibate is no easy matter. Celibacy goes against the instructions of our genome. Holy celibacy requires a change of heart and mind, and not surprisingly seminaries failed to bring about that 'deep internal metamorphosis in all priestly candidates' that is required.[187] Celibacy is more than a negation; it is a gift, something one accepts and integrates into one's whole personality. Ultimately celibacy is for heroes, something one embraces and not suffers. As such, holy celibacy is rare.

To feed students into Springwood philosophy classes, in 1942 the Marist Brothers began offering secondary classes through to the Leaving Certificate on the seminary site at Springwood. Students as young as 12 began arriving at the seminary to commence their studies for the priesthood. Chris Geraghty was one. Life was not easy for the young boys placed in these minor seminaries. Pressure from Church officials, poverty (often as a result of big families), and the perceived honour of having a son a priest, convinced parents to grant permission to the Church to care for their children. I have a friend who was in such an institution in Ireland; he refers to himself as one of the stolen generation – a term in Australia reserved for Aboriginal children removed from their parents.

At Springwood in the mid-1950s, students noticed a young man behaving oddly. There were sudden outbursts of anger. He frequently sat alone in class and began chewing the skin on his hands until they bled: 'He used to bite hard on the thick butt at the base of his thumb or on the dorsum of his hand, close to the wrist.' Clearly the student needed help, but professional psychological help was not the first choice of action. Even for boys who were little more than children, seminary life was survival of the fittest. If people broke down then there was a weakness and they were unsuitable. One of the deans, Doctor George Joiner, asked the young Chris Geraghty, aged about 16, to help his fellow student. Joiner told Geraghty that he was moving the disturbed young man from his table in the refectory to sit next to him and he urged Chris to befriend him. Chris managed to get the young man to talk to him, watched him chewing his hand and encouraged him to break out of his depression. There was an improvement and some months later the student went home to his parents. He later attended university, married, had children and became an expert in his profession.[188]

A serious problem for young boys joining minor seminaries was the loss of their teenage days and the natural development of their sexual maturity. Little wonder they began work in parishes as child-adults. Geraghty went to the Springwood minor seminary in February 1951. Chris was prepubescent, an innocent child, ignorant of most things sexual. Sex hormones surge at the onset of puberty. Testosterone levels rise about eighteen fold in boys and twofold in girls. The seminary system will oversee this turbulence by ignoring it and threatening eternal punishment for those who sin.

Geraghty was surrounded by older men who might have helped him, but no one did. His spiritual director, whom he saw once a month, should have been his mentor, but Father George Meredith felt more comfortable talking about college rules. Sex education, even with his parents at home, may not have existed. Most young Catholic men and women grew up in the fifties without any serious or sound sexual education. But the added problem for the likes of Geraghty was the religious atmosphere in which they lived. Impure thoughts and masturbation were serious sins. It was too easy to become scrupulous in the hothouse atmosphere of a seminary where most things relating to sex and sin became exaggerated. To sit quietly in the pew at morning Mass while everyone around you stood and went to communion was a public embarrassment and an acknowledgement of sin, probably of a sexual nature. Sinful souls could not receive communion.

But there was some sexual 'education'. George Joiner was called upon to explain to the young boys the facts of life in his biology class:

> Anyway, anyway, this class is not to be, anyway, a source of amusement. Anyway, there's to be no giggling. This is serious, anyway, and must be treated so. Now, anyway, copy this down.

Anyway, a rigid penis ... a rigid penis, anyway penetrates ... penetrates anyway ... a receptive vessel anyway ... receptive vessel (spitting out the 'ive' like 'receptiffe') ... called a vagina, anyway, v-a-g-i-n-a, anyway.

Recently, I spoke to Geraghty about how he could be sure George said the above. He told me he took copious notes as a student and these are George's exact words.[189]

There were variations of the Springwood model for minor seminaries. In the 1950s and early 1960s, Saint Patrick's Secondary College in Ballarat, Victoria, placed likely lads in a minor seminary on the college site. The minor seminary in Ballarat was therefore part of the school community, unlike the school at Springwood, where the young boys were part of the seminary. And the notorious seminary in County Wexford, Ireland, Saint Peter's College, had a secondary school with three hundred boarders attached. The authorities at Saint Peter's frowned upon any fraternisation between the school boys and the seminarians. The authorities should have kept an eye on the fraternisation between priests and students.[190]

Life for young boys in Australian minor seminaries was probably no worse than it was for young men hoping to be priests in England. In 1953, John Cornwell, British academic and author, entered a minor seminary aged thirteen.[191] In his outstanding memoir, *Seminary boy*, Cornwell details his agonising experiences with issues of sex and masturbation. He notes that semen and seminary come from the same Latin word: *seed*. The irony of the etymology should not be lost. The word *seminary* originally referred to 'a garden plot where seeds were grown, protected from harsh weather'. Much later on it became a word signifying a place where children and young men were protected from the world while they pursued their schooling and priestly studies.

In his minor seminary, Cornwell was influenced by a religious world cut off from the streets and violence from which he had escaped. Along with his secondary school studies, Cornwell filled his days with devotions to the Blessed Virgin Mary, Saint Thérèse of Lisieux and Thomas à Kempis.

At Christmas, Cornwell travelled home to London. Leaving Cotton College, he caught the train from Oakamoor station in North Staffordshire and when the train stopped at Derby he noticed a young girl aged about 16 close to his window:

> She was slight of build and wore a well-cut navy blue coat and neat black shoes. Her dark lustrous hair was cut short and parted in the centre of her head. She seemed to me to be the most beautiful, delicate creature I had ever seen, and I was surprised by my sudden sense of wonder. I thought: I shall never forget this girl and this moment for as long as I live.

These were dangerous thoughts for a young man looking ahead to the celibate life. Back in the seminary Cornwell was plagued with scruples and temptations. Unlike Geraghty, he was offered both bad and good advice. In his desperation to stop *wet dreams* and possible masturbatory events, Cornwell, aged 14, took the cord from his pyjamas pants and tied his wrists; with the slack he tied it around the back of his neck. He wrote that he did this 'to prevent my hands straying downwards while I slept. My last thoughts were of Our Lady – Our Mother and our refuge.'[192] He awoke, confused, to find his hands tied.

Saint Pius X, pope from 1903–10, was to blame for my monastic life in the bush along with the monastic existence of most seminarians around the world. In New South Wales, Pius was ably assisted by two cardinals: initially by Cardinal Patrick Francis Moran of Sydney, who bought this land for our bush hideaway in 1908, during the reign of Pius X, and then in the 1960s by Cardinal Sir Norman Gilroy, who had imbibed deeply at the well of Roman culture, and who was responsible for my seminary training.

These three men intended to not merely isolate me from the world, but through my training to convince me to focus my spiritual development on a God who exists outside this world. Pius X saw the world and its people as a distraction. My spiritual development, of necessity, must now take on a vertical shape. I am to look up to the sky for inspiration. To become a priest, I have first, it seems, to become something of a monk. I am to be alone with my God. There is nothing in my background that has prepared me for this. All my previous religious experience and understanding had God at a horizontal level, alive in the world and living in all people to the extent that He had made them all in His image and had invited them to love Him.

But Pius X had a different view. Pius was a reactionary in politics and religion. As a sign of his thinking, one of his first decisions on becoming a cardinal in the See of Venice was to close down a college for lay students attached to his seminary. This was to prevent seminarians from contacting lay students. Pius wanted his clerics to breathe in clear clerical air in isolation from the laity.

Pius was a pope for clerics, a pope for tradition, a pope for class distinctions. The separation of the classes was part of the natural order. Despite his peasant background, when he became pope he forbade any clergyman to use language which could cause in the poor an aversion to the upper classes. In this he followed his distinguished predecessor, Leo XIII. Pius believed in an ordered world of hierarchies, which must remain undisturbed. Both Leo and Pius X were unashamed supporters of the ruling class.

Under Pius X, Catholics involved in social, economic and political change had to work under the direction of the Church or face serious consequences. Pius deplored democracy, liberalism and socialism. He believed in three things: first, a God who was a practising Catholic; second, authority, which he exercised with his bishops; and three, obedience, performed dutifully by the faithful under his care.[193]

In one sense, Pius X was little more than a parish priest acting out the role of pope. Unlike his aristocratic predecessor, Pius was a pastoral pope. His father was a village postman and his mother a seamstress. He was the first peasant pope for three hundred years. He 'had never worked in the curia, had no experience of Church diplomacy, and was neither a theologian nor a canon lawyer'.[194] All, or some of which, could have worked in his favour, but it wasn't to be. His background and the legend that built up around him would have him as simple-minded. This is to underestimate the man. He was autodidactic and intelligent.

Unlike Pope John XXIII, who opened himself and the Church to the world, Pius greatly feared the world and its liberal ideas. Outside his self-imposed prison within the Vatican, Pius thought he could see the Antichrist at work. Preyed on by dark visions of catastrophe, he imagined he saw the beginning of those evils which are reserved for the last days. He did not lack courage and he had a clear agenda. Pius would save the Church by eradicating it of its clerical intellectuals, who, foolishly, thought that perhaps the Church had something to learn from the new religious, political, economic, philosophical and social ideas that had led to the secular attacks on the Church. Pius never trusted intellectuals. He thought that a learned priest, 'stood in danger of being a proud and potentially unfaithful one'.[195]

Pius greatly valued the priestly vocation: 'The priesthood that Jesus Christ instituted for the salvation of souls is by no means a human profession...' Pius would reform Catholicism to meet the new secularism and he would begin with the clergy and their formation in seminaries. He insisted on greater discipline amongst the clergy, on greater mental obedience and on a strict allegiance to papal teaching. Seminary directors were urged to eliminate insubordination and the spirit of independence. The Catholic laity must hold their priests in high regard, and the clergy themselves must hold themselves in high esteem. Pius didn't invent clericalism; he merely insisted on it.

The transformation of seminary training was Pius's priority. He believed that a major internal problem for the Church was, in part, due to poor initial training of priests. He insisted on a 'monastic-style regime to ensure life-long holiness and dedication'. Seminaries were to be in remote places cut off from the world. Seminarians must wear cassocks and Roman collars at all times and, where possible, every priest around the world should wear the cassock in public. He urged that vacations from the seminary be limited. He stressed that the clergy be conscious of their separation from the world and that they follow standards not expected of laymen. He wanted bishops to ordain only those men who had reached the required high standards he set. In his letter, *On the clergy in Italy,* Pius instructed the Italian bishops to reject candidates for the priesthood whose inclinations demonstrated 'a disregard for discipline and that pride of mind which fosters it'. The chief virtue he wanted in both seminarians and priests was obedience. The clergy should exhibit 'external signs of piety, purity and innocence'. Much of this policy dated back to the Council of Trent.[196] What we know now is that practices of obedience and the absence of personal autonomy in clerical life must be considered significant in helping to explain the causes of clerical abuse in the Church:

> especially if obedience becomes an instrument of oppression in the hands of Church leaders who work in a spirit of power and control rather than a spirit of guiding leadership.[197]

Pius would have loved our seminary. He said that seminaries should exclude outside influences. Lay teachers, secular books and newspapers were to be banned. (After 1930 and the 1950s, radios and televisions were also excluded.

Seminaries for young boys 141

At Springwood, we also had no access to telephones.) Pius forbade the clergy to edit newspapers or periodicals. Seminarians were no longer allowed to attend courses in secular universities, nor were lay students allowed inside the seminary. Women must not enter the enclosure and seminarians must not be involved with the local community. In the presence of women (God forbid such an event), seminarians were advised to practise 'custody of the eyes'. They must also avoid special or particular friendships within the seminary community.[198]

Forty years after his death, Pius X was canonised a saint.

Chapter 11

Decade of change

In the early 1960s, Prince of the Church, Cardinal Norman Gilroy, Archbishop of Sydney, leader of our seminary in the bush, a man overladen with earthly decorations and honours, began his preparations for the Second Vatican Council, convened in 1962–65. Rome requested a list of topics from Norman for discussion at the Council. Content with the status quo – truth does not change – Norman, nevertheless, decided something must be said, and consulted with his senior brains trust at Manly seminary overlooking the beach. The 'grey heads' got together and thought and thought and eventually came up with ... nothing:

> Everything in Australia was sweet. Steady as she goes. Plain sailing ahead. Perhaps there could be a bit of tidying up some minor matters which had been overlooked at the first Vatican Council ... Maybe some fiddling at the edges, some fine tuning of the administration of the sacraments, but nothing radical. It should be all wrapped up in a few weeks. The Roman Curia could be trusted to let them know what they should think.[199]

But Norman had a good idea for the Council Fathers, which he shared first with Pope John XXIII:

> Here we set great store on having the priest visit the home; and we cannot help but notice when we come to Rome that the parish-clergy are less devoted to that work. I would strongly recommend regular and methodical visitation, because it always proves fruitful, and one would have to say the Communists hate and fear it. The pastor who visits his own people will keep the wolves of Communism at bay.[200]

But all is not well. The 1960s will be the decade of change. God's Church will be threatened socially and spiritually. The Church and the notion of the cultic priesthood will be redefined. The clergy will fall from their pedestal and become an integral part of a humbler pilgrim Church called the People of God. In this decade the Church will lose its triumphalism and begin a tentative reaching out to other religions. The Mass will be said in the language of the people and those in the pews will become players not spectators. The laity will learn they are sharers in a royal priesthood, but while the concept will confuse the vast majority, those like my mother are happy simply to shake the hands of those around them and smile: 'And peace be with you.' Some priests will leave their presbyteries and marry. Nuns will remove their white coifs, their long-flowing black habits and emerge as women. They will wear skirts and dresses with heads bare and become professionals. Some will leave the convent and look for partners. I will marry one.

Humanae vitae appears in 1968 and a majority of Catholic married couples reject its rulings on birth control. Sexual mores can never be the same following the medical approval of the contraceptive pill in 1960. Millions of women are on the pill by 1965. With fears of pregnancy behind them, married women enter the workforce. Families become smaller and the days of offering excess children up to the Church are over. Vocations to religious life freeze.

The world is suddenly mobile. Beginning in the 1950s, young men and women are on the move. Cars, bought on time payment, carry them away from their small towns to regional centres on Saturday nights. Small local dance halls close. Cars bounce on their rubber at the new drive-in theatres. Drive-in theatres are an American idea that caught on in the mid-fifties. Local parish church groups founder. Mobility is the catchcry. Aspirations broaden and education shifts from its factory model of educating the poor. Working-class kids want to complete Year 12, become doctors, and study at universities. Young people in schools are asked their opinions. Many religious teachers jettison the *Truths* enunciated in the catechism and encourage their students to find Jesus at the centre of their lives. Everyone has a view on everything and authority crumbles. The Catholic ghetto crashes open. In churches, guitars replace organs and in the streets, universities, workplaces and homes the sisterhood is on the march. Sex, drugs and rock-n-roll throw

Australian conservatives like Bob Santamaria into a lather.[201] Well-bred young women at universities begin to sound like shearers. They look you in the eye and tell you to 'Fuck off'.

Veechy and his team don't know it yet, but the old Church paradigm, which set the tone for our seminary back in 1563, and was revitalised by Leo XIII and Pius X, is fraying. It's hard work when you possess the Truth. The Church gave the finger to science and Galileo in the seventeenth century, trembled with rage at Voltaire's wit, and failed to understand the cheers that greeted the bloodied head of an absolute monarch and the crash of a prison gate in Paris in the eighteenth century. She ignored the cries of the poor crushed by the new factories while she gathered her cassocks around her celibate legs in the nineteenth century and declared the prisoner of the Vatican infallible in matters of faith and morals. Yet there was a limit to this self-obsession.

The old paradigm staggered into the next century with an authoritarian and misguided man, Pius X, waging a futile war against what he saw as the latest evil threatening the Church. He branded it *Modernism*. He was followed by a good man called Benedict whose offering of mediation in the Great War was rejected. Then came the disappointing Pius XI, autocrat and conservative, dining with the aristocrats and powerful in Milan, allowing the fascists to drape his Duomo with their ugly symbols. As pope he went on to choose Mussolini over one of his own, Luigi Sturzo, and Fascist trade unions over Christian unions.[202] Next was Pius XII, the clerics' cleric, an ascetic man and a Germanophile who tragically chose Fascism over Russian Communism. Both were abhorrent – he did not have to choose either. Pius allowed his Catholic values and concern for the Church to override fundamental human values. He wouldn't be the last.[203] But was it all too late? After Treblinka and Auschwitz, even God was silent.

The old paradigm cracked and broke in the 1960s. I missed much of it, but inside Saint Columba's seminary our little group of singers, knocking out the beat in the ablution block with our guitars and folk songs, went on as if little had changed. But for some of us, the fresh winds blew through our mountain range bringing with them new sounds and a promise of change and hope. The times were changing.

More immediate for the Catholic bishops than societal changes in the 1960s was the commencement of the Second Vatican Council. The Council would shake the four-hundred-year-old paradigm of the Church. The Council challenged, in particular, the preconciliar model of priesthood and, indirectly, the value of mandatory celibacy. But challenge was one thing. Winning was another. The Council Fathers were frustrated in their attempts to discuss celibacy. Pope Paul VI, sensing danger, moved to stop any public discussion. He sent a letter to Cardinal Tisserant to be read to the Council. The pope said he did not wish to restrict the freedom of the Council Fathers, but he did just that. He requested that celibacy be not discussed and all those with questions should address them directly to him. Evidently some issues were too important to be left to the Council.[204]

Nevertheless, celibacy became an issue when the Council indirectly redefined priesthood by forcing the earlier cultic model of priesthood into a creative balance with a 'servant-leader' model of leadership. The clear understanding priests had of their vocation, certainly their role as mediator between God and other humans, their 'unquestioned status and exalted privilege' – features that had helped priests deal with the sacrifices and crosses inherent in their vocation – began to blur. For some priests:

> the council's emphasis on the dignity of baptism and the universal call to holiness raised questions about the discipline of celibacy's ascendancy, at least on the level of practice, over the sacrament of marriage.[205]

But we should not get too excited. This subtle shift away from the supremacy of celibacy must not be overstated. Hans Küng, Swiss theologian and author, writing in 2014, concluded that Church attitudes regarding marriage and celibacy have changed little.[206]

The Second Vatican Council dipped its toes in the flowing waters of change. Minor seminaries were an anachronism in 1965, but that did not stop the Council Fathers – in their decree on priestly training – endorsing the idea of minor seminaries for young boys. The decree argued that such institutions were needed to 'develop the seeds of vocations'. Minor seminaries provided a place where young boys could be prepared by 'special religious formation, particularly through appropriate spiritual direction...' The year could have been 1563. But some positive reforms were passed on minor seminaries. In something of an admission, the decree acknowledged that 'proper cooperation with parents' was necessary and that the daily routine of these young boys should be in accord with their age; further, that there should be, 'fitting opportunity ... for social and cultural contacts and for contact with one's own parents'.[207] We should be thankful for such small mercies.

Towards the end of 1965, Pope Paul VI proclaimed the Second Vatican Council's decree on priestly training. We knew nothing about it, but it would turn seminary training on its head. The move away from Thomism was striking. Thomas rated only one mention in the decree and that was in the study of theology. The decree was critical of the separation between philosophy and theology. In our system we studied philosophy for three years at Springwood and then theology for four years at Manly. The Council decree argued that philosophy and theology should be suitably aligned and ecclesiastical studies should be taught to all students on entering the seminary. These introductory ecclesiastical studies should have as their focus the end product. This excellent reform meant that the work of the priest was to be placed at the very front of priestly formation. Students should 'perceive the meaning, order, and pastoral end of their studies'.

Philosophical training will change. Philosophical studies will be broadened and students will receive a:

> solid and coherent knowledge of man, the world and of God, relying on a philosophical patrimony which is perennially valid and taking into account the philosophical investigations of later ages.

The words 'perennially valid' were as close as Thomas got to the action. Importantly, the problems identified in philosophy were to be related to problems in real life. Seminarians should receive a 'humanistic and scientific training', which young men in their countries would expect to receive as a foundation for higher studies. These were significant reforms. There was also a new emphasis to be placed on learning. Teaching staff must be highly qualified in their disciplinary field and were to have pedagogical training. Greater emphasis was to be placed on individual learning with lecturing merely one aspect of the learning process. Lectures were to be complemented by discussion groups and seminars. Students should be encouraged to develop their own study patterns and learn to work in small groups with other students. They should be encouraged to *rigorously* search for the truth while recognising the limits of human knowledge.

The decree placed great emphasis on work experience, in this case pastoral experience. Pastoral training must be integrated into the whole of seminary life. Students were to have pastoral experience from the outset, both during the academic year and during vacations.

Strict regimentation and the emphasis on external behaviour and appearances were intended to disappear, but despite many excellent reforms, the essentials remain in place. In particular, although shaken, the essentials of clericalism will survive. The priesthood will continue to be understood as a 'divine vocation'. Priests will continue to be 'divinely chosen' by God. Celibacy will be central to the notion of priesthood, and while students will learn to recognise the 'duties and dignities of Christian matrimony', they must also be taught to recognise 'the surpassing excellence of virginity'.[208]

I see now that my arrival to study for the priesthood at Springwood in 1964 was at the end of an era. The old Church of Trent and the First Vatican Council was ready to fall into a sinkhole. The Second Vatican Council lifted the Church up and out and gave it a chance, but the Polish Pope, Saint John Paul II, and his successor, Pope Benedict XVI, pushed it back into the hole and there it lies, humiliated and shamed following the world-wide clerical sexual abuse scandal.

By the time of the Second Vatican Council, the Catholic religion had become a parody of the Gospels. In the second half of the nineteenth century and the first half of the twentieth century, Catholic believers in Australia lived in a Catholic ghetto; they had become enclosed in their own social form – a closed environment with their own world view. At the time I was so trapped in my paradigm I could not see it. David Foster Wallace, American author, has a modern parable that explains my entrapment. There was once an old fish swimming alone downstream. He met two younger fish swimming upstream. 'Good morning,' he said to the two young fish, 'how is the water downstream?' 'Good,' they replied. Once the old fish had swum on, the two young fish looked at each other and one said, 'What's the water?'[209]

Sunday afternoon is letter writing time. All mail can be censored. We hand our open letters to the bursar for postage. We write in our rooms or join others in the major classroom where for the first time I hear folk music being played. I write home every week to my mother. I also write to my friend, Kevin Lee, in Terang. Each Sunday night, Kevin cuts all the Victorian football results from the pink paper. The slim cuttings put the censors at Springwood off the scent. This way I learn if Melbourne, my football team, has won.

One of the Deans of Discipline, probably Walshy, censors the music we have started playing. An appropriately named group called Peter, Paul and Mary is acceptable. When I finish my letter I go down to listen to the music and talk with friends. Bob Dylan advises us that the answer is blowing in the wind. May it blow through these gullies and gorges, Lord.

Within a decade this counter-cultural wind, reflected in this music, will blow this seminary and others like it out of the water. The gathering forces, both religious and secular, will bring the Divine Church to its knees. But where will it blow me? I am lifted up in this new wind. My inability to make a decision weakens me, stripping me of weight. I float through my days waiting for something to happen.

I arrived at Springwood with a history of political and social activism. Camus says we each live with two or three ideas which guide our lives. We polish and transform them when we must. He thought it takes about ten years to make them our own.[210]

I had two big ideas in 1965. They related to what it meant to be a Catholic. My ideas had nothing to do with Pius X's paranoia or Thomas Aquinas's philosophy of Being. In 1965, without knowing it, I was, philosophically, a personalist. My attitude to religion was, first, based on the dignity of the human person and, second, on an indivisible link between the spiritual and the temporal. These two ideas, especially the idea that in loving people I was loving God, were in conflict with the clerical and elitist ideas informing our seminary.

I abhor the total control, the rules that determine my every movement, but, unlike Tom Keneally, I find I can live within them. I dislike intensely my isolation, but the rules I manipulate, and when I want to, I ignore them. My greatest problems are long-term – the nonessential trappings that attend the priesthood: clericalism, mandatory celibacy and the Church's anti-world view.

Perhaps I have lived too long in the world. The call to the priesthood is all-embracing. To be a priest I have to turn away from the world and the people in it whom I love. The Church demands that I give myself wholly to her and forgo all else. In becoming a man of God, which I think I am, I have to forsake all else. Why does it have to come down to this, this absolutism, this all or nothing? My seminary God would separate me from everything I love and desire. This institution has its God and it would seem I have another. At heart I am a layman.

How did I get to think like this? It was due to my education in Catholic Action. In the Young Christian Workers' Movement (YCW), I was taught to love the world and the people in it. I learnt that God lived in the world and I had a mission in the world. In loving people I was loving God. God was love and love was indivisible. The distant seminary God was a selfish God. He sought me out for himself. But my God was an internal God – the risen Jesus who sent his Spirit to live within me. Even now, fifty years on, I can't help thinking that perhaps I lacked the necessary strength of mind and will. Perhaps I was overly simplistic in my thinking. Perhaps I lacked humility.

There was a related issue. I was aware of a tension, which tore away inside me and which followed from my experience in Catholic Action. It was the tension between persons and souls, this artificial separation of body and soul, this dualism at the heart of Catholic doctrine. The lay mission, as I saw it, was directly concerned with persons – undivided persons. The clerical mission appeared to get it half right with its concentration on souls and their salvation. Clerics, it seemed, saved souls not people. Disembodied souls at that. At the point of death, the Church taught that the soul left the body and went to its particular judgement. On the last day, at the general Judgement, the soul and body were once again to be united.

This clerical mission worried me greatly. The Church taught that God directly created souls. Whatever about the evolution of bodies, the Church insisted on God's creation of individual souls. Souls were the business of the Church and its priests. And the salvation of souls was intimately connected to notions of sin, forgiveness and our true happiness in Heaven. The clerical caste worked as shepherds. They guided and protected their flocks from the evils and errors of the world. I was a restless shepherd. Rather than protecting people from the world, in 1965 I wanted to bring about the Kingdom that was central to the teaching of Jesus. This Kingdom was the reign of God here on Earth. In the YCW we saw it as the transformation of earthly life and a continuation and eventual completion of the work begun by Jesus prior to his death and resurrection. Its constitutive elements were built on justice and love. Political involvement was a necessary concomitant. The Kingdom that I believed in stood in opposition to worldly kingdoms.

The Kingdom for me, however, was never a grand universal strategy for conquering the world. In terms of action, its scope was small and natural, encompassing no more than the whole of my life. The wonder of the YCW was its ability to convince an uneducated working-class kid growing up in a tiny country town that he had a unique mission and could make a contribution. In thinking about it now, I am reminded of a conversation between a poor, innocent Jewish man named Yakov Shepsovich Bok, charged with the murder of a small boy in Bernard Malamud's novel *The fixer*. Yakov is defended by a lawyer B. A. Bibikov.

Bibikov worries that he will fail Yakov, which puzzles Yakov. Naively Yakov asks, 'Why should you fail me?' Bibikov replies:

> Partly it is our situation in this unfortunate country that causes me doubt. Russia is such a complex, long-suffering, ignorant, torn and helpless nation. In one sense we are all prisoners here ... There is much to be done that demands the full capacities of our hearts and souls, but, truly, where shall we begin? Perhaps I will begin with you?[211]

Where shall we begin? That is the question. When I first read that many years after I had left the seminary, I thought of the Kingdom and the YCW and our efforts as young men and women to build it. For better or for worse, when I entered the seminary, saving souls for happiness in some future life always seemed to be something of a diversion.

'Where life overflows without ambitious plans'
... our seminary buildings, reminiscent of a rich man's mansion ... A pointed tower, more Arabic than Christian, sits three floors above the squat block of stone with its Romanesque entry into the courtyard. These are signs of civilisation. (p.46)

All souls
... I follow the traditional practice of making a short visit to the chapel, then out and back in again ad infinitum, to pray for the souls in purgatory ... Donnelly is aghast. He says it's all nonsense. Is Donnelly a Catholic? My brain is filled with hocus pocus. (pp. 94-5)

Oral examination
With Veechy. At night. First door on right. *... the lights of Sydney are blinking ... A few of us line up outside his door ... What's he asking? Dreyfus! It's Dreyfus. Jesus, Mary and Joseph! (p.103)*

Presocratics
... I realise philosophy is going to be a problem ... Either these ancient Greeks were mad or I am mad. Looking out the window into the courtyard I see cloisters, small trees, green grass and a sandstone building. Not a fire or a number in sight. (p.19)

Spiritual exercises
... we dug holes and filled them in. After some time, Say decided to give me a serious job painting the railings along an overhead path that linked the private quarters of the building ... and the chapel. (p.99)

154 Trapped in a closed world

Top: The bush
Clinging to the trees are the abandoned shells of cicadas. On the red ground black ants scurry in frantic busyness. If I walk far enough I can hear farm noises. I hear a man shout away in the distance and a dog barking. There is another world and I am comforted. (p.61)

Insert: The mail
We wander down to the rec hall built by previous students, collars off, soutanes undone, scungy t-shirts, some of us positively louche-like, and waited for the head prefect to come with the mail from loved ones, which he delivered frisbee-like into the raised welcoming arms of children at a circus. (p.48)

Top: Mum and Dad visit the top field
Filled with the milk of human kindness, they are as sweet as the spring grass I sucked on when bringing in the cows at Maureen's and Pat's farm. Full of uncertainty about my future, the one certainty in my life is that I am greatly loved. (p.208)

Insert: The nuns' convent
Forbidden to converse with them, we never manage to meet with them, to thank them. ... One of the sisters drives a car and sometimes we meet her coming along the road up from the front gate. We all wave and to our great joy she waves back. That is the extent of our communication. (p.62)

156 Trapped in a closed world

Above: Mary and the Romanesque arches
She is an apparition. She meets a student and asks demurely if she can see Kevin Peoples. I see her now in my dreams. Her short skirt is above her knees, her hair has streaks of grey, her eyes, always beautiful, have long eyelashes, and dark pencil shades highlight the blue. (p.63)

Top left: Memories and Des Welladsen
We both played rugby there with the excellent ball skills of Victorians. 'You remember how we practised a move, you at fullback and me five eight'. He looks at me, waiting for a reply. I shake my head. 'Well one day I looked over my shoulder to throw you the ball and you were gone' ... An old man now, once a seminarian and fullback, who one day disappeared and didn't say goodbye. (p.164)

Lower left: The breakfast door
After Mass ... we were drawn by another bell to gather in pairs outside the refectory for breakfast at 8.00 am. No talking. The great silence, which began after late evening prayers the night before, continues until after breakfast. (p.48)

Leaving
I had not failed. I had done what I had to do and it was over ... I would not sneak off. I would say goodbye to my friends, and I would drive out into the good world through the sandstone heritage gates more confident than I had been for years. (p.14)

Chapter 12

Friends and ghosts

I meet Donnelly on his way to the chapel. He's carrying his music. J. S. Bach.
I have a question for him, but he gets in first.
'What do you want?'
'Do zoologists know anything about ants?'
Donnelly looks amused. A natural inclination.
'Depends.'
He waits for me.
'I've been watching ants.'
'And?'
'Well, they're feverish little buggers,' I say. 'They appear to have a plan. One lot dashes out of a small hole and another lot dashes in. The ones dashing in carry things down the same hole.'
'Things?'
'Well, sometimes it looks like white things. Little lumps of things. Like small bits of sugar.'
He moves Bach from one hand to the other. Red hair, face flushed.
'Of course they have a plan,' he says. 'They live in colonies. The queen lives under the ground and the infertile female ants fossick for food and store it down the hole.'
'Ants have a queen? Like bees?'
I see he's pleased I know something about bees. He waits.
I ask him what males do.
'Not much. Bugger all.'
He begins to walk away.
I need to know what males do. 'Is that all? What do males do?'
'You wouldn't want to know. Queens are born at a certain time and

take off with their new wings looking for a winged male. They have sex, the queen bites off her wings and the male dies.'

Right now, given a choice, I think I'd choose to be the winged male. There is nothing Donnelly doesn't know. After a while I hear from the chapel the steady beat of Bach. The up and down of it. The rise and fall of it. Like riding a horse trotting – like riding Dad's mare, Dainty. Fifty years on it's the magical incongruity of it all – of Donnelly and me, Sydney and Terang, Bach and the bush.

Veechy continues to entrance. I want to teach history like him. He sweeps in, gathers himself and eventually speaks: 'Talleyrand, Gentlemen,' an ironic smile from centre stage, 'was at one time a bishop.' Veechy's teaching method has nothing to do with the principles of learning outlined earlier. And yet it has a magic and works brilliantly. There appears to be no introduction and no end. There is simply a dramatic whole built on storytelling. No conclusions are drawn, no references are given, no reading is required and no follow-up instructions are necessary. His stories are like the parables of Jesus. They scatter in the wind and we make of them what we will. Some fall on paths, others on rocks and thorns, but others take hold in rich soil and spring forth a hundred fold. With me they fell on rich soil.

In 1965, I've never heard of Charles-Maurice de Talleyrand, who was the bishop of Autun, a bishopric in Burgundy, at the onset of the French Revolution. Typically, I'm fascinated by the sound of his name and I have never forgotten one story Veechy told us on that day.

Talleyrand, aristocratic and clubfooted, secular not spiritual, has become important in the turmoil sweeping France. Talleyrand is flexible; his mind slips and slides. He is not to be trusted. He takes bribes. Napoleon, consistently sabotaged by Talleyrand, claimed he, 'never knew anyone so entirely indifferent to right and wrong – a shit in silk stockings'.[212]

Extraordinarily sharp and subtle of mind, self-serving and ambitious, Talleyrand has an uncanny ability to see the direction of the wind and to race ahead before it arrives. He supports the 1789 uprising and, against papal instructions, supports the Civic Constitution of 1790, which democratises the Church. More importantly, his subtlety enables him to suggest a happy solution to the vexed problem of Church property. He proposes that all Church property be sold with funds going to the State; in its turn the State will pick up all financial expenses of the Church including a wage for the poorest curés. Talleyrand has nationalised the Church! Talleyrand is clever and for his cleverness, the pope excommunicates him in 1791 and laicises him in 1801.[213]

But it's another of Veechy's stories that really sticks in the mind. Late one night, Talleyrand's grand carriage swings through the bishopric of Autun. The faithful sleep quietly in their beds unaware that their bishop is passing through. In the dark, Talleyrand looks out at the scene for the first time. His carriage suddenly hits a wet patch on the road and the wheels on one side begin to sink slowly down to the axle in the black mud. The horses strain but gradually come to a halt. Eventually the bishop finds himself precariously perched on an angle, stuck and unable to move. Talleyrand instructs one of his men to go to the nearest village, to wake up the locals and bring them here to rescue their bishop, who is after all their shepherd and in desperate need of help. The villagers fall in behind the idea if for no other reason than the desire to see their bishop. The men step into the mud and lift and heave and push. Progress is slow but for his part the bishop stays warm and dry. Once out and on dry ground again the whip cracks and the horses race off into the night. The locals are left to watch their bishop gallop out of their lives. It was the first and last time they would see him.

In 2008 our tourist bus drives through the magnificent gates of the Chateau de Rochecotte in the Loire Valley. Once inside I learn this is where Talleyrand, voluptuary and womaniser, spent much of the latter years of his life. Tomorrow the tour will visit other bigger and more important chateaux in the valley, but without me. The ghost of Monsignor Veech and I will spend the day exploring and reading. I know more about Talleyrand than I did in 1965, but Veechy has forgotten more than I know. The hotel staff provide me with every available piece of reading on the history of Chateau de Rochecotte. I visit the small chapel built by the Duchesse de Dino for Talleyrand, her uncle, and possibly her lover. The Duchesse rightly worries about Talleyrand's soul as he approaches death. He is thirty-nine years her senior.

In the afternoon Veechy and I traverse the gardens and settle under a tree reminiscing. We are away from the main buildings and surrounded by a forest of thin, white birches. Veechy, not a man to sit on the ground, is uncomfortable. With great reluctance he had lifted his long soutane and settled himself in the lush undergrowth. He is carrying a white handkerchief in his right hand. I know nothing about him. Where was he born? Who were his parents? What was their background? Did he have siblings? Where did he first go to school? I remind him that his friend Balzac also stayed here. He gives a low snort but says nothing. Late in the day we go inside for the serving of tea. There is an American woman sitting alone. Her husband is looking at paintings in the next room. She smiles hello to me and then explains that she was far too tired to go on a sightseeing tour today and besides this is such a wonderful place and have you seen the pool and besides there is this absolutely a-may-zing person called Talleyrand who lived here and who even spent time in America. I sensed his importance rested on the latter. Veechy looks askance and takes a seat in the corner. Tea is served by a servant in gloves. After a time she asks me if I have heard of Talleyrand. From the corner I hear a Veech snigger. 'Yes', I reply. Then in a loud voice she calls to her husband: 'Darh-ling, there's a man here who knows something about Talleyrand.' It is the case I have a view about Talleyrand, but I choose instead to tell them a story about the Bishop of Autun whose carriage was bogged one dark night and his flock pushed him out. They like the story but I can see they are disappointed. There must be more. I suspect Veechy is happy enough that I remembered his story and as for me there is nothing more to say. *Ah, no, Veechy, you never knew the whole of it ...*[214]

Back in Springwood, Father Bede Heather, scripture scholar, has become a friend. We are drawn together because of our friendship with John Molony. In 1947, John's first year at Propaganda Fide College, he met Bede. There was an annual division of students into small groups at Propaganda and Bede and John found themselves the only Australians in a group of thirty. Some years later, when John became a cleric, Bede gave him a wild-looking tonsure and after they were ordained, four close friends including John and Bede bought an old Ford car and travelled around Europe.[215]

Bede commences his lectures to us on the scriptures. He begins with the prophets – Isaiah, Jeremiah, Hosea and Amos. Bede is a teacher; he reads Greek and Hebrew and has given his life to biblical scholarship. The students call him Bede the Venerable. A half century on, he will be asked by the Royal Commission into Institutional Responses to Child Sexual Abuse to explain why he destroyed certain documents when he was Bishop of Parramatta. I find it virtually impossible to think ill of him. He treats us with respect, gives us space and involves us in the process of learning. With the exception of a new young philosophy lecturer, Father Paul Ryan, whom I admire, Bede is unlike all the others. He tells us that one day we will do more serious work on the prophets, but for me this is as serious as it will get. Fifty years on I remember Jeremiah and Bede.

On Sunday nights, Bede occasionally invites me to his room. He tells me about Molony. Bede is a tall, dignified man who speaks in a measured voice: 'I saw John, today Kev,' he begins. 'He sends you his best regards.'

'How is he?' I ask.

Bede has no desire to distress me with bad news, nor does he avoid John's stressful state. John is progressing. He is working as a gardener at a reception place owned by a friend and cleans up after wedding parties. 'He'll come through this, Kev.'

On some Sundays, Molony makes his way from Sydney and meets Bede. They go for a drive and a talk. Ian Burns, a secretary to Cardinal Norman Gilroy, is another mate from Roman days and may have driven John to Springwood. These men cling together as brothers. When they were newly-ordained in Rome they decided they would be priests for the people, but, first, they would begin by being brothers to each other. Back in Australia, fifteen years later they proved they were still brothers.[216] I am not a priestly brother to John in the manner of Bede and Ian. But I am a brother of sorts – we were brothers together in the YCW. With Bede I am careful with my questions about John and do not pry. Whatever the Church might say or do, I will stand with Molony. I'm pleased I saw him in Sydney.

At first I am the only Victorian at Springwood, but in 1965 I am joined by the nineteen-year-old Des Welladsen, ten years my junior. Des is a working-class boy from Barnawartha near Wodonga. His dad is a ganger on the railways and a returned soldier. We have much in common. He left school after Year Ten and became an apprentice in Wangaratta. When ordained he will belong to the Sandhurst diocese. He is a reserved, sane country boy, but Springwood will bring him down. After lights out he sneaks into the bush and goes for walks. He feels put-down, not valued. He feels he doesn't belong. Yet he is giving his life to this mob. One night he meets with a couple of friends in someone else's room. They sit in the dark and share a cuppa and cake. The Dean, John Walsh, springs them. Some days later, Walshy interviews them individually in his office. Des has a cut on his head. In the dark he clashed heads with a friend. 'What happened to your head?' Walsh asks. But Des is not believed. He is not taken seriously. It's the tone. Private school polish and years of privilege meet Barney from Barnawartha, an apprentice hairdresser from Wang Tech. The other boys are punished, but Walshy lets Barney off with a warning. As Barney turns to leave Walsh says to no one in particular, 'You wouldn't know any better.'

I spoke to Barney recently. His desk is covered with papers and books and he tells me he's doing a Masters in Theology. He is a much loved parish priest and has bought himself a home out of town. His parishioners did the renovations and one of them turns up while I'm there. Photographs of successful Geelong football teams decorate the walls around our table on the back verandah. 'I hated the place,' he tells me, 'the worst years of my life.' We both played rugby there with the excellent ball skills of Victorians. 'You remember how we practised a move, you at full back and me five eight?' He looks at me, waiting for a reply. I shake my head in silence. 'Well one day I looked over my shoulder to throw you the ball and you were gone.'

My eyes are suddenly filled with tears. I don't fully understand. I try to write notes as Des talks on in his back garden. We are surrounded by his water tank, water display and watering system in his new orchard. But I can no longer write. I have stopped hearing, filled with a rush of emotion. Perhaps memories of memories as Chateaubriand would have it. I am playing rugby on a green field surrounded by bush on two sides. In his cassock and cape, Veechy, white hair, red face, stands on the side watching. Loud voices compete with screaming cicadas. 'Hold it in, Kev. Hold it in.' Instinctively I look to give the ball off. An old man now, once a seminarian and fullback, who one day disappeared and didn't say goodbye.

I asked Des what happened after I left:

> I became depressed and I couldn't even spell the word. They sent me to a psychologist in Sydney. It was about a month before we

went home. At the end of the year. I didn't tell anyone at home but when Mum got the bill from the doctor she knew.[217]

Eventually, Des felt well enough to try theology at Manly but lasted three weeks. He met the rector, Monsignor Jimmy Madden, for the first time when he went to tell him he was leaving. Unlike me, Des wanted to be a priest. His bishop sent him to Glen Waverley seminary in Melbourne and that's where I called in to see him one Sunday morning in the late sixties or early seventies. There was a casual feel about the place that surprised me. Students were sitting around having coffee and reading newspapers. Des asked me if I'd like a drink. 'Come up to my room,' he said. I tentatively crossed the threshold. From under his bed he dragged out a flagon of sherry. 'Are you happy here, Des?' 'Better than Springwood, Kev,' as he passed me a sherry in a tea cup.

The Second Vatican Council is into its third year. In our seclusion we hear little to nothing. If the *Sydney Morning Herald* has a front page story of the Council, George Joiner reads it out. Our life goes on unchanged but a storm approaches. I hear that *Time* magazine has a story on the Council. One of my friends is going into Katoomba and asks if I want anything. I request the latest edition of *Time*. The following Sunday, after High Mass, I wander down to the hole in the ground which will become our new swimming pool. We have free time before lunch. I lie on the grass and read about the Council. That night I have another visit from my mate Peter H. The senior prefects have met and discussed my brazen behaviour. Could I not have read *Time* in my room? Why did I break the rules in such a public display of disobedience? I was, after all, a prefect too. I am becoming careless. I apologise and promise to be more prudent in future. I think the rules are stupid but that is beside the point. My pragmatism ensures I will never have a nervous breakdown. I have music in my head, I am greatly loved, I have faith, I have friends and in the end all will be well.

While Peter berates me for reading *Time* magazine in public, other young Australians of his age are randomly chosen by ballot to perform two years National Service. They are conscripts and some make it to Vietnam. Two hundred and ten of them will die. We live on the other side of the moon. Blow wind, blow.

Chapter 13

A cultural problem

The Church's burning fear of women, its obsession with sexual morality, and its celebration of celibacy are evidence of what Richard Sipe calls a *homosocial society*. Homosocial is the opposite of heterosocial. It is not related to sexuality and implies neither heterosexual nor homosexual. The Catholic Church as a broad community is heterosocial. Its hierarchy, however, is homosocial. Sipe's view has negative implications.

Because some members of this homosocial society have behaved so abominably, it is essential to question this clerical caste. The Church's homosocial society has a serious cultural problem and the sexual abuse scandal proves it. Sipe has recently concluded a twenty-five-year ethnological study of celibacy and sex among Catholic priests in America. In 2014 he was asked to outline the main reasons for the high percentage of Catholic clergy who sexually abuse minors. His verbatim reply was:

> Many reasons can account for this particular deviance among a group of men who are publically sponsored as sexually safe – clerical culture is a haven for underdeveloped and psychosexually maldeveloped men:
>
> a) the clerical culture demands perfect lifelong sexual abstinence and obedience from any man ordained to the priesthood;
>
> b) celibacy is maintained as a means of institutional control;
>
> c) priesthood excludes women and thus establishes a homosocial society;
>
> d) effective training for celibacy is deficient or entirely lacking in seminaries and religious houses;

e) celibacy is not well practised within the system by superiors – bishops, rectors, confessors, etc. – this establishes a dissonance between stated doctrine and actual practice that in turn encourages the development of a sociopathic atmosphere...[218]

Prior to the Second Vatican Council, the seminary system around the world was noxious. It is clear to me now that no-one should enter a seminary until they reach the age of twenty-one. The minds of the young were twisted and torn by the Church's paranoid obsession with sex and sin. Sexual sin was the dominant topic of the moral textbooks that seminarians were required to study in the 1950s and 1960s. Catholic morality was fixated on the sixth and ninth commandments. The task of the seminary curriculum was to root out from the minds of the young the notion that pleasure and sex were in any way related. Pleasure was the antithesis of sex. Catholic sexuality, as distinct from human sexuality, has never been a thing of beauty, but an ugly, utilitarian and misogynist thing entangled and mired in sin. Sex can be many things, but its potential to be celebrated as the joyful, physical expression of the love shared between two people, of its capacity to help overcome the radical oneness and loneliness we often feel as individuals, of its ability to renew and support a relationship, of its deep and profound goodness and holiness, of the way it completes and makes us feel whole – all of this was lost on a Church intent on celebrating virginity.

Seminarians were taught that the possibility of serious sin was involved when 'wilful pleasures' were had, not merely 'from words, thoughts, or deeds involving the illicit exercise of the sexual act, but also from wilful words, thoughts, or deeds that might *lead* to such pleasures'. In one text, the section on masturbation ran for five pages, whereas rape rated a third of a page. The point hammered home was that orgasmic enjoyment for men and women was sinful 'whether the orgasm was voluntary or not, alone or aided by another, by the married or the unmarried'. Trapped in its theory of natural law, the Church taught that enjoyment from sex was 'against Nature ... in that the pleasure of the sex act being procured is detached from its true purpose – legitimate procreation.'[219]

In 2011, the Conference of Catholic Bishops in the United States received their report from John Jay College of Criminal Justice on the causes of sexual abuse by their clergy. The report should have brought big smiles to the faces of the bishops. Not that they would have been surprised. Every six weeks the John Jay sociologists conducting the inquiry met with the bishops and reported on their activities. The bishops told them what to look at. The same bishops were making sure that the divine Church of Christ would be protected.[220] Surprise! The report concluded that the bishops and their Church were not to blame for the scandal that had rocked the Church. The researchers found that the phenomenon of sexual abuse by the Catholic clergy was a one-off historical event, and had virtually nothing to do with Church culture. Not only was Church culture blameless, but the bishops were congratulated. It was their fine initiative that brought the phenomenon of sexual abuse to a sudden halt: 'Although no specific institutional cause for the increase was found, factors specific to the Catholic Church contributed to the decline in the mid-1980s.'[221]

The report went on to say that the decline in cases of abuse, which was noticeable after 1985, was brought about by the work of the bishops in reforming their seminaries. Importantly, behind this finding is another. The training of priests, therefore, was regarded as a serious problem and directly related to the sexual abuse scandal in the United States. The bishops' central reform of their seminary system was aimed at a more holistic development of seminarians – one that sought a balance between human and spiritual development.

Also importantly, however, John Jay found that the male priesthood and celibacy were not causes of sexual abuse, and not even contributing factors:

> Features and characteristics of the Catholic Church, such as an exclusively male priesthood and the commitment to celibate chastity, were invariant during the increase, peak, and decrease in abuse incidents, and thus are not causes of the 'crisis'.[222]

John Jay looked at clerical sexual abuse through the narrowest of lenses, and their conclusions ignored Catholic culture and Church history completely. The Ferns Inquiry (2003) in Ireland arrived at the opposite conclusion. That Inquiry appointed an Expert Panel to assist them in their deliberations. The Expert Panel was 'unanimous in its view that the vow of celibacy contributed to the problem of child sexual abuse in the Church'.[223]

The John Jay researchers wrote a report that never strayed outside their narrow timelines. Their research question was restricted to a consideration of 'the reasons for the increase of sexual offences from 1950 to a peak in the late 1970s, as well as reasons for the sharp decline after 1985'.[224] This question ignores the responses of the American bishops, which appear on the surface to be as inadequate as the responses were in Australia.

The narrow brief and the bishops' oversight of the project allowed the John Jay researchers to avoid the hard questions of a religious nature that might well have thrown light on the Church's role in the sexual abuse scandal. As far as John Jay was concerned, the American bishops and the institutional Church were sacrosanct. Their concern was with individuals who happened to be priests and who also happened to be Catholic. The words *clericalism*, *misogyny* and *authoritarianism* were not mentioned in a report that was five years in the making and cost the bishops $1.8 million American dollars.

There is general agreement that there is no *single* cause for the sexual abuse of minors by Catholic clergy worldwide. Church culture is just *one* important factor that must be considered when determining causation. If Church culture is eliminated as a possible cause, then causes will relate to individual weaknesses. John Jay, however, were forced to look beyond individual weaknesses. They asked themselves two questions: what happened in American that led to an outbreak of sexual abuse in the 1960s and 1970s and what led to its sudden decline after 1985?

John Jay concluded that societal changes in the United States in the 1960s and 1970s were most likely the principal cause for this one-off historical outbreak of sexual abuse by the Catholic clergy in that country. If the Church was responsible in any sense, John Jay argued it was its failure to support those older men, who were trained prior to the Second Vatican Council in seminaries that:

> concentrated too heavily on intellectual and theological studies to the exclusion of human, spiritual and pastoral formation. These seminaries were characterised by tight external control with little emphasis on the seminarian's interior growth.[225]

John Jay is, therefore, highlighting two essential points. The first relates to the failures of the seminary system to adequately train Catholic priests, and the second relates to societal changes in the United States that triggered the outburst.

John Jay, however, leaves the reader with the clear impression that if societal change had not occurred in the United States in the 1960s, then these poorly-trained clergy would not have become sexual abusers. Societal changes as causal factors in the rise of sexual abuse are difficult to assess. They should not be discounted, and they did provide an important background which may well have provided an environmental trigger for some at-risk vulnerable clerics. But to rate societal change as high on the causal scale as this research does, and to ignore completely cultural aspects of the Catholic Church, apart from seminary training, as if seminary training itself did not reflect Church culture, is simplistic.

The John Jay (2011) report then only takes us so far. It was important in helping to explain, in part, why some 'individual clerics' failed, but ignoring Catholic culture will never get to the heart of the problem. It is impossible to accept that such an all-embracing, deviant Catholic culture did not have some influence on the behaviour of its abusing clerics and misguided bishops.

In the 1960s, the liberation movements, sexual and feminist, ignited an increase in premarital sex and promiscuity, an increase in drug use and alcoholism, and an increase in crime and violence along with a growing number of divorces. All this represented a dramatic change in American society. John Jay would have it that the Catholic clergy, working away steadfastly in their parishes, baptising babies and hearing confessions, suddenly became overexcited at the changes in society, turned their clerical backs on celibacy and sobriety and took to the streets with the hedonists, revellers and criminals.[226]

The John Jay brief meant it could ignore completely the deliberate pattern of stealth and secrecy employed by the American Catholic bishops. As in Australia, the American bishops moved abusing priests from one parish to another. They strove to protect the good name of the Church at any cost. They failed to recognise the role of civil society and the right of secular States to punish criminal offences. They failed to acknowledge the harm done to innocent children and they failed to offer them the love, compassion and support they deserved. The same bishops felt no compunction in enticing lay Catholics, in particular, Catholic lawyers and others, to assist them in their secretive actions and skulduggery. All of this, the John Jay team would argue, was outside their brief. It is impossible, however, to separate into two neat boxes, firstly, the institutional responses of the bishops and (through them) the papacy and the Vatican bureaucracy, and, secondly, the behaviour of individuals who belong to that same institution.

Culture forms moral mindsets. Culture assists or retards psychological maturity. The American bishops followed a cultural, moral mindset which was centuries in the making. Bishops around the world followed the same moral mindset. The consistency of this global pattern of behaviour is no accident. It was a Catholic moral mindset – a Catholic cultural mindset. This fact alone proves a systemic, institutional problem. It was inevitable that once clerical abuse became public, the Church would bunker down in her shell-hole, and like a besieged mother fight to protect her own. Francis Sullivan, CEO of the Australian Truth, Justice and Healing Council admits, as much:

> In almost every one of the public hearings looking at the Catholic Church institutions, we have seen how rigid, closed, defensive and combative the institutional Church can be when it is threatened. It has been ready to use all its might, resources and social position to prevail over abuse survivors looking for justice.[227]

Sex abuse by Catholic clergy has never been solely dependent on external, contemporary societal conditions. The Catholic Church has a long history of attempting to keep its clergy chaste. Neither the behaviour of the Catholic hierarchy, nor the criminal behaviour of its clergy, can be explained solely by wider social changes, either in the United States or in other countries that experienced much the same social changes. Recent sexual abuse is not the first time that the Church has faced this problem.

The sexual violation of children and adults by clerics has been a tragic part of the Catholic Church's history since the early days of the Church. The first teaching document of the early Church communities, which refers to sex with young boys, dates from 98CE. The Didache states that 'Men shall not engage in sex with young boys and nobody shall engage in illicit sex with anybody else'. These teachings were made against a Graeco-Roman cultural background that allowed such behaviour.[228] From the early fourth to the twenty-first century, there has been:

> a constant flow of monastic rules and canons promulgated by individual bishops, gatherings of local bishops, councils of all the bishops, and papal decrees attempting to regulate the sex lives of the clergy.

Condemnations of the sexual abuse of minors by members of the clergy and the solicitations of sex by priests in the confessional feature in the history of the Church. Such condemnations are found in 'the unorganised decrees of local churches that were promulgated before the first comprehensive collection of laws and commentaries' in the middle of the twelfth century.[229]

Saint Peter Damian (d.1072) reported on sexual abuse by the clergy in the eleventh century. A secret report, commissioned by Pope Paul III (d.1549) on the need for a Church council in 1536, contained the following on sexual abuse in the Church: 'So much abuse and such grave diseases have rushed upon the church of God that we now see her afflicted almost to the despair of salvation.'[230] The Fathers at the Council of Trent in the sixteenth century were forced to invent a confessional box to protect women from assault by their confessors. Up to that time women knelt at the feet of Father and at times rested their heads on Father's lap. Saint Charles Borromeo put an end to that, although not to the continuing abuse. Sexual abuse of women increased after the introduction of the box. In 1561, Pope Pius IV (d.1565) gave permission to the Spanish Inquisition to prosecute what he called the 'crime' of priests seducing women in confession.[231] The John Jay inquiry, sticking to its timelines, could safely ignore Church history. Importantly, it ignored similar inquiries into sexual abuse around the world.[232]

Not surprisingly, Sipe was critical of the John Jay report. It had ignored various institutional elements that were peculiar to Catholicism but not to the United States, and the study ignored secrecy, clericalism and authoritarianism. From 1962, the papacy has insisted on a high degree of secrecy in the Church's handling of sexual abuse issues. Even witnesses and complainants could be excommunicated for breaking the code of secrecy.[233] Sipe claimed that not one of the research team had any experience within the Catholic Church as a seminarian or priest. Important lay voices, who had 'intimate knowledge of the dynamics of the hierarchy' were ignored, along with the 'substance and conclusions of Grand Jury reports' that had investigated the scandal. Sipe claimed that 'the structure, pattern, and practice of the Church's response revealed in civil and criminal cases and trials were not taken into account'. Sipe was also critical of John Jay for failing to accept an aspect of the official definition of paedophilia, i.e. thirteen years as the age of puberty, not ten.[234]

Another critic is Thomas Doyle. Doyle is an American Dominican priest. Doyle, former Air Force chaplain and canonist at the Vatican embassy in Washington, has been an expert witness and a consultant in over a thousand civil and criminal cases throughout the United States, in Canada, Ireland, England, Belgium, Australia and New Zealand. He was a witness at the Australian Royal Commission in Sydney. He has been an expert witness for several of the grand jury investigations in the United States, including the Philadelphia grand juries of 2005 and 2011. He has served as a consultant or expert witness for government commissions in Ireland, beginning with the Ferns Commission, and for the Cornwall Inquiry in Canada. Doyle's support for victims and his criticism of the institutional Church has led to virulent criticism of him by supporters of the US bishops.[235]

Doyle told the Australian Royal Commission that the cause of the sexual abuse scandal in the Catholic Church was essentially theological. The Church's clerical leaders and its faithful followers demanded that the institution be protected at all times, especially from those scandals which reflect badly on its divine origins. Any such scandals are a direct reflection on God himself. They must therefore remain hidden. And why? Because Catholics believe their Church was founded by Christ. It is the One True Church. The pope is a monarch and Vicar of Christ on earth. The bishops trace their office back to the twelve apostles. The priests in God's Church are sacred persons. Within such a context, a ten-year-old child raped by a sacred person does not stand a chance.[236]

Doyle is highly critical of the John Jay report. He argues that the report 'didn't come close to examining the true causes [of abuse]'. He believes these causes:

> are in the sacrosanct domain the institutional church goes to every length to protect but it is the domain where we will begin

> to find the answers: the clerical sub-culture and the narcissistic hierarchical elite that has allowed this nightmare to happen and has failed to comprehend the profound depth of the damage done, not to the Church as institution, but to the most important persons among God's people, the victims. This dark and toxic side of the Church will only [begin] when popes, bishops, priests, religious and laity understand that when we say 'Church' we refer not to the hierarchy, the government or the power structure, but those harmed, abused, marginalised and rejected by a Church that ... forgot that before all else it is the People of God.[237]

In Australia, when Patrick Parkinson asked himself why Catholic priests and religious brothers committed sexual abuse offences against children at higher rates than other faith communities, he ignored wider, societal reasons. And he did not separate the institutional Church's response to sexual abuse from the crimes of individuals belonging to the institution, as had the John Jay report.

Parkinson outlined two reasons and both pertain to Catholic culture. The first was that the Catholic Church had become a law unto itself. This argument goes directly to the failure of the institution. Acknowledging a generally weak commitment to Canon Law in the life of the Australian Church, Parkinson argued that at the level of culture and practice:

> it is likely that bishops and other leaders saw themselves as first bound to obey the Pope and Canon Law, and only secondarily as citizens of a country in which they have civic responsibilities and obligations. The culture that child sexual abuse cases were to be dealt with internally by the Church was alive and well in Australia ...

Parkinson argued that the influence of the Vatican played no small part in explaining the behaviour of national churches. When the Irish bishops developed a new policy on handling sexual cases in 1996, which included mandatory reporting to the police, they were severely rebuked by the Vatican and told that 'procedures established by the Code of Canon Law must be "meticulously followed"'. In 2001, the Vatican issued instructions that sexual abuse cases which may be dealt with under Canon Law should be referred to the Congregation of the Faith (CDF) in Rome. And the 2011 document issued by the CDF in Rome read as if Canon Law is primary, and civil law secondary:

> or at least that the duties of bishops are limited to obeying mandatory reporting laws and cooperating with the police, not that they should encourage victims to go to the police or themselves initiate police involvement.[238]

The Church was indeed a law unto itself.

Parkinson's argument is supported by Geoffrey Robertson, QC. Robertson contends that in the matter of sexual abuse by its clergy, the Vatican operated as a separate quasi-State:

> The Vatican's pretensions to statehood cannot be separated from its child abuse crisis, because that crisis has exposed the fact that the church has operated a parallel, para-stratal jurisdiction, forgiving sins that host states punish as crimes.[239]

Parkinson offered clericalism as the second cultural reason for the higher than normal rates of sexual abuse in the Catholic Church. This argument brings together both the failed response of the institution and the individual crimes of the sexual offenders. The Vatican's CDF 2011 document stated that: 'The bishop has a duty to treat all priests as father and brother.' This was interpreted by some bishops 'as involving an obligation to protect priests and religious brothers from the criminal law'. And as we now know, that is exactly what many bishops around the world did.[240] When the Cardinal Prefect of the Congregation of the Clergy, Cardinal Dario Castrillón Hoyos, addressed the Irish bishops in 1998, he insisted that their primary obligation was to defend their accused priests. On the Irish bishop's visit to Rome in 1999, Hoyos told them they were to be fathers and not policemen to their priests. When the French bishop, Pierre Pican, was given a three-month suspended sentence for not reporting a serial abuser to the police, Hoyos drafted, and had approved by Pope John Paul II, a letter congratulating Pican, 'for not denouncing the priest to the civil administration'. A copy of this letter was sent to all the bishops.[241]

By acting as 'father and brother', the institutional church prolonged the abuse of individual clerics. This becomes very clear when considering the evidence given by Gerald Ridsdale, probably Australia's worst clerical sex offender. When questioned by the chair of the Royal Commission, Peter McClellan, QC, Ridsdale answered the following questions:

Question: 'Mr Ridsdale, do you agree that someone with your issues should never have been a priest?'

Answer: 'Yes. I accept that now. I'm sorry that there was nothing –'

Question: 'What should have been in place with the church to stop you from becoming a priest?'

Answer: 'There should have been a better screening process that was much more thorough, a psychological process that was much more thorough than anything that was conducted then.'

Question: 'If, when you discussed your offending behaviour with the Bishop, he'd gone to the police, that would have brought it to an end wouldn't it, as far as your role in the church was concerned?'

Answer: 'It would have, and I am now sorry that it didn't; that it didn't happen.'

Question: 'You might be sorry, but the offending –'

Answer: 'It would have saved so many others.'[242]

In considering Ridsdale, it is important to say something about paedophilia. Church culture cannot be blamed for Ridsdale's abuse, although it must be blamed for allowing his behaviour to continue. Gerald Ridsdale should never have been ordained. Those responsible for selecting men for ordination should have seen to that. That he studied at three different seminaries should have said something to the authorities.

When researching another topic years ago at the archives of the Catholic Church in Ballarat, I came across a letter from the rector of a seminary where Ridsdale was studying. The rector was advising James P. O'Collins, Ridsdale's bishop, that he had considerable doubts about the suitability of Ridsdale for the priesthood. The bishop replied requesting the rector to give Ridsdale more time. I did not take a reference to these documents, but I presume they still exist in the archives.

Men who suffer from a medical paraphilia disorder are not dependent on cultural factors for offending against children. Nor are they dependent on dramatic social changes as the John Jay 2011 report makes clear. Their disorder is individual and personal and there is no known cure. Not all paedophiles, however, are sexually active and not all child sexual offenders are paedophiles. Much sexual abuse of children is performed in families by so-called normal people with no apparent disorder, mental or psychological, and it is rarely or never reported. Paedophilia is not something chosen but is a mental disorder and if acted out causes harm to children. People who commit child sexual abuse sometimes exhibit the disorder, but child sexual offenders are not paedophiles unless they have a primary or exclusive sexual interest in prepubescent children. Popular usage which brands any sexual interest or act of child sexual abuse as paedophilia is imprecise usage of the term.[243]

Paedophilia is a technical psychiatric term. Experts generally use the term paedophilia to describe the sexual abuse of a prepubescent child. The diagnostic criteria for this disorder are a constellation of fantasies, urges or behaviours involving sexual activity with a young child (often aged thirteen or younger). The individual in question must be primarily sexually attracted to prepubescent children and must be experiencing these fantasies, urges or behaviours for at least six consecutive months. Additionally, the individual must have either acted on these fantasies or urges with a child, or the fantasies and urges are excessively distressing to the point where the individual's personal life or occupation is negatively affected.[244]

A second necessary and useful technical term is ephebophilia. This label distinguishes between two groups of non-adults – one prepubescent, the other postpubescent. Ephebophilia is a clinical term denoting an abuser whose sexual attraction is for adolescent or postpubescent children. The word *minors* is often used here to describe the victims of abuse. Minors are adolescents generally under the age of 18. Some researchers and clinicians have further specified that ephebophiles are attracted to adolescent males. Some experts in the field think ephebophilia is an unhelpful concept, and the American Psychiatric Association does not include it in the latest *Diagnostic and Statistical Manual of Mental Disorders* (DSM-5, 2013).

Richard Sipe estimates that 2% of all Catholic abuser priests in the United States are paedophiles and that an additional 4% involve themselves sexually with adolescents.[245] The John Jay research found the number of medically-defined clerical paedophiles who abused in the 1960s and 1970s was a very small minority of the total number.[246] The diocesan vicars in the States estimate that 90% of priest abusers targeted teenage boys as victims.[247]

This means that most Catholic priests in the States are more likely to be ephebophiles than paedophiles.

The Australian evidence is clear that the average age of victims when first abused is younger than in the States. In her opening address before the Commissions in February 2017, Gail Furness said that the average age of people who made claims of child sexual abuse, at the time of the alleged abuse, was 10.5 years for girls and 11.6 years for boys. Statistics for the age range will not be available till December 2017. We must wait to see the numbers of teenagers targeted. Did Australia have more paedophile priests, in the medically defined sense, than in America? We must wait for the Royal Commission to release its final report.[248]

To complicate the matter further, the Australian Royal Commission defines a child as one under 18 years. The Church is vague about how it defines a child. Canon Law, on the one hand, allows 14-year-old girls and 16-year-old boys to marry in a Catholic Church, but another canon states that the bishops must follow the civil law of a particular country.[249]

Available research indicates that most Catholic priests who have sexually abused young people have abused males. In the States, John Jay puts the figure at 81%.[250] In Australia, where the gender of people making a claim was reported, 78% were male and 22% were female.[251] This high figure of males as victims may be due to the ready access priests had to boys as altar servers, particularly when they worked as chaplains to Catholic schools and other Church institutions. John Jay found that when the Church's Canon Law changed in 1983, allowing young girls to become altar servers, there was a substantial increase in the late 1990s and 2000s in the percentage of female victims.[252]

It is also the case that psychosexually immature priests – and Kennedy and Heckler found any number of them – are likely to find an emotional congruence with adolescents rather than with mature adults. Some commentators have argued that the increasing number of gays in the American priesthood helps to explain the sexual abuse scandal and, in particular, young males as victims.[253] Sipe argues that at any one time since the 1960s, about one in three priests in the States have a homosexual orientation. In the general community the figure is closer to one in thirty.[254] It should be noted, however, that John Jay found that gay priests were more likely to have sex with gay adults than with children or minors.[255]

It is most unlikely that satisfactory answers for the causation of sexual abuse in the Catholic Church will be found by separating the institution from the offenders. Such a separation suits those persons who would focus attention on the weakness and failures of individuals and thus ignore systemic failure with its implied notion of a cultural problem.

Men who have been close to the issue of sexual abuse in the Catholic Church for decades, such as Thomas Doyle, argue that Church culture lies at the heart of the sexual abuse scandal. For Doyle, culture explains why the institution responded as it did, and culture helps to explain why some clergy offended. He believes that the abuse came from 'a dark and destructive force that had its roots deep in the essence of the institution itself'. More specifically, he believes the reasons are a combination of the Church's ideological thinking. The first relates to theological definitions about the nature of the Church, the second is Canon Law, and the third is the Church's theology of human sexuality. The Church proclaims itself to be the One True Church 'directly established by the Almighty...' Doyle names this as an unsubstantiated claim. Canon Law has failed the Church because of its 'fundamental nature as a legal system in service to a monarchical government'. Third, Doyle argues that the completely inappropriate responses of the bishops and the clergy – and their failure to realise the serious effects of molestation and abuse – can be partially explained by the Church's traditional teaching on human sexuality and the impact of mandatory celibacy on the emotional and psycho-sexual formation of clerics. Doyle believes that the Catholic Church's teaching on sexual matters derives from the thoroughly-repudiated notion of natural law.[256]

Tom Doyle should have the last word. The sexual scandal issue for the bishops and the papacy was not fundamentally about sex; it was not about the victims, the parents of victims or even the Christian community. It was, says Doyle, about the institution and power and a seriously flawed image of Church as an institution governed by the hierarchy:

> ... the abysmal and treacherous abuse of power – ecclesiastical power, church power, power that has been given by the Creator only to do good but power that has been selfishly perverted by those to whom it has been entrusted and which has brought some of the most despicable harm imaginable to the most innocent and vulnerable members of Christ's Church. The harm has been sexual, emotional and physical but I believe that in the end, the most devastating harm has been the assault on the spirit.[257]

Chapter 14

My narcissistic Church

Specially chosen, we are trained for narcissism. Apart from God, we need no-one. Our Church is self-sufficient. We are self-sufficient. If our isolation at the foothills of the Blue Mountains National Park isn't self-centred enough, the Church then insists we develop our personalities in keeping with our future celibate state. Intimacy with others is forbidden. Theoretically, we must develop a spirit of independence that will take us through life, content in the knowledge we need no other. But there is a terrible irony. Our training leads directly to dependence. Sufficient for our sanity is a relationship with an invisible God in the sky. This will be our single, meaningful relationship.

John Cornwell's book, *The dark box: A secret history of confession* (2014), is disturbing. It's a book about the history of confession, the formation of the clergy, the exaggerated emphasis the Church places on sexual morality and the development of narcissistic mindsets. Empathy is lost in the development of narcissism. Empathy and narcissism are opposites.

Cornwell analyses interviews conducted by Dr Marie Keenan, the Dublin sociologist and psychotherapist. Keenan interviewed nine convicted priests who served jail terms for sexual abuse crimes. What she found lacking in the priests was their failure to recognise the consequences of their action on others – a sign of narcissistic personalities.

Cornwell read all nine interviews and found nothing in them to suggest any empathy for the abused children. How could this be possible? Something shocking and incomprehensible to most people had led to this moral failure. Their feelings for others had calcified.

There are others who have found the same tragic phenomenon. In his work as a diocesan vicar in the United States, Donald Cozzens investigated dozens of reports of clergy sexual misconduct. This included interviewing the accused clerics. Cozzens did not find one priest who suffered any form of moral torment for his behaviour. He found 'something amiss at the core of their personalities' and 'sensed little guilt for their seductions':

> The only regret I could identify was associated with being caught. For the most part, the men I worked with were more concerned about themselves and their futures than for their victims.[258]

Brother Sean Sammon, former Superior-General of the Marist Brothers, writes that many child abusers are 'me-first individuals who find sexual relationships with children and minors safer and less threatening than relationships with peers'.[259]

This lack of empathy is directly related to the Church's clerical culture – or what Sipe calls the celibate/sexual system – and in particular to the seminary formation of the clergy. Human beings find it difficult to live moral lives without empathy. Hatred eventually fills the gap left by empathy. Without empathy, people are robbed of their humanity; the other becomes an object to be used. The loss of empathy is a form of death, and persons without empathy live on within themselves, becoming increasingly narcissistic. Inevitably, the human heart loses its ability to share in the sorrow of another and when that happens we not only rob others of their humanity, we begin to destroy ourselves.[260]

With their loss of empathy, the nine convicted Irish clergy replaced the hole in their hearts with something they inherited from the institution which formed them from the time they were children. They demonstrated a narcissistic self-centredness and a concentration on sin, in particular sexual sin, which they saw solely as a personal offence against God.[261]

The nine men informed Keenan that they found the celibate life impossible to live. They told her their young lives were obsessed with the dangers of impurity. Such obsession enshrined sexuality at the heart of their identities. Impure thoughts, repeated ad nauseum, haunted their early adulthood. One fatal attraction of the priesthood for the nine was that it would shield them from their unhealthy and sinful sexuality. These men told Keenan they feared intimacy with other adults as it might 'excite dirty urges'.

They felt consigned to loneliness, and in their emotional immaturity, they believed that only with children could they control their evil thoughts and find some form of intimacy.[262]

At the same time there was a remarkable failure to acknowledge the injustice done to innocent victims.[263] What upset these priests more than anything was their own weakness and failure to take the necessary steps to avoid their sinning. Confessing their sins to another priest provided them with the comfort of renewing their relationship with God and continuing their work as priests. They appeared to have lost touch completely with real people living in a real world.

While one priest spoke initially of his guilt, shame and a fear he might get caught out, '[his] consciousness of what he had done was entirely self-centred'. He regretted he had not taken steps to deal with the compulsion which had caused him to sin. 'I was quite upset with myself and the way I was going,' he told Keenan. He dwelt on his weaknesses, yet took comfort that God 'was the father of the Prodigal Son'. He saw himself as fitting into the parable. Keenan interviewed another priest who told her: 'I did not think about justice to the individual … it was about how far did you go with yourself in the process before committing a sin. The individual was not considered.'[264] There is a serious pathological problem here that is clearly related to culture.

Dr Keenan wrote that making 'celibacy mandatory for all Catholic clergy no longer serves anyone well'. She concluded her study of the nine men by directing attention to Church culture, in particular:

> … to the dynamics of priestly formation with its extreme denigration of the body, its over-intellectualising of morality, its failure to equip seminarians with sufficient knowledge of the way modern life is lived and understood, its neglect of the personal and emotional development of the curious young men training for priesthood, its unrealistic expectations about the sublimation of sexuality.[265]

Many of the commissioned reports into the clerical abuse of children and adolescents fail to see beyond individual weakness. Too many miss the systemic problem. They measure and count and fail to dig down deep and look at the culture that made them what they are. Too often, Catholic priests get bundled into the general mill of abusers. They are, of course, very different.

Sexual abusers from the general community don't normally undergo seven or eight years of formation isolated from the world of women and children. Neither do they undergo training that leaves many of them psychosexually immature. Nor are they taught that on a special day human hands will be placed on their heads and they will be changed forever, ontologically changed, new beings, supernaturally charged to bring salvation to their inferiors. Nor are these same sexual abusers from the general community taught they belong to a divine institution; that they alone, amongst all the faiths in the world, possess the truths that all humans crave. Nor have they been forced to reflect on and analyse every imaginable sin against the sixth and ninth commandment to the point that tension and anxiety about autoerotic sins can drive them to distraction.

Crimes of abuse committed by Catholic priests are a special case. Their very celibacy is intended to set them apart. Cornwell concludes that:

> The evidence from the huge circuit of depositions, police and official diocesan reports, court accounts, interviews with victims and perpetrators, journalists' investigations, and academic sociological research is that the clerical sexual abuser of children, as portrayed in the media, ill accords with clinical and criminal definitions of paedophiliac behaviour in men who are not members of the clergy...[266]

The idea that Catholic culture and seminaries are not, in part, responsible for sexual abuse by Catholic clerics demonstrates a degree of ignorance. Seminaries, since the Council of Trent, have been an extension of the hierarchical system of the Church. They participate, as Sipe argues:

> ... in the church's structure and its essence: only male figures have power, and the ultimate justification for this power structure is that God is sexed. The Ideal for whom one gives one's life is Jesus Christ, masculine and divine.[267]

The Church's narcissistic culture is well-demonstrated in the way Catholic bishops reacted globally to the sexual abuse of minors by their clergy. Up until the 1950s, sexual activity in a priest was viewed by the Church hierarchy as a moral/spiritual problem. By the late 1960s, the hierarchy, at least in the United States, became aware that children were being abused. They labelled this problem as deviant and personal and sought psychological answers for the individuals concerned. Church culture was not part of the equation. In Ireland the situation was much the same. Some senior Irish clerics saw the abuse of male children as homosexual behaviour rather than child abuse per se. Their emphasis focussed on the moral implications for offenders, and priests were urged to seek the forgiveness of God through their confessor. The victims of abuse were not considered, and apparently few, if any, bishops considered that Church culture might be a causal factor.[268]

Preoccupied with sin, the Church was blind to love. The nine Irish priests were inculcated from the age of five to reflect on their sins. In primary school, aged seven, they made their first confession. From the time they were children, the Church had bathed them in a consciousness of sin. There was a terrible tension between, on the one hand, normal human beings steeped in sin and its consequences, and on the other hand, humans treated as special persons – superior, entitled, chosen by God to act as his celibate ministers with the power to forgive the sins of a fallen people. There was the potential for pathological madness in this contradiction.

After decades of working with clerics and victims, Richard Sipe is convinced that while priests may be ordinary men, they do not exist in an ordinary social-moral culture:

> Theirs is a culture apart. It is an exclusively male world bounded by mandatory celibacy, where power, control, employment, and even financial reward are dependent on the exclusion of women and the appearance of a sex-free existence. No one can say that this culture has nothing to do with the problem of child sexual abuse. Experience demonstrates clearly that cultural factors inherent in the celibate/sexual system are crucial and pivotal in some instances of sexual abuse not only of minors but also of adult men and women.[269]

Narcissism in the Church came from the top down. When Saint Pope John Paul II decided to speak publicly about the sexual abuse scandal in 2002, he did so in the most narcissistic way:

> We are personally and profoundly afflicted by the sins of some of our brothers who have betrayed the grace of Ordination in succumbing even to the most grievous forms of the *mysterium iniquitatis* at work in the world ... a dark shadow of suspicion is cast over all the other fine priests who perform their ministry with honesty and integrity.

The pope's first thought was his own sense of affliction, not the victims, and his second thought was for the image of the Catholic priesthood. When it came to the nature of the crime, John Paul drew on the 'mystery of iniquity' from *2 Thessalonians 7*, 'which speaks of the end of the world and the coming of the "wicked one". Clerical abuse is not therefore the work of men, it is the work of Satan.'[270]

Sections of the research completed by John Jay in the United States in 2011 reinforce the findings of Dr Keenan in Ireland. The abusive American clergy lacked empathy for their victims. They claimed they were sexually and emotionally immature, had little or no experience of intimacy and their emotional needs were not met within the Church. Some of the priests interviewed claimed they were responsible only to God and to the practice of seeking reconciliation. They claimed the right not to be judged by others. Victims were thus ignored, as the abusers claimed they had already been forgiven. Some blamed Church leaders for their poor seminary training which left them ill-prepared for life in the priesthood. John Jay labelled this latter as a technique known as 'condemning the condemners'.[271]

The fatal dualism that exists in the Church – body and soul, Heaven and Earth – found its way into the minds of some of the abusers. Some presented a divided self to the John Jay researchers. They recognised within themselves a 'bad self' and a 'good self'. Sin was related to their human self not their spiritual self. The wrong they did was not their sexual sin per se but rather a subversion of the higher authority or the subculture to which they belonged. They explained that a sin must first be mended with a higher authority, namely God. Many could not see they had done any great harm to the minors they abused.

What is extraordinary is that John Jay saw all these comments by the offenders as mere excuses, unrelated to the institution to which the men belonged. The possible influence of a culture that isolated them from the world for seven or eight years was apparently not considered. A formation that left a high percentage of them psychosexually immature while claiming they were sacred persons was ignored. A culture with a sex-and-sin obsession was unworthy of serious thought. A culture that valued virginity over married life, that denied equal rights to women, and that sought happiness in another world was either dismissed or considered irrelevant.[272]

The global Catholic Church entered the 1960s with a mental illness that infected its whole body. Narcissism is a mental illness and the Church was narcissistic. Many practising Catholics will reject these hard sayings. However, Hans Küng's latest book has sickness as its leitmotif. Despite his bitter criticism of the Church, Küng remains a determined Catholic. He continues to love the Church, which has given him much sorrow, and to which he has given his life. And there is another Catholic. In his conclave address before being elected pope in 2013, Francis, then Cardinal Jorge Mario Bergoglio, identified what he believed was the Church's fundamental illness: 'ecclesiastical narcissism'. This was a Church, said Francis, 'living in itself, of itself, for itself'.[273] Francis also used a sickness metaphor when he referred to clericalism as a 'cancer' in the Church.

But earlier popes so glorified the priesthood that any change in the future will be difficult. In his hierarchical scale, Saint Pius X, whose influence on the training of the Catholic clergy in the first half of the twentieth century was critical, placed priests above the angels – wherever that might be! Pius X was one to fret about priestly chastity. 'The priest', he wrote, 'must fear the insidious attacks of the infernal serpent. Is it not all too easy even for religious souls to be tarnished by contact with the world?'[274] These extreme otherworldly views permeated the whole Church prior to the 1960s. Such views represent a deliberate turning away from what it means to be human. What was lost was something grounded in real life – something earthed, solid and sane. And in the process of turning their backs on real life, some priests and religious lost a sense of the otherness of people. It was relatively easy for compassion and empathy to slip away.

In my narcissistic Church, many of its seminarians were drained of their best human instincts. When I entered the seminary, the Church was self-absorbed, sucked into its own black hole, filled with little more than its self-importance. In its closed world, criticism from within was not tolerated. It demanded loyalty from its religious with an oath to the pope. Its clergy alone could restore the faithful to a state of grace. It was triumphant, patriarchal and authoritarian. It was obsessed with obedience and power. It was sectarian in jealously guarding its claim as the One True Church constituted by Christ, with salvation reserved for its members, and with a barely-contained contempt for other Christian churches.

It was quick to reject any scientific discovery which threatened its understanding of the world. It was fundamentalist and literalist in its view of the scriptures and punished its own scripture scholars who dared embrace the new learning. It rejected developments in theology and philosophy that didn't match the truths it had discovered centuries earlier. Only its clergy received their vocations as a direct gift from God; its laity were subservient with no acknowledged independent role of their own. These were some of the signs of a narcissistic Church. This was a Church that didn't belong, a nowhere Church with no place to live, balanced somewhere between Heaven and Earth.

By 1960, the Church had become an end in itself. The culture of the institution was toxic and its toxicity had the power to infect its clerics through its teachings and its seminaries. Garry Wills, Catholic historian, author and long-term seminarian studied the sexual abuse by priests in the United States. His conclusion is an indictment of the Church and its manner of training its clergy:

> The infantilism of priests, the combined sexual inexperience and prurience resulting from celibacy, the belief that a celibate male is more attuned to spiritual reality than a married man – all this created a framework where sins, when they occurred, had to be denied, the victims had to be blamed, the solution to the problem was simply praying harder. Where therapy failed, the confessional would take the sinner with spiritual force beyond the worldly wisdom of psychiatrists.[275]

Hardly surprising then that Angelo Giuseppe Roncalli, when elected pope in October 1958, called an Ecumenical Council within three months of being named John XXIII. The new pope called on the Church to open wide its windows. Let the Church breathe. Let the Church see out. Let the world see in. Let the fresh winds blow. Let the winds cleanse the Church of its illness.

With its cold arms, my seminary embraced the unholy trinity of clericalism, misogyny and celibacy. In our isolation the seminary had the potential to produce an inhuman and distorted view of life and for some of those who endured it to the end it did. For a relatively small percentage of ordained priests, Catholic culture and the particular identities and personalities of some individuals was a dysfunctional mix. But human instincts can never be totally destroyed. The Church and its seminaries set out to make us in her image. But to their everlasting credit, some young men went in one end of the seminary sausage system and came out the other end much the same as when they went in. One such priest, from my hometown, warned me not to take my seminary training too seriously. It was, he said, something to be worked through. He is now a very old man, long retired, who when called on still drives his car to small country centres on a Saturday to say Mass for the local farmers. His best mate in the priesthood became a sexual abuser. This man was also my friend. Many a Sunday night was spent in his company around the winter fire with friends singing, reciting poetry and telling stories. This man should never have been ordained. Celibacy was not for him. He embraced my nineteen-year-old sister once. A warm embrace that surprised her. I asked her what she felt about that now he was jailed. She shrugged her shoulders. 'I think he just needed a hug,' she said.

John Cornwell gets it right by concentrating on the 'moral mindset' of the nine Irish priests who lost sight of what it meant to be human. Their moral mindset, he writes:

> ... is that of a person who habitually neglects to consider the otherness of people – a failure to consider consequences in the real world in which people live and have their being; a rule-bound ethic with no developed sense of individual, authentic conscience; a person trapped in a moral stage of infancy. At the

same time the mindset is typical of a view of human nature that is essentially dualistic – recognising a split between body and soul – with the body being held of less value than the soul. The predicament is reminiscent of the unfeeling personality of the psychopath, although in the case of the priest, we are dealing with years of learnt behaviour in the institutionalised environment of the seminary.[276]

Cornwell is describing the imprint of Catholic culture on the moral mindset of these Irish priests. Moral mindsets relate to values. They influence the way people behave. They influenced the way that both clerical abusers and the bishops who protected them behaved.

Chapter 15

Undivided heart

Celibacy requires ongoing vigilance. The will must be trained and disciplined from the onset of adolescence. That is one reason why we are here isolated from our communities, our sisters and our mothers. As young men we must pray to the Blessed Virgin for purity. Jesus is our model – unmarried and celibate. If we love Jesus we must commit to his mission in the same way he committed to the mission of his Father. The priesthood is for real men, strong men. According to *Matthew*, the apostles once asked Jesus if it was better not to marry. He replied:

> Not everyone can accept this word, but only those to whom it has been given. For some are eunuchs because they were born that way; others were made that way by men and others have renounced marriage because of the Kingdom of Heaven. The one who can accept this should accept it. (*Matthew 19:11*)

This is as close as Jesus gets to talking about celibacy. Surrounded by married men as his closest followers, he did not see celibacy as a burning issue. The above quotation is no ringing endorsement of mandatory celibacy. Jesus is clearly opting for optional celibacy, and despite calls from the papacy for clerical sexual abstinence for the first four hundred years of church history, the call fell on many deaf ears and was generally unenforceable.

Religious celibacy is a charism (not charisma as personal charisma, but rather as a gift from God). No one can impose a charism. Some, like Richard Sipe, think mandatory celibacy is untenable. To attempt to force or legislate celibacy is a perversion.[277]

But the perversion lingers. Celibacy for the priesthood was reaffirmed by the *Decree on the Priesthood* promulgated at the Second Vatican Council:

> Through virginity, then, or celibacy observed for the Kingdom of Heaven, priests are consecrated to Christ by a new and exceptional reason. They adhere to him more easily with an undivided heart ... (n.16)

Undivided heart. There's the rub. According to the Council Fathers there is no place in the priestly heart for another. Love of God alone is absolute. Success depends on a gift and the gift of celibacy is what *God bestows on his Church*. The Church ropes the will of God into *its* will. The Church has only one spouse and that is Christ. But does God bestow His gift on every individual in my seminary where mandatory celibacy is the law? We have no choice.

The Church is aware of the difficulties, but is confident the sexual urge can be suppressed. Nearly one thousand years of a celibate priesthood stand behind the modern Church, but the tradition crumbles. Celibacy was encouraged from the earliest days of the Church, but the battle to win the day took Rome nearly seven hundred years. Numerous early laws enjoined the clergy to be celibate. Women, the argument went, were a distraction. There were also property settlement issues. Celibates leave no heirs and with the growing wealth of monasteries and other cloisters, the papacy sought to ensure that wealth stayed within her embrace.

Compulsory celibacy received a boost at the beginning of the eleventh century by Pope Leo IX (d.1054) and in particular by Pope Gregory VII (d.1085). While Leo and Gregory built on a strong tradition in the upper echelons of the Church, there was equally strong opposition from married clergy within the Church. Gregory's strategy was to direct attention to the laity. His encyclical in 1074 absolved the people from their obedience to bishops who allowed married priests.[278] In 1075 he commanded the laity to accept no official administrations from married clergy and to rise against all such priests. At the same time he endeavoured to deprive all such clergy of their revenues. In 1139, at the Second Lateran Council, Innocent II (d.1143) voided all marriages of priests, and anyone wanting to be ordained had first to divorce his wife. The battle for the absolute control of the clergy was won, and along with that victory the separation of the clergy from the laity.[279] The Church had created a new social order and clerics became a class apart.

One of the main arguments in favour of celibacy was based on this exclusive and heroic giving of self to God without worldly distractions. I was not convinced about the need for celibacy in 1965, but I was in training and I was already one of the specially chosen. Since God had chosen us above all others, this was, apparently, His will for me. Being specially chosen made it doubly hard to leave. It meant rejecting God's personal and extraordinary offer and in a sense rejecting God Himself. Or if not that, certainly leaving with the likelihood of guilt feelings overriding the decision.

Oddly enough, I cannot recall any serious discussion about celibacy in the seminary at Springwood. To the best of my knowledge it was never mentioned. It was, apparently, just assumed that the priesthood and celibacy went together and the matter was never raised.

The one certainty was that we budding celibates were special. Our special status was explicit in Pope Paul VI's 1967 encyclical *Sacerdotalis Caelibatus*:

> This law [i.e. celibacy law] should support the minister in his exclusive, definitive and total choice of the unique love of Christ; it should uphold him in the entire dedication of himself to the public worship of God and to the service of his Church; it should distinguish his state of life both among the faithful and in the world at large. (n.14)

Another argument for celibacy, deeply embedded in the thinking of the Church, was its attitude to women and sex. Church representatives in the eleventh century had no difficulties in stating it. Cardinal Humbert (d.1061), Pope Leo IX's delegate to Byzantium, condemned the Eastern Churches for allowing priests to marry in these terms:

> Young husbands, just now exhausted from carnal lust, serve the altar. And immediately afterward they again embrace their wives with hands that have been hallowed by the immaculate Body of Christ. This is not the mark of a true faith, but an invention of Satan.[280]

Evidently, God and marriage don't mix. In 1130, Pope Innocent II declared that:

> Since priests are supposed to be God's temples, vessels of the Lord and sanctuaries of the Holy Spirit ... it offends their dignity to lie in the conjugal bed and live in impurity.[281]

It always gets back to sex. Sex is unclean. Women are unclean. A ritual purity for priests was therefore required, one that was modelled on the Levitical priesthood as described in the Hebrew Bible.

Celibacy and clericalism are intimately linked. Clericalism has eaten away at the heart of Catholicism. As Küng argued in 2013, the Church believes that the clerical state is superior to the lay state:

> The clergy of the Western Church, by contrast [i.e. with the Eastern Church] were separated from the laity by their celibate state, implying a higher moral perfection making them superior to the laity and better qualified to rule.[282]

At Springwood, George Joiner tells us that the two strongest drives in humans are for food and sex. If George is right then we have a problem. The food in this place is poor and the second is unavailable. Even if it were available it is forbidden. I have too many memories, too much history. I am too enlivened with thoughts of a home with a wife and children. Too much unfinished business. I have a recurring image of a small blonde boy throwing his arms around me and holding on as if I mean the world to him. It is not the priesthood that worries me in 1965. It is celibacy. I am attracted to the work of a priest, but not without a wife and family. It is clear I cannot have both.

It seems to me now that mandatory celibacy and the concept of a total institution fit neatly together. It comes down to a question of clerical power. That is why mandatory celibacy is so important for a clerically controlled Church. Those who marry and have families are less amenable to clerical control.

For nearly three years, I was a member of a clerical institution where we gifted our adult self-determination and autonomy to the institutional Church, and where our freedom to act as individuals was severely curtailed. Sociologists have a phrase for institutions that resemble the seminaries of the 1950s and

1960s. A Canadian sociologist, Erving Goffman, made famous the concept of the 'total institution' in his paper of 1957. 'Total institutions' impede the growth of individuals as mature and responsible citizens. Their impact is to:

> ... disrupt or defile precisely those actions that in civil society have the role of attesting to the actor and those in his presence that he has some command over his world – that he is a person with 'adult' self-determination, autonomy, and freedom of action.[283]

Goffman divided total institutions into five different types:

> 1. Institutions established to care for people felt to be both harmless and incapable: orphanages, poor houses and nursing homes
>
> 2. Places established to care for people felt to be incapable of looking after themselves and a threat to the community, albeit an unintended one: leprosariums, mental hospitals and tuberculosis sanitariums
>
> 3. Institutions organised to protect the community against what are felt to be intentional dangers to it ... concentration camps, POW camps, penitentiaries and jails
>
> 4. Institutions purportedly established to better pursue some work-like tasks and justify themselves only on these instrumental grounds: colonial compounds, work-camps, boarding schools, ships, army barracks and large mansions from the point of view of those who live in the servants' quarters
>
> 5. Establishments designed as retreats from the world even while often serving also as training stations for the religious: convents, abbeys, monasteries and other cloisters.[284]

There is considerable difference between my total institution and many of those on the Goffman list. We had imprisoned ourselves and we were free to leave.

Goffman is right to argue that people in such institutions were 'reconstructed' to fit with the demands of the organisation and to an extent 'which could never be achieved in more open social contexts'. He is also correct to argue that there was psychological damage done to both supervisors and those supervised.[285] Happily, Goffman found that the 'inmates' normally found some scope to develop an 'inmate culture'. Hence my development of close friends, who, despite the rules forbidding particular friendships, gathered to sing songs in the ablution block before study, and on Sunday afternoons escaped into the bush, I with my guitar case filled with contraband.

The seminary was not my first experience of a 'total institution'. I was compulsorily called up to complete 176 days of military training when I turned eighteen. I joined other *Nashos* at Puckapunyal, an army camp outside of Seymour in Victoria, for ninety-nine days of full-time training in the spring of 1955. To say I was a very bad soldier would be a serious understatement. Being something of a Gomer Pyle, I was unable to hold the rifle at the correct angle on my shoulder. This led to a roaring Sergeant-Major selecting me out of 3000 soldiers on the parade ground on the day the three battalions marched out. I was quickly set upon by a regular soldier who, muttering blasphemies in my ear, valiantly tried to correct the angle of my rifle. I had problems with weapons. When practising to shoot the Bren gun, I managed to set the sights too high and nearly wiped out a herd of sheep quietly grazing above the shooting range. I was in a transport battalion, the 20th, but I was fortuitously one of the few who didn't hold a driver's licence. I discovered that made me somewhat irrelevant, which is precisely where one wants to be in the army. I learnt two things in the army: never volunteer and always aim for a legitimate task *outside* the mainstream.

The army and the seminary had much in common. At Puckapunyal we were deliberately isolated from the wider community. We were drilled and trained to automatically obey orders and respect authority. We were never encouraged to think for ourselves. The idea was: 'Don't think. Act.' We lived in alphabetical order just as we did in the seminary. The army and the Church knew best and both institutions worked on the premise that if we were not fully occupied discipline would collapse and chaos result. In the first three weeks at 'Pucka', I found myself running from place to place to keep up. I was conscious of people with power bending and shaping me to their will. They shouted, bellowed, threatened and set impossible timelines. Peace eventually came at the end of the day, when I collapsed on the wire-framed bed in our twenty-six-man tent. The army filled our days and when given *free* time we polished brass and cleaned boots. With our pull-throughs, we made sure the barrels of our rifles, when held up to the light, glistened in the Pucka sun.

Both the seminary and the army worked according to a regular routine. The army moved us in numbers – 'one, two, three, one, two, three, one' – and the seminary moved us with bells. Bells have a fine tradition in the Church. Before telephones and electronics, chiming bells were the Vatican's way of communicating across the city.[286] In both places, we marched to meals and the food in both places was hardly cordon bleu, but in quality and quantity the army was well ahead. The army took criticism of its food seriously — armies after all march on their stomachs. In both institutions we were instructed and trained, not educated. We were trainee soldiers and trainee priests. In the seminary I was Domine Peoples, in the army, Private Peoples. In Pucka and Springwood, I was a cog in a very big machine.

But predictably, I settled. I didn't enjoy the army and they bent me according to their whim. But, as in the seminary, all was not lost. There was a life outside the routine and I was saved by sharing the pain with my friends. Within the frenetic madness an extraordinary bond united us. We were in it together and we would survive. I once asked a question of our corporal, a regular soldier and a good man. We were gathered around him in a Nissen hut and Corporal Jefferies was explaining how to load the 303 rifle – 'our best friend'. Enthused and fooled by the intimacy, I ventured an opinion to the corporal (Gomer Pyle would have done the same) that it might be better to push the bolt of the rifle back into the closed position after loading with the palm of one's hand, rather than with the thumb and finger as he was instructing. Audible breaths were sucked in and a long silence followed. I realised, too late, I had made a cardinal mistake. Corporal Jefferies, who normally didn't swear at us, told me in a quiet but serious voice that he would cut off my fuckin' hand if I didn't shift the bolt according to his instructions. I never asked another question.

I was more content in the army than the seminary. I could see to the end of the army, but the seminary and Church stretched out forever. And the Church worked away inside my head with a set of values and attitudes that left me feeling uncomfortable. Both institutions were patriarchal. Women and sex were also a problem, at least for me, for both the seminary and the army dealt with two extremes. The seminary system was obsessed with sex and celibacy. The army was obsessed with sex and debauchery. Exploding levels of testosterone disturbed our beds, vibrated our tent and shook the green hills of Pucka, a poetic couplet lending itself to the mayhem. We were awash with sex. Mighty exploits of others with the opposite sex filled my days and imagination. I found it hard to look my mother in the face when I came home on leave after six weeks. But there was a certain relaxed pragmatism about me in 1955. When I lay down along the side of the road for a break from marching, I went to sleep. By the time I reached Springwood in 1964, my Pucka experiences were a distant memory.

Goffman looks at how various people adapt in 'total institutions'. One form of adaptation is the 'inmate' who appears to take over the official staff view and sets out to become the 'perfect inmate'. We had a number of them and one was a young man we call Speed. When the bell rang at 6.00 am it was the signal to get out of bed and be down in the chapel by 6.30 am. One second late and you were 'rung off' by a prefect who stood in the foyer of the chapel waiting to snare you. This meant you sat in the back seat and reported to the dean.

When the 6.00 am bell goes, Speed flings open his door and with a whish and a whoosh, black soutane flying, dashes to the chapel. Most of us struggle to do our ablutions and get dressed in the thirty minutes, but old Speed is up and about before any of us and waiting to roar into the day. The thing that's different about Speed is that he's absolutely genuine. A happy young man, he appears to be in his element. He spends more time on his knees or doing the Stations of the Cross than any of us. Whatever he is asked to do he does with alacrity and energy and appears to enjoy it. Yet I never gained the impression he was trying to impress. Speed is the 'perfect inmate'.

When I interviewed Des Welladsen, I asked him if he remembered Speed. He said he saw him recently, in Peru, all dressed up in his black 'clobber', caring for the inmates of a jail where he has worked for years.

We finish a Saturday morning class and Speed stands quietly staring out of the window into the courtyard. I'm slow moving and one of the last to leave. I wander over to Speed to see what he's looking at. 'Everything alright Speed?' I ask. I break his reverie, but like a light switched on he immediately glows and gives me his full attention. 'I'm wondering, Kev, if there is a real tree there.' Smiling.

I look out the window, somewhat bewildered, and stare at the tree. I distinctly remember this as a moment in my life. Saturday mornings at home came back to me. The excitement of a football game or a cricket match in the afternoon or taking Heather to the pictures on Saturday night. Brendan Ryan, a poet from my tribe and place, calls this excitement 'Saturday morning optimism'.[287] My life now is reduced to looking at a tree and wondering if it really exists, or is it a mere representation in my mind.

'What do you reckon mate?' I say.

'Well, it looks to me like an existing tree, Kev,' says Speed enthusiastically, 'but can we be sure? Will it still be there if we walk away?'

We have been studying the philosophy of that man from Kilkenny, George Berkeley, who worried about the real existence of a world outside his head. If the world is not observed, he thought, we cannot be certain it is really there.[288] And if it is there it is because God is keeping his keen eye on it.

I can't recall now how our conversation continued, but for certain we strode off with purpose – Speed did everything on the run – leaving the tree to its 'treeness', as Thomas would say, and me thinking of Heather and other Saturdays.

Chapter 16

I can't go on, I'll go on

One big disadvantage for me in 1965 was my lack of understanding of Church history. We had no historical texts in our syllabus at Springwood and the limited history we did learn came from Say Carroll's waffle about the beginnings of civilisation in Egypt, and Veechy's dramatic eccentricities on eighteenth and nineteenth century European cultural history.

What fed my soul in 1965 was not history but spiritual reading every afternoon in the chapel. I remember Thomas Merton's *The seven storey mountain*, Eugene Boylan's *This tremendous lover* and Teilhard de Chardin's *The divine milieu*. The first two men were Trappist monks; Merton was American and Boylan was Irish. Teilhard was a French Jesuit, palaeontologist, biologist and philosopher.

I found it difficult to read in the afternoon. Normally I dozed off. It was hot in the chapel and we had just finished sport and showered. Our clothes heated up already warm bodies. We were covered from top to toe in black soutanes and around our necks was a tight white collar. I see it clearly. I reach inside the collar with my finger and shake it to get some air.

I sit at the same dining table as Donnelly. His sanguine disposition rests comfortably with his red hair and fair complexion. Australian soldiers are fighting communism in Vietnam. We talk war and peace, communism and anti-communism. My head is filled with Santamaria's right-wing propaganda. Calmly, Donnelly queries Australia's involvement. I regard all those who march for peace as compromisers and fellow-travellers. Donnelly is surprised at my aggression. He grows red in the face but stays measured and logical. The other members of the table remain silent as the two older men argue.

Donnelly is a professional zoologist; I am a professional anti-communist. He mentions Bertrand Russell as a sane voice campaigning for peace. I say Russell is a 'stupid old bugger' who is always rabbiting on about something and who probably supports the communists. Donnelly goes quiet. After some time he says sotto voce to me, 'You know he is one of the great mathematicians in the world. He is also one of the great philosophers in the world.' I have no idea what Russell does apart from demonstrating in the streets. The discussion has become personal. Donnelly cannot understand why I speak so. Anti-communism, while reaching fever pitch in Victoria, never reached great heights in New South Wales. I back off when I realise Russell is important for Donnelly.

Why these dark shadows of memory now come into focus I cannot know. Perhaps lighter shadows are so transparent, so unimportant they have become invisible and lost to my memory. I have two copies of Russell's *History of Western philosophy* in my library. Recently, I became so excited on seeing a new edition of his *History* going cheaply that I couldn't resist buying it. It keeps company with the copy I bought soon after I left the seminary. Next to them is Ray Monk's biography of Russell. Monk, I have learnt, did not like Russell. I cannot think of Russell without thinking of Donnelly. Russell writes with a speaking voice and great clarity on complex philosophical issues. I admire him greatly. As a young man, Russell lost his faith in God. In a sense, Russell's faith was not faith at all, but something based on a rational belief of the necessity of such a being. When John Stuart Mill argued persuasively in his autobiography that the argument demanding a 'first cause' to explain the existence of the universe made no sense, Russell was forced, logically, to agree. Russell's loss of belief resulted in great personal sadness that impacted on his ideas about nature, the world and his place in it. He concluded that nature must be sad in itself and the universe some dreadful mistake.

Donnelly is marvellous. He's interested in photography and he and Doc Joiner drive off together with cameras. A most unlikely couple, but Donnelly gets on with everybody. Did we have a dark room? I think we did. I think Donnelly did his own prints. On rare Saturday nights we watch a film in the *rec* hall. We see a very tall man named Jacques Tati in *M. Hulot's holiday*. I think the film appalling. Donnelly loves it along with the other Sydney sophisticates.

I wear my working-class values on my sleeve. I wear my ignorance hidden deep inside in some dark corner where I feel sorry for myself. Bertrand Russell says that the problem with the world is that the ignorant are cocksure and the intelligent are filled with doubt. Donnelly is intelligent and he doesn't seem to have doubts. I am ignorant and in general not cocksure. My closest friends are country boys just out of school. Most of them were students at Saint Stanislaus's College in Bathurst. They appear to be here on an extended holiday. Compared with them I am lucky. This is their precious youth and each day they recklessly squander it without, apparently, a second thought. The loss may well come back to haunt them.

When I raise a question about philosophy they look at me in wonderment. Leo says, laughing: 'And, what would be the use of the answer to your question, Kev, even if you knew it?' I say it's got nothing to do with use.

'Think of it this way, Kev; you're a priest. You're driving your car, a hundred miles in the bush, and you break down. Now what's the use of philosophy? Where's your Plato and Socrates out the back of Burke?'

It is as if he's read this in Aquinas's *Summa*. Doug, from Coonabarabran, thinks Leo has a point. Frank, who will one day be a spy and work for ASIO in Europe, smiles to himself. I think he's with me.

These blokes are my mates. I don't care what they think because I don't take them too seriously. Together we empty my guitar case and fill it up with contraband and go into the bush and sing and talk and relax. The Rhinestone Cowboy carries the golden guitar while someone else heaves the heavy case. The tops of my fingers are developing hard calluses from the guitar strings. The handle of the case is showing signs of strain.

Somewhere deep down inside all of us seminarians is a place, a human place, where the seminary system can't go. It is where that spark of life reaches out to some few others whom we instinctively know we can love. Without them I would be lost. Without them I would have to leave. They are my close friends. I trust them and I enjoy being with them. I seek them out when I can. With them I can be myself. We have things in common that draw us together.

The Church Fathers at Trent had it all wrong. Trent was part of the cultural transition from the medieval to the modern world, but despite an eye to the future, the ideas of the Council Fathers looked back. Their seminary system is now four hundred years old. Whatever wind it had, it is well dead. The Church locks us in this mountain retreat cutting us off from our families and loved ones. And then, once here, it demands that we live separate lives. We are not trusted to grow inwardly and develop friendships. We do not participate in our development. Some of those who are young will struggle to reach maturity. Those who are older are in danger of losing what they had. We are in danger of becoming other than what we are. We must not walk with one another. We must not 'break the threshold', i.e. enter another's room. We must not have 'pfs', i.e. particular friends. But in all of this the system will lose. If we were to obey the authorities we would lose our humanity:

> The man with no friends has already abandoned himself to the fate of his own self-destruction. Psychiatrists realise from clinical experience what poets have proclaimed in inspired verse, that to retreat permanently into the loneliness of one's own soul is to surrender one's claim upon life.[289]

My seminary ran on auto-pilot. Its computers were set by Pius X and the men of Trent. Veechy's touch on the administration was ever so light. The staff were told what to teach and then left to get on with it. Apart from Doc Joiner, the rest of the staff emerged from their offices to lecture us and then retreated back to their cubby holes – small units comprising office, bedroom and bathroom. On Thursdays a few of them played golf. Others disappeared in their cars.

At the time, we knew nothing about how the place was managed. It seems there were no organised meetings or committees advising or working with the rector. Individual members of staff had informal meetings with Veechy, but formal structures that gave rise to institutional questions that drive a normal educational institute never existed. There were no processes in place to test the morale of staff or students; there were no educational discussions about, for example, the suitability of the library; no official spaces to raise questions about the effectiveness of teaching methods, or the suitability of the curriculum or the spiritual or educational development of the students. All questions raised by staff were on a private one-to-one basis with Veechy. Whether anyone learnt anything was of secondary importance, compared to the overall aim of developing obedient students who would come to know their place in the hierarchical structure of an autocratic Church. Veechy had no idea what was being taught on a day-to-day basis. With staff he didn't trust, he would sniff around students to find out what was happening. He warned one new young member of staff never to mention celibacy in his classes.[290]

The immutable seminary existed to weed people out. The only change that occurred was in the numbers of students. Either we weeded ourselves out or the authorities weeded us out. We were never asked to contribute to the overall organisation of the place or to our educational or spiritual development. In our medieval paradigm, we offered nothing and nothing was expected. The thought of students protesting was outside the paradigm. We understood that the system was set in concrete and troublemakers were asked to leave.

The Catholic community in the early 1960s still had a strong sense of its exceptionalism. We were superior because we belonged to the One True Church led by an infallible pope on matters of faith and morals, who also happened to be the Vicar of Christ on Earth. Locally, our bishops led us at a diocesan level and priests at the parish level. No mere student would dream of ever challenging our clerical leadership. Institutions that believe they have the truth require only one thing from their adherents – obedience. The biggest complaint I heard from the students concerned the quality and quantity of food.

Every six months or so the staff met, but nothing of substance was discussed. Veechy had a couple of staff members who were trusted and these men could be consulted on a particular issue. The place ran itself around the set routine of college rules. The Deans of Discipline and student prefects kept our seminary-plane in the air. Veechy did meet regularly with the Head Prefect, who then reported back to us on our Saturday night meetings in the recreation hall. The prefects were his eyes and ears. I have no recollection of Veechy ever addressing the student body on any issue of substance. I do distinctly remember him addressing us in the chapel prior to visiting days. His message was to remind those without visitors to keep well away from the front of the college and in particular the front field where visitors had their lunch.

The year after I left, Cardinal Norman Gilroy appointed a new member of staff, Father Chris Geraghty. Veechy wrote a note to Geraghty advising him he would teach two subjects, which, as it happened, Geraghty knew little about. He had no teaching qualifications and there were no negotiations about what he might like to teach. For six months Veechy never spoke to him. The Cardinal arrived for a three-day visit some months after Geraghty's appointment. Norman Gilroy made no personal overtures to talk to Geraghty. Norman had appointed him yet he never sought to ask Geraghty, a man of twenty-nine, if he was happy or how he was coping in his new role as a professor. At no time in the three days the Cardinal was at Springwood was there a staff meeting to either discuss issues of importance or learn what the Cardinal thought about the place or thought about anything. On the morning of his departure back to Sydney, the Cardinal, addressing staff, began a sentence with, 'I couldn't help but notice...' – the staff held their breath waiting for Norman to say something. Norman, with set smile and red socks, concluded his sentence '... how shiny the students' shoes were during Mass.'[291]

Nothing could be more Australian than our bush setting. Yet we are trained in the Roman mould.[292] Our timetable is Roman. Thursday is a free day with sport and recreation. Saturday is a normal working day. Our curriculum is Roman dating back some hundreds of years. Our philosophical text book is written in Latin and authored and printed in Rome. Many of our lecturers were trained in Rome. Our leader, Cardinal Norman Gilroy, whose first loyalty is to the pope in Rome, trained in Rome. Cardinal Patrick Francis Moran, who purchased this land for the seminary, was educated and lectured in Rome. And Veechy, whose lectures mesmerise me, is more European than Australian. I have no recollection of him ever referring to Australian history or literature.

I discover our rector has a love other than Emma Bovary – it is Doctor Samuel Johnson. He has a copy of Boswell's *Life of Johnson* next to his bed and assures us this is the greatest biography ever written. He brings it into his classes and reads slabs of it to us: 'Johnson is wise, gentlemen,' he announces.

Boswell records Johnson like no other, but, 'Gentlemen, Boswell is a dreadful scoundrel.' Huffing and puffing follows as Veechy shares a private joke with Johnson and I'm left to wonder why Boswell is a scoundrel. Before going to sleep at night, Veechy opens up a page at random and fills his soul with the wisdom of Johnson. It seems to have replaced both Emma and the New Testament in his life.

In Sydney, when I eventually leave here, I take a bit of Veechy to Terang with me. I buy Boswell's *Life of Johnson* in two volumes. What will the locals think?

Boswell tells a story about Johnson coming out of church one morning. Johnson and friends begin a conversation (as was their wont) about George Berkeley, the same Berkeley who so troubled Speed. Johnson wants to illustrate his point about Berkeley's philosophy. Johnson looks around and finds a solid stone, not as big as the one Sisyphus pushes up his mountain but sizable enough. Waddling over to the stone, Johnson gives it a hard kick and, possibly regretting his action, proclaims, 'I refute it thus: *Argumentum ad lapidem*.'[293] Veechy huffs and puffs hilariously and, led by Donnelly, whose mind moves like lightning, we all join in. I'm still working on the Latin!

Socrates had a story about cicadas. Perhaps the cicadas I hear screaming in the seminary are in fact singing. Socrates thought they sang. I first met Socrates at Chevalier College in my final year of schooling. We studied Ancient History, and the only lay teacher on the staff read to us Plato's story of Socrates' trial and tragic end. But was it so tragic? Socrates believed in the immortality of the soul. Four hundred years before Christ, he embraced his last moments and looked with equanimity, even eagerness, to the unity of his soul with Plato's archetypal Forms.

On a summer's day, hearing the cicadas' singing, Socrates related to his companion the problem enthusiastic singers and musicians face – the problem of not knowing when to stop singing and focus on the really important things in life – like, for example, eating. According to Socrates, cicadas were originally an early group of human beings who fell in love with music and became so enamoured with it they forgot to eat and drink and in their forgetfulness they died. But some time later, they returned to earth as cicadas and messengers to the Muses. They continued with their singing as cicadas and reported back to the Muses on how human beings were honouring song, dance and the other arts.²⁹⁴ Did they hear me singing? I listen to them!

As 1965 comes to an end, I am full of doubts and contradictions. To the best of my ability I am doing God's will. With Samuel Beckett I can say: 'I can't go on. I'll go on.'²⁹⁵ So I persist. Thursdays are free days. We go into the bush on a long walk to Grose Valley. George Joiner will meet us later for lunch. In the back of his utility he carries the buns, cold sausages and cordial prepared by the nuns. Many of us walk carrying thick walking-sticks. We walk on a single red road and meet no one. The bush surrounds us. I feel its menace and stay close to my mates. The bush can drive a man mad. The bush is dangerous. The seminary can drive a man mad. The seminary is dangerous. Some of our younger students fool about. One is pushed into freezing water. We pull him out but he goes blue and stops breathing. Someone gives him CPR while others run back for help. He is revived and we are all shaken. The next day it's as if nothing happened and our lives and his resume their normal course. The system reigns, but Thursdays and recreation each afternoon provide us with a chance to make decisions. With these small bursts of freedom we develop our individual selves.

Sometimes we have cricket, football matches or foot-running carnivals. Some third-year philosophers want to keep fit and look good! They specialise in body-building following an exercise plan developed for the Royal Canadian Air Force called 5BX. Tennis courts are popular and each year we run a knockout competition. With my new Maxply I fancy myself to survive a few rounds, but the Dean of Discipline, John Walsh, runs over me without raising a sweat.

Some would like to play golf but there is no golf course. At one of our Saturday night meetings in the *rec* hall I ask why we don't use the Springwood Golf Course which adjoins the seminary. General laughter greets the suggestion. After further discussion I move that the Head Prefect raises the issue with Veechy. The request is that a small number of interested golfers be granted permission to use the Springwood Gold Course on a Thursday morning with the permission of the club.

Months pass and Veechy is still considering our request. Each Saturday evening someone asks the Head Prefect what is the news about the golf. Each evening the same reply. I argue that all this hesitation is positive. Obviously it is under consideration. On one of our perambulations between classes, our group is joined by Peter H., who instructed me to take down the curtains. Peter is a keen golfer. He says to me with a grin 'If we win this, I will suggest we put up your statue on the premises.'

The answer comes back. Veechy has agreed, with qualifications. Access is limited to second and third-year philosophers and a small number at any one time. What I remember is going down to the Springwood Golf Club on the back of a ute driven by Father Lenny Wholohan with about half a dozen other golfers. No statue was ever built, and Veechy advised the Head Prefect he wanted no more 'trade union deputations'. Did he see what I would become?

On another Thursday in 1965 I saw my father suddenly walk around the back of the main building. I had known my family was coming but didn't know when. Dad is tall, thin, raw-boned and resembles Chips Rafferty. He could well have left his horse tied around the front of the building. He is dressed up wearing a tie and a green cardigan. I see him now. Fittingly, he has made for the back entrance. I shake his hand. Dad's generation neither hugged nor cried. I never saw my father cry, which does not mean he didn't.

Seeing my father is the only image I have of the day my parents came to visit me. My cousin, Rusty, drove them from Terang in his Ford Customline, along with my friend, Maureen Bourke, who made my white curtains. Maureen and I are now the only survivors of that day. I rang her recently and asked what she remembered. 'Not much,' she said.

Then: 'I know I wore a brown hat with white lace that I made and a brown suit with a white blouse!'

'Apart from what you wore is there anything else?' She replied that we went down to some 'bush land' at the front of the main building, lit a fire and had a meal. She said, 'I took photographs. They're still around the house somewhere. I'll see if I can find them.'

When she spoke an image came back, just a picture of us standing around the fire and Thomas McNiven Veech himself, who had wandered down to have a chat. He would have hated it but he came – just as he visited every parent group on the two or three visiting days in the year. For an obsessively private man, he pushed himself to the limit.

What did we talk about? Rusty could have engaged Veechy in a discussion on trucks and cars. Rusty loved big cars and Veechy owned an old, comfortable Oldsmobile. Rusty is a bitumen man, a semi-trailer driver. His mother waves goodbye to me in her pink dressing-gown when I leave Terang on the train. He is 33 years old in 1965. Before I leave Terang after the Christmas holidays, he goes around his mates in the local pub asking them for a donation to help pay my way back to Sydney on a plane. He hates trains. In grade six he began practising backing semi-trailers in Hank Cole's back yard. At fourteen he developed mathematical precision in reversing the tray up against the ramp. Once Hank took him to Melbourne, as a kid, for company, to bring back 44 gallon drums of petrol. On the way home, Hank thought he needed a snort at the Moriac Hotel. Sometime later he gave Rusty the keys to get them home. Hank needed a sleep. The police pulled them up between Moriac and Colac. A police car drove past and turned back when they thought they saw a semi on auto-pilot; they couldn't see the driver!

Mum and Dad are becoming fragile. Mum has angina pains and carries tablets in her bag. Worried about a heart attack, she has asked Maureen to accompany them on the long journey. Mum comes from Kirkstall of Irish stock. She lost her mother and father when she was twelve. Her mum died giving birth and her dad was banished on the same day as his wife and dead child were buried. He was thought to be incapable of caring for his four little girls. Mum helped bring up her three younger siblings with relatives.

Dad worries privately about his shortness of breath and occasional dizzy spells. His mother died in 1913 when he was nine and his older brother at the Great War in France three years later. He survived the Great Depression, but his heart is bruised and his expectations of life are minimal. The briquette dust from the milk factory where he works is slowly choking him. The best thing in their lives was finding each other, but next year that will come to an end. They are brave, unpretentious working people, educated in life and know what it means to suffer. Filled with the milk of human kindness, they are as sweet as the spring grass I sucked on when bringing in the cows at Maureen's and Pat's farm. Full of uncertainty about my future, the one certainty in my life is that I am greatly loved.

Dad might have told Veechy the story of Adam Lindsay Gordon jumping his horse over the fence at the Blue Lake in Mt Gambier or might have recited *The sick stockrider* for him, but I doubt it. Maureen is attractive and charming, confident and intelligent. She will engage with Veechy. She has overcome multiple sclerosis, thrown away the wheelchair she was married in and given birth to seven children. She too is brave and strong.

I asked Maureen how I was dressed. 'You were in your black soutane,' she said. I suspect Mum and Dad were proud of their son, the would-be priest who happened to be their eldest; they had not seen him before in his priestly clobber and would never see it again. What I didn't know at the time, and what I only found out recently, was that both knew I was unhappy.

I next asked Maureen did they go to Sydney. 'No,' she said, 'your Dad wanted to go to Bathurst to see what memorials, if any, were there honouring Ben Chifley and then he wanted to go to Jerilderie, but I can't remember why.' I can guess why. He wanted to see the bank that Ned Kelly held up in 1879 and the place where Ned wrote his famous letter. I am my father's son.

I am a tenor in the choir – from my first year! In the first few weeks, all new students visited Father John Walsh in the *rec* where he questioned us about our musical experience, played a few notes on the piano and asked us to sing. I'm a Nat King Cole man, a *Mona Lisa* man, a singer of love songs. Walshy is looking for something else, but he takes me on. Practice sessions are frequent and the liturgy becomes alive. Each Sunday we sing the Mass in Latin using Gregorian chant. I become adept at reading the small black squares. Ordinary chants of the Mass for the *Kyrie, Gloria, Credo, Sanctus, Benedictus* and *Agnus Dei* are easy, but most Sundays we learn a motet, which we sing in parts at the Communion. Donnelly plays the organ for us and sometimes he plays Bach and we sit quietly and listen. *Veni Creator Spiritus*. I grow into the liturgy. My mould is changing. I'm taking on a clerical shape.

On Good Friday I had made my second visit to the Grotto. Warren, the head prefect, is our leader. We do the Stations of the Cross, ignored by the bush. On Easter Sunday we surprise ourselves. *Haec Dies quam fecit Dominus*. In three parts we lift our voices in joy and thanksgiving. Walshy is delighted. We process out from the chapel in pairs into the sunshine, white surplices, black birettas, red sashes; we carry our missals. Speed walks in front of me singing with radiant happiness. Waiting outside in the courtyard, under the balconies, are the families of the students. Easter Sunday is the first visiting day of the year. Those with visitors will go down to the front paddock and spend the day. Those of us without visitors must stay away from the front of the building. Apart from families, fraternising with people from outside is strictly forbidden.

Performing on stage in the old *rec* hall becomes part of my life. These events are important. They represent an expression of our limited freedom and are thus treasured – along with sport, one of the only times when we are free to express ourselves. But even here our creativity on stage is curtailed by the paranoid nature of the institutional Church to sex. The Church not only wants to separate women from our lives – it wants us to grind them out of our lives, expunge them from our very thoughts. The love between a man and a woman, it seems, is at odds with the love we must have for our seminary God.

I sing the *Goodbye* song from *The whitehorse inn*. There is a line which I must watch: 'Although I know that I'll be sometimes missed by the girls I've kissed.' Our drama director and third-year student, a fine tenor named Keith, changes those words. He warns me, 'Whatever you do, don't sing the original line.' The problem is when I get into the song I forget. On the night we perform, Veechy and his staff come to see the entertainment. In a loud voice, I tell them all, boldly and proudly, that I *will* be sometimes missed by the girls I've kissed. Keith is embarrassed and Veechy's head drops even lower.

Of course this is all silly, but it reflects a deep malaise in the teachings of the Church where men and women and sex are concerned. We run the risk of becoming psychologically unhinged, of losing a sense of what is human and good, decent and normal; of devaluing the beauty of women and children and family life.

When we perform *Oklahoma* I sing one of the male leads. Keith sings Curly and I sing a song called *Kansas City*. It has a wild verse about an overweight girl who disrobes on stage and proves to those watching that everything she has is real. Keith, who had some doubts about me, said: 'You can't possibly sing that.' He deletes the verse. We censor ourselves. I understand that to sing such a verse may well become an occasion of sin for our audience.

In the dark, after night prayers, young men, specially chosen by God, walk piously to their cold beds. Indelibly fixed on their minds is the image I have implanted – a huge, buxom girl, round above and round below, disrobing before their eyes. Private mortal sins may follow that could result in eternal punishment in the fires of hell. Jesus, Mary and Joseph!

Female roles for our plays and concerts were never a concern for we could always find a young man who liked dressing up – after all, ritual was our business and long black dresses were popular. On Sundays for High Mass we added a touch of colour with red sashes to contrast with the black and our white collars. On our heads we wore a dashing black hat from the fourteenth century called a biretta. They were square with three peaks and some had a titchy little pompom in the middle.

Sometimes we dress up in white linen bed sheets and do comic sketches. Stan Freberg's *Rinse the blood off my toga* is one. Towards the end of the year we perform a nativity play. I'm one of the wise men and paint my face black. I'm such a ham, very much part of the place.

I missed the 1964 Melbourne Cup. Father Say Carroll had me on a working party. So in 1965 I began making arrangements. Jimmy Lawrence lived in a small home on the property. He had worked as a general handyman at Saint Columba's for decades and was known to generations of students. He had retired and his best mate was Doc Joiner; most afternoons Doc had him in the front seat of his ute. I spoke to Jimmy about the Melbourne Cup and wondered if I just happened to wander past his place on the first Tuesday in November whether the television might be on. And so I watched Light Fingers, ridden by Roy Higgins and trained by Bart Cummings, win in a titanic struggle to the post. I missed Jean Shrimpton, who was more suitably attired on Melbourne Cup Day than she was on Derby Day, when she shocked the Melbourne racing establishment by wearing a mini dress and displaying the longest of legs minus stockings, and leaving gloves and handbag back at her hotel.

Another year behind me and I am seemingly no closer to making a decision about staying or leaving. Years later and well into my teaching career, I learn about the Myers-Briggs personality test. I'm a big 'P', i.e. a person who hates closure. All options remain open. I float ideas which others think I actually believe and intend to follow up. I'm not good at making decisions and instinctively avoid making commitments that might tie me down. I hate timelines. I like flexibility. I drift into things and drift out of them – eventually. I'm not a stay-in-and-fight person. I tend to walk away and look for greener pastures. At the same time I'm also capable of making sudden decisions that surprise everyone including myself – without considering the consequences. I'm the sort of person who likes to go on a holiday by driving out the gate without a plan and thinking, which way? So with this priestly business, I will make a decision when I must. I've discovered I run about ten years behind most people. 'You're slow, sir,' a waiting taxi driver said to me once as I sauntered out to meet him in our driveway while he tapped his anxiety on the steering wheel.

I have reached the end of my second year and my fourth as an adult student. On my way home I call in to see the Molony family in Canberra. Denise and John meet me at the railway station at Yass and we drive to their two-bedroom *govie* home in Narrabundah. John has obtained work translating ancient Latin manuscripts at the Australian National University.

John was automatically excommunicated for his marriage to Denise in a registry office. They wanted a church wedding, but Cardinal Sir Norman Gilroy, for reasons best known to himself, sat on John's laicisation papers from Rome. Norman eventually passed them on and with delicious irony, Father Ian Burns, the Cardinal's second secretary, then married John and Denise in Norman's private chapel. Perhaps the Cardinal was in Rome at the time. The couple never received a marriage certificate from the Church. John was told it was locked away in the secret archives in Sydney at Norman's orders.[296]

I stop off at Chevalier College in Bowral. Father Paul Strangman, MSC, asks me if I'm still being taught that 'Thomist nonsense'. Father Frank Fletcher, MSC, more to the point asks, 'Why don't you come and join us?' Frank was responsible for my success in History. Father Brian Gagen, MSC, my inspiring English and Economics teacher, tells me I'm the best raw material he has come across for the priesthood. He was a good man and a good friend. Halfway through my final year at Chevalier, he encouraged me to add Economics to my list of subjects. He tutored me in his office at night and my A pass in November was due to him.

In Melbourne I take the Warrnambool train to Terang. It's a stop and start affair. The train gets to Geelong and stops. Young men dash to the cafeteria to satisfy two hungers: one for food and another for the sight of beautiful young country women selling tea, pies and sauce. We no sooner leave Geelong than we stop in Colac and then Camperdown. Each time we stop, people dash from the train into the railway cafeteria – 'cuppatay, piensauce please'. For the last fifteen years on this line I have been aware of these working-class girls. Nothing has changed. Celibate as I am, my heart reaches out to them in solidarity. It's their laborious work, their femininity and a sense I have of their limited life opportunities. Perhaps it's something more. Do they await a tall handsome stranger to step from the train and take them away to a place where the sky is always blue and the grass green? Their faces are flushed from the urgent demands placed on them by the customers and the steam from the boiling water. They wear railway uniforms and on the back of their heads biretta-style caps sit precariously. On small white plates marked with a blue *VR* they shake red blobs of tomato sauce. If they would permit me, I would take each one in my arms and tell her how beautiful she is and how one day someone will step off the train and rescue her from pies and sauce. It is more than solidarity.

From Camperdown we're on the home stretch, then over MacKinnon's bridge where as children, my brother and sister and I always held our breath when looking down onto Emu Creek where Clarrie Carmody fished with Alan Marshall, and where by this time Wagner's *Tannhauser* is running inside my head, keeping pace with wheels and whistles, and out the train window fences are dipping and rising, dipping and rising:

Once more dear home
I with rapture behold thee ...

The jagged Blue Mountain range of Springwood has given way to the volcanic richness of the Western District with its low-slung hills, which we call mountains. Harvesting has begun and bales of hay litter the paddocks. In recent years I've earned good money from Curly Moloney stacking bales onto his semi-trailer for twelve to thirteen hours a day. And I sang my way through those days too, at ten bob an hour with *Tom Dooley* hanging down his head while we drank cold black tea holding a silver top thermos in our raw hands as we sat under the tray of the semi to avoid the hot sun.

Change is in the air. As we come into the Terang station, *Tannhauser* has competition. I am aware of new songs, new sounds, soft, yet sharp, like my father's scythe, slicing and swishing grass outside our home as with perfect timing, he swings and fells the tall grass for Dainty. Something has changed in me. Inside my head Peter, Paul and Mary are singing something about a hammer and a bell and a song to sing.

At home my parents have a new television set. It sits in the front room, which has become a television room. I watch this other Mary who sings and shakes her long blonde hair in a most disconcerting fashion. I think I might have a new song to sing. Wagner may have run his race.

PART THREE
1966

It is apparent that perpetrators are more likely to offend when an institution lacks the appropriate culture and is not managed with the protection of children as a high priority.

Royal Commission into Institutional Responses to Child Sexual Abuse. *Interim Report, Vol 1, Executive Summary,* 3.5

Chapter 17

Ballarat's disgrace[297]

Whatever decision I reach about the future, these Christmas holidays are my last as a student at Springwood. Every January we organise family trips with Rusty driving his big Ford, and if another car is needed we use Dad's green Falcon. When I left for Chevalier College in 1962, I gave Dad my sports Triumph, a cheap car which he disliked. When the opportunity came, he traded it in for a real car with six cylinders. In the country, real men drive big cars.

We endeavour to organise trips to coincide with Dad's Sundays away from the milk factory. He often works on Christmas Day. When he does he brings home a gift from management – a jar of cream. We head north to Ararat, Stawell and the Grampians. On a clear day from the highest hill in Terang, where we played football as kids with the Arundells, two of whom became priests in the Ballarat diocese, I was fascinated by the Grampian's serrated spikes resembling a giant handsaw leaning into the blue sky.

When work stopped Dad from joining us on our long Sunday drives, we took Mum and two of her sisters, Eileen and Beryl, and Auntie Poll back to the Irish district where they were born and lived as children – Tower Hill, Killarney, Koroit, Crossley and Kirkstall. These women have moulded me with the love and lore of Ireland and as we get closer to Kirkstall, Polly's brogue becomes contagious. Memory collapses all those visits down to one image – the laughter and smiles of going, and 'Jesus, Mary and Joseph' on arrival. The three big women laugh and cry, legs out, unbecoming, as they struggle and slide to lift themselves out from the soft back seat of the car to see their broken old home leaning in on itself to remain upright, where they once lived and where their mother died with her dead baby, and their father disappeared out of their lives, and all on the one day, so to speak, in 1911 when they were children.

I make my regular pilgrimage to see my bishop in Wagga and give him a report on progress. Francis Henschke is well over six feet tall. He invites me into his small chapel to pray with him. I think he admires me as much as I admire him.

'We could send you to Rome, you know. You've done well. Do your best, that's all we can ask. God will let you know what He expects of you.'

He shakes my hand and says, 'God bless you.' He never once pressured me. How can I abandon him?

In January 1966, I drive the eighty miles to Ballarat looking for work. This is open flat country, sheep country dotted by volcanic hills. Winds blow the whole year round tearing at the tall gums lining the narrow bitumen road that stretches and narrows to a piece of string in the distance.

I drive through Darlington, Derrinallum and Skipton, and into the scratchy pig country of Scarsdale close to Ballarat. My YCW friends still continue the *Wash-N-Shine* company we had started back in 1961, but the jobs are reduced to cleaning windows at Saint John of God's Hospital. Unfortunately for me, these windows were cleaned before Christmas and the only available job is cleaning the floor at Saint Patrick's Hall, part of the Cathedral parish. My friend, Jim, tells me he has given the Monsignor-administrator a quote for the job, so if I want it it's mine: 'Just go and tell the Mons you're working for us and he'll get you started.'

I know the Monsignor well enough and he knows my family. He comes from a small farming community just out of Terang. We talk about the seminary and I ask him about his life here at the centre of diocesan life. An important man, handsome and tall, he sits behind his paper-littered desk and asks me about the health of my mother and father. I explain why I'm here and he's delighted to give me the job of cleaning the floor of his huge hall.

'We have to agree on a price,' he smiles his banker smile. 'Before you start.'

'No, the price is agreed. It's the price Jim Ross gave you.'

'But Jim's company is not doing the work. You are, and his price was for the company. I suggest we come to a private arrangement.'

I am shocked, 'I think I need to discuss this with Jim.'

'Please yourself,' says Handsome.

Back at Jim's office, I explain the Monsignor's problem with the price.

We agree he's a mean bastard: 'Either he pays you the same price as the quote or he gets someone else to clean his hall.' I need the job so I go back with Jim's ultimatum. Reluctantly, Handsome agrees and I clean his floor. With each swish of the mop I wonder about the generosity of some of the servants in the Lord's vineyard.

In 1966, when I arrived to mop-up Handsome's dance floor, I knew Ballarat well. From my days in the YCW, I had met many of the diocese's younger priests who worked as chaplains to the groups. In 1961, I had moved in with the Ross family in Sebastopol, an outer suburb of Ballarat, and became a window cleaner. Sometime in that year I cleaned windows at the Sacred Heart Girls' college across the road from the gothic red brick presbytery and grey granite stone church next to the primary school run by the Christian Brothers. This was the parish of Saint Alipius. It would become the most dangerous place for young children attending school in Australia.

What would the original Alipius have thought? Not a well-known saint, Alipius was a lawyer and friend of Saint Augustine. Both were baptised by Saint Ambrose (d.397) in Milan and both were ordained together in Hippo, North Africa. Alipius became the long-serving bishop of Tagaste. Ambrose had an extremely negative view about sex, seeing it as part of a sinful world, 'and a wound everyone must wear'. Virginity, said Ambrose, 'was the goal of all believers'. He linked women to sexual temptation that 'ultimately led to sin and death'. Alipius, undoubtedly, thought much the same.

The three friends knew about the canons the early Christians had agreed on at the Council of Elvira in Spain (309CE). Apart from legislation promoting celibacy, Canon 71 condemned sex between adult men and young boys: 'Men who sexually abuse boys shall not be given communion even at the end.' While the canon did not mention clerics, the prohibition of communion on one's deathbed indicated the seriousness of the sin.[298] Sodomy of boys by Catholic clerics began well before the sexual revolution in the 1960s. If Alipius could now see this parish named in his honour, he would weep and mourn and demand justice for the rapes and assaults on its innocent children.

In March 1961, on the other side of the city, I had called in to visit Father John Molony, chaplain to Saint Patrick's Boys College. My aim was to convince him that B. A. Santamaria was vulnerable and the National Catholic Rural Movement could be saved for genuine Catholic Action. *Big George* Pell, footballer, actor, debater, and all-round leader of boys had recently left the same College to study for the priesthood at the Jesuit-run Corpus Christi seminary, Werribee. Before *Big George* left he called Father Molony to his bedside at Saint John's Hospital with a problem. George had promised Richmond, a famous Melbourne Australian Rules football team that he would train with them in 1960. *Big George* idolised Molony. But George also had decided he would study for the priesthood. He could not do both and he was in a pickle. Molony reassured him there was no problem. Time would solve the issue. You might decide not to go to Werribee and you would be unwise to break your links with Richmond at this time. Wait and see, said the priest.

Towards the end of 1961, or was it 1962 – Alex Southwell, QC, said there was some doubt about the year – *Big George*, then a seminarian aged about twenty, volunteered to accompany a group of altar boys from the parish of Braybrook in Melbourne to a holiday camp on Phillip Island. Forty years later he was accused of sexually abusing a twelve-year-old boy, Phillip Scott. Scott alleged that *Big George*, by then Archbishop of Sydney, had thrust his hand down the young boy's pants and got 'a good handful of the boy's penis and testicles'. Scott also alleged George had tried to guide the boy's hand into the front of his own pants and on another occasion, while walking in Indian file at night, *Big George* had grabbed Scott from behind and put his hand down the inside of Scott's pants. The Archbishop denied the allegations, branding them as lies. Scott, by then a reformed alcoholic with criminal convictions (in the main relating to drinking and driving and more latterly trading in amphetamines), in turn claimed: 'I will stand by what I said till the day I die.'

Scott told his ex-wife, some fourteen years after the alleged events, that he was molested by a 'big bastard called George'. Later, he also told his children. Nothing happened for another fifteen years. Then in 2000, Scott recognised *Big George* again – this time on television as the Archbishop of Sydney. Scott spoke to one of his friends in Alcoholics Anonymous who advised him to speak to his parish priest.[299] This priest advised Scott to take his complaint direct to the Church. But Scott first approached Broken Rites, an online not-for-profit organisation dedicated to exposing and denouncing cases of sexual abuse in the Catholic Church. Then he tentatively contacted the Bishops' National Committee for Professional Standards, which was responsible for *Towards healing*, a 1996 process document prepared by the Catholic bishops and leaders of religious institutions. The document set out the principles and procedures to be followed in response to individual complaints of sexual abuse by the Catholic clergy. The Church officials advised Scott to take his complaint to the police, an unlikely course for someone with a police record, so he did nothing.

It wasn't till 2002 that Scott made a formal complaint and the allegations were heard by a retired judge, the Hon. A. J. Southwell, QC, under the auspices of the National Committee for Professional Standards, a body established by the Australian Catholic Bishops Conference. The Committee instructed Southwell, by the terms of the enquiry, to determine, 'whether or not the complaint has been established...'

From the outset, Scott made it clear he sought neither compensation nor police involvement. Scott said he merely wanted the Church authorities to know about the offences, which he alleged had happened to him. Southwell would later find there was no malice or any reason other than the claim of molestation that led Scott to make the claim again the Archbishop. Pell stood down for nearly three months from his role as Archbishop and the enquiry was heard in private in the boardroom of Rydges Hotel in Melbourne over four days in September 2002. Both men were represented by a QC.

During the enquiry, Scott claimed that Pell had also attempted to molest another boy, Martin Foley, who had died in 1985. Scott told Southwell he heard Foley say to *Big George*, 'fuck off'. Scott said that Foley had run into the bush and when joined later by Scott, the two boys, fed up with the abuse, agreed to set fire to the camp. The enquiry was told the Country Fire Authority had attended a fire near the camp on 13 January 1961. Another person, who attended the camp in 1961, told Southwell that Scott had told him to 'watch out for Big George'. Southwell questioned Scott's ex-wife, who confirmed that Scott had told her some fourteen years after the alleged events that the man who molested him years before was the same person he saw on his television screen as Sydney's Archbishop. Southwell found her an 'honest witness'.

The lawyer for Pell, Mr Sher, QC, accused Scott of lying, but Southwell concluded that such an argument does 'not persuade me that he [the complainant] is a liar'. He went on, 'I do not form a positively adverse view of him [the complainant] as a witness'.

In the end it came down to two protagonists arguing over an alleged event that had occurred forty years earlier. Pell's credibility was not questioned but Scott, according to David Marr, 'survived forceful attack almost unscathed'. The unfortunate Southwell found it difficult to make a definitive decision one way or other. He found the case too evenly balanced to bring down the 'grave, indeed devastating' consequences of preferring Scott's complaint to Pell's. In his conclusion, Southwell wrote:

> In the end, and not withstanding that impression of the complainant, bearing in mind the forensic difficulties of the defence occasioned by the very long delay, some valid criticism of the complainant's credibility, the lack of corroborative evidence and the sworn denial of the respondent, I find I am not satisfied that the complaint has been established, to quote the words of the principal terms of reference.

Pell's solicitor claimed, 'We have been vindicated'. Pell said, 'I am grateful to God that this ordeal is over and that the enquiry has exonerated me of all allegations.' Some years later, Pell claimed in a statement to the Royal Commission into Institutional Responses to Child Abuse that Scott's claim was 'unfounded'. Individuals who read Southwell's report will make up their own mind on that point.[300]

Father Gerald Ridsdale, paedophile priest and local Ballarat boy, was ordained in the same year as I cleaned windows opposite to what became his presbytery at Saint Alipius, East Ballarat. By 1993, when he was arrested, Ridsdale had raped, abused and assaulted his way around the diocese. His bishop from 1971 was Bishop Ronald Mulkearns, coadjutor bishop to Bishop James O'Collins from 1968–1971. Ridsdale was convicted of some 138 offences against children, involving 53 victims. There were undoubtedly more. Bishop Mulkearns, apart from sending Ridsdale to New Mexico for treatment, moved him from parish to parish, apparently without dissent from the members of his College of Consultors, who demonstrated not only a remarkable lack of courage and curiosity, but a degree of clerical subservience to their bishop that many would name as criminal.[301] In 1971, the bishop and his consultors sent Ridsdale as chaplain to the Christian Brothers Primary school next to the presbytery and church at Saint Alipius.

A young Father George Pell had returned to Australia from studies in Rome and Oxford in 1971. His bishop sent him up country to Swan Hill for two years and in 1973 Father Pell returned to Ballarat and moved into the presbytery with Ridsdale at Saint Alipius. He could not have come at a worse time. Four Christian Brothers, Best, Dowlan, Farrell and Fitzgerald, and Father Ridsdale, were sexually abusing the children. Father Pell had moved in with a paedophile ring. Pell would later say he knew nothing. So began a pattern of behaviour over decades of Pell not seeing, not hearing, not noticing, not interested, not told, not responsible, not having authority or being deliberately deceived. It was as if Pell didn't want to know. On one occasion he told a newspaper reporter:

> If a priest comes to me, I don't want him to tell me if he is guilty or not guilty, unless he insists on telling me. In which case I would have to act on the information.[302]

On the final day of October 2016, the Royal Commission into Institutional Responses to Child Abuse published submissions from counsel assisting the Commissioners. The Commission does not have to accept the findings of these submissions, but, 'it would be unusual if they were ignored'.[303] Some of the conclusions, drawn from an analysis of the evidence presented to the Commissioners, is critical of the now Cardinal Pell, although some of the claims made under oath by witnesses to the Commission regarding Pell were dismissed as unproven by counsel assisting.

Two areas of concern for the Commission where Pell's evidence is questioned relate to the period in the Ballarat diocese when Pell was the Episcopal Vicar for Education (1973–1984) and director of the Aquinas campus of the Institute of Catholic Education. Pell was also a member of the College of Consultors (1977–1984) advising Bishop Mulkearns on the governance of the diocese in various matters (property and finance) and in particular on the appointments of priests. Areas of concern for Pell after he left Ballarat to become a bishop in Melbourne are not discussed here.

The first area of concern in Ballarat relates to the paedophile behaviour of a Christian Brother, Edward Dowlan. In an article in *The Age* newspaper in 2002, Pell is alleged to have said 'he did not remember hearing rumours about Dowlan at that stage'. Counsel assisting said that if Cardinal Pell:

> ... made the statement attributed to him in *The Age*, it could not have been an accurate statement unless Cardinal Pell had at that time entirely forgotten the matters upon which he has since given evidence.

Counsel assisting argues that Cardinal Pell's sworn evidence before the Royal Commission indicated 'he was aware since the 1970s of allegations that Dowlan had engaged in sexual infractions with minors ...'[304]

Counsel submitted that the evidence established 'that between 1973 and 1975 Father Pell was told by at least one student and one or two priests about Dowlan's infractions of a sexual nature with minors'.[305] Counsel submitted that Father Pell had not taken sufficient action to ensure these infractions were dealt with properly. Pell had told Father Brendan Davey, the Chaplain at Saint Patrick's college, about the rumours he had heard. Father Davey told Pell that 'the brothers were looking into it'. In fact, the response by the brothers, in particular the Principal and Superior at the College, Brother Nangle, was reckless in regard to his students' welfare and unconscionable. Within the college, Dowlan's behaviour was 'very common knowledge' and there was 'a lot of talk in the school yard'.[306] Counsel accepted the evidence provided by an ex-student at the college, Timothy Green, to the Commission. Green said he told Pell at the Eureka Swimming Pool, when he was a young lad, that 'Brother Dowlan is touching little boys'. 'Father Pell said, "Don't be ridiculous and walked out".'[307] Cardinal Pell told the Commission that 'while he did not suggest Mr Green', who appeared before the Commission 'was lying to the Royal Commission, he did not accept Mr Green's evidence was accurate'.[308] Counsel assisting, however, chose to believe Green.

Counsel submitted that Father Pell should have at least consulted with Brother Nangle. Cardinal Pell conceded before the Commission that he should have done more and in particular he should have consulted with the school principal, Brother Nangle. When asked why he didn't, Pell said, 'I didn't think of it and when I was told that they were dealing with it, at that time I was quite content.' The Cardinal said he did 'not tell the Bishop because it came under the control of the Christian Brothers...' In conclusion, Pell said, 'I regret that I didn't do more at that stage.'[309]

The Cardinal is vulnerable here and the final report of the Royal Commission will have more to say about the Dowlan affair.

The second area of concern where counsel assisting the Royal Commissioners questions Pell's evidence relates to what he knew or didn't know about the paedophilic behaviour of Father Gerald Ridsdale. Some media reports have tended to exaggerate the strength of the submissions of counsel assisting against Cardinal Pell.[310] Counsel evaluated the case against a young Father Pell, inside his role as a member of the College of Consultors in Ballarat. His membership of the College covered the period July 1977 to 1984, after which he left for the archdiocese of Melbourne to become a bishop.

The vast majority of the decisions by the Consultors relating to Ridsdale were made before Pell joined the College. At the Consultors' meeting of 19 July 1977, Ridsdale, who had been acting as Administrator of the parish of Edenhope, was promoted to parish priest. This appointment followed a pattern of sexual abuse dating back to 1963. This meeting was the first that Father Pell attended. From my reading of the relevant transcripts of evidence presented to the Commission, and my reading of the report by counsel assisting, it is apparent that Father Pell had joined a consultor's group where a majority of its members knew what Ridsdale was up to.[311] What Pell himself knew at the time remains uncertain. Throughout a series of long interviews before the Commission, Cardinal Pell remained adamant he did not know about Ridsdale's paedophilic behaviour. In light of Ridsdale's long history of sexual abuse in the diocese and what other clerics knew, plus some Catholic lay communities, counsel struggled to comprehend how it was possible for Father Pell not to have known.

There are various levels of knowledge, and some members of the College of Consultors knew more than others. There is little doubt that senior priests close to the bishop, e.g. Monsignors Fiscalini, O'Brien, O'Keeffe and McKenzie, knew more than other members. There is also good evidence that in some ways the consultors' meetings under Bishop Mulkearns were something of a farce. Decisions were sometimes made prior to the meeting. Members were thus little more than a rubber-stamp. On some occasions members were encouraged to discuss issues; on other occasions they weren't. The bishop controlled his clerical world and secrecy was second nature.[312]

The Ballarat diocese is geographically large, covering the western one-third of the State of Victoria, but numerically small. In the year 1969–1970, the diocese had just 84 priests working in 52 parishes. In comparison, in the same year the Archdiocese of Melbourne had 188 parishes and 442 priests.[313] Following Ridsdale's sexual abuse of children in Warrnambool (1970), Ballarat East (1972), Apollo Bay (1974), Inglewood (1975) and Edenhope (1976–7), it is difficult to believe that the relatively small number of priests throughout the diocese did not know something about his sexual abuse of children.

Counsel Assisting, Gail Furness, submitted to the Commissioners 'that there had been some rumours or talk about Ridsdale's sexual abuse of children in the Catholic communities' of Apollo Bay in late 1974 and early 1975 and Inglewood parish in late 1975 and early 1976.[314] Cardinal Pell, however, gave evidence that it did not come to his attention at the time that it was 'common knowledge' at Inglewood that Ridsdale was interfering with children. When asked if he subsequently discovered that it was 'common knowledge', he replied with a throwaway final sentence which he surely regrets:

> I couldn't say that I ever knew that everybody knew. I knew a number of people did. I was – I don't know whether it was common knowledge or whether it wasn't. It's a sad story and it wasn't of much interest to me.[315]

Priests belong to an all boys' club. Priests have no families to discuss the day-to-day happenings in their lives. They network and they gossip. Some play golf together. Some drink together. Some gamble at the races together. Others holiday together. They have no one but themselves. There are innumerable examples in the transcripts published by the Royal Commission that prove strong networks exist in most dioceses, and much talking, even if in whispers and rumours, is the norm. The Cardinal was perhaps above such gossip.[316]

At Father Pell's first meeting with the Consultors on 19 July 1977, Ridsdale was appointed as parish priest of Edenhope. Counsel assisting submitted that those who made that decision, and who were present at an earlier meeting, knew Ridsdale had a history of child sexual abuse. Father Pell was not one.[317] When questioned about the Edenhope decision, Cardinal Pell told the Commission that nothing was said about earlier allegations against Ridsdale. Paedophilia, in particular, was never mentioned. Cardinal Pell agreed that he should have been told about earlier charges against Ridsdale, but he wasn't. He went on to claim the bishop deceived him. When asked why, he replied:

> Because he would realise that I didn't know and he did not want me to share in his culpability. And also, I think he would not have wanted to mention it to me and some – at least some other members of the consultors because, at the very minimum, we would have questions about the propriety of such a practice.[318]

In his evidence from Rome, the Cardinal could not remember whether any reasons were given for Ridsdale's original appointment as administrator to Edenhope in April 1976. When pushed on this point, Pell said there may have been 'generalised explanations' as to why Ridsdale was an administrator and not a parish priest. He listed a range of possibilities including such mundane problems as being restless and disagreeing with the school principal. Counsel assisting took strong exception to this answer and has submitted to the Commissioners that Cardinal Pell 'deliberately excluded the most likely possibility, having regard to the evidence at the time, which was that Ridsdale was removed due to child sexual abuse'.[319]

That particular submission by counsel is the only negative conclusion relating to Pell from this his first meeting. Counsel made a number of submissions, but had nothing to say on Pell's knowledge about Ridsdale's history of abuse. Father Pell attended another meeting of the consultors in September 1979, where Ridsdale was given a year's study leave from Edenhope. Counsel made no submissions against Pell, who in evidence insisted 'that in the period 1977 to 1979 he never heard anything in relation to the misbehaviour of Ridsdale'.[320] Perhaps it was fortunate for Father Pell that he was absent from a crucial meeting of consultors on the 16 January 1981 when Ridsdale was appointed as parish priest of Mortlake. Ridsdale later admitted to being 'out of control' at Mortlake and was forced to leave the parish after twenty months.

⋘

Terang. November 1981: my hometown, although I am well gone. The presbytery overlooks the dry lake. The Ballarat senior clergy hide their dirty secrets behind the protective walls of their city-state. But Ridsdale's multiple sins and crimes are so horrendous that a breach has opened up. Ridsdale is out of control in Mortlake. He was 'out of control' in Inglewood. He was forced out of Apollo Bay and Edenhope. Mrs BPF tells the Royal Commission that her two sons stayed overnight at the Mortlake presbytery with Ridsdale. Mrs BPF meets one of her sons the following day at Saint Colman's School fete. The boy is distressed and refuses to look her in the eye. Has Ridsdale touched you? He holds his head down and does not answer. That same evening Mrs BPF and her husband drive to Terang, a distance of fourteen miles. Monsignor Leo Fiscalini is the parish priest and Vicar-General. He is a member of the College of Consultors. The boy's mother told the Commission:

> We met Monsignor Fiscalini at the front door of the presbytery. I don't think we went inside. I said to him, 'we've got a problem in Mortlake.' That was as far as we got. We didn't even get a chance to say that it was Father Gerry who was involved. He told us that Bishop Mulkearns was not in the diocese at the time. He said, 'I will deal with it' and dismissed us. He did not ask us any questions.[321]

The couple drove back to Mortlake. Counsel assisting submitted that Mrs BPF's evidence should be accepted.

Warrnambool. Ballarat Diocese. Twenty-nine miles from Terang. Ridsdale is a curate and abusing young boys. Mr BPL, an altar boy in the early 1970s, requests a meeting with the parish priest, Monsignor Fiscalini. The two meet at the Warrnambool presbytery after school:

> I told Monsignor Fiscalini what Ridsdale had done to me and I told him that I thought it was happening to other kids. I told him I knew something had happened to Michael [his brother] and that I'd spoken to Father Bongiorno about Ridsdale's behaviour. Monsignor Fiscalini said that there was a problem with Ridsdale

and said the Church was dealing with it. I told Monsignor Fiscalini that I had tried to speak to the Bishop about it, but I was not allowed to.

Mr BPL stated that Fiscalini told him not to spread the story to anybody, and it was important for him to protect the Church, the parish, other boys and himself. Counsel submitted that Fiscalini's reply was both believable and consistent with other evidence about the culture in the Ballarat diocese.

Two or three days after this conversation, Mr BPL returned home from school and his mother said that Monsignor Fiscalini had been around that day and that he would get a hiding if he talked about these things again. Mr BPL told his mother that what he told the Monsignor was true, but his mother replied, 'Well, Monsignor thinks they're lies.'

When he was nineteen or twenty, Mr BPL had a breakdown and ended up in Brierly Mental Hospital for a week in Warrnambool. His mother arranged for him to meet Monsignor Fiscalini. On meeting, Mr BPL called the Monsignor a liar. The Monsignor assured Mr BPL that the Bishop had Ridsdale under control. The Monsignor then gave Mr BPL 'a very stern lecture about my soul going to hell for not following the guidance and teaching of the church...'

In 2006, Ridsdale pleaded guilty to sexually abusing BPL.[322]

Ballarat. Consultors meeting, 14 September 1982. Father Pell attends. The Bishop announced 'that it had become necessary for Fr Gerald Ridsdale to move from the [Parish of] Mortlake' and 'negotiations were underway to have him work with the Catholic Enquiry Centre in Sydney'.[323] The bishop told the meeting the diocese had a problem with 'homosexuality' and he referred directly to Ridsdale. There was no general discussion. The bishop made clear it was his decision to remove Ridsdale from Mortlake.[324]

When questioned about this meeting, Cardinal Pell said he could not remember 'explicitly asking why it had become necessary' to remove Ridsdale from Mortlake, but he agreed it was 'entirely possible the reason given was homosexuality'. He said paedophilia was not mentioned. He also said it was:

> completely misleading to nominate a person with a record like Ridsdale to the Catholic Enquiry Centre ... and that if he had known for a minute that there were five or six charges (complaints)

against Ridsdale he would not have tolerated the legitimacy of such an appointment.³²⁵

Father Pell will have an opportunity to do just that some months later.

Following this meeting, it is hard to imagine how any of the consultors present could claim they were unaware of Ridsdale's sexual abuse of children. Cardinal Pell again defends his position that at the time of this meeting he knew nothing about Ridsdale's paedophilia.³²⁶ Counsel assisting makes submissions at this point but is cautious regarding Pell. While naming a number of consultors who knew Ridsdale's history, counsel does not name Pell.³²⁷

The next meeting of the College was on 30 December 1982. Pell was an apology. A special meeting was called for the 8 August 1983 to discuss an extension of time for Ridsdale with the Catholic Enquiry Centre (CEC). Pell attended. The minutes record the following:

> Fr G. Ridsdale, C.E.C. Fr J. Fitzpatrick, O.M.I. Nat. Director C.E.C. requested that Fr G. Ridsdale remain for a second year with the Catholic Enquiry Centre. It was moved Fr. P. Downes, seconded by Mons McKenzie that permission be granted. Carried.³²⁸

Was the decision unanimous? Did Father Pell protest at this decision? The minutes don't say. Whatever Father Pell knew about Ridsdale before the meeting of the 14 September 1982, he surely knew much more after it. It appears the Cardinal is vulnerable here.

And there is another aspect that the Royal Commissioners will find interesting when they come to write their final report on what exactly Pell knew about Ridsdale. A little-known priest then, now Parish Priest of Stawell in Central Victoria, seemed to have greater insight into the Ridsdale affair than did Father Pell in 1982. Father Eric Bryant was a young priest when he joined the College of Consultors in 1982 – five years after Pell. After the meeting of the 14 September 1982, which Pell attended, Bryant recognised that something 'was going on with Ridsdale'. He told the Royal Commission he was 'shocked' when the bishop mentioned homosexuality and said that Ridsdale had to move from Mortlake. Father Bryant said his presumption at the time was that Ridsdale was being sent to Sydney where he'd be away from children. Counsel submitted that Father Bryant's 'evidence that he believed Ridsdale was being moved to the CEC to be away from children should be accepted as being his understanding at the time of the meeting'. Bryant expressed great regret that he had not spoken out about Ridsdale. He said he was 'young and naïve' at the time:

> I feel great guilt for what happened to people personally. I didn't do the right thing as far as Ridsdale was concerned and perhaps I didn't know how to handle it and I was presuming all the time that the Bishop and others were doing what was seen to be right.[329]

The Commissioners may well compare the reactions of both Bryant and Pell. The Cardinal is walking on quicksand at this point and what the Commissioners make of the Ridsdale affair we will learn towards the end of 2017.

Chapter 18

Sisyphus returns

It takes seven years to become a priest, but for me it will take nine. Counting my two at Chevalier, this will be my fifth year. So Sisyphus returns for the last time to Springwood having waved goodbye yet again to the women in his life, some of whom gather together yet again in their vegetable garden bordering the railway tracks, while others stand yet again in the centre of roads with one arm waving a white handkerchief over their heads, and their other arm clasped around waists holding tightly to dressing-gowns.

    This time I return on the correct day and discover I am the deputy head prefect, one of the senior men, living on the top floor, looked up to by the newcomers. Do the authorities not know I sneak down the road to watch the Melbourne Cup, and meditate on a blonde Mary who flings her head about disconcertingly while singing about the disadvantaged in the world? Do they not know my guitar case is used to carry magazines, books and cakes into the bush? I have a new room facing the mountains. Some of my old mates are missing. Donnelly and Blake, the two scientists in our year, are in Rome. I will miss them both. My soutanes and white collar wait for me exactly where I left them before Christmas. Before entering our rooms we stand outside our doors in the corridors until everyone is ready. Then a prefect introduces a prayer appropriate for the time of day and we all join in: 'Remember, O most loving Virgin Mary, that never was it known, that anyone who fled to thy protection ...'

The lord of our seminary, responsible for our spiritual and intellectual development, the Cardinal Archbishop of Sydney, Sir Norman Thomas Gilroy, makes his annual trip to Springwood. Norman appointed Veechy and his staff and they answer to him. My bishop in Wagga, Francis Henschke, has no seminary so we study here with Norman's agreement.

When we are told Norman is coming, the Sydney boys get ready for private audiences. Norman was a student here in 1917 before going to Rome in 1919 to study at Propaganda College, where the best and brightest go. How Norman made the cut is anybody's guess, but in 1924 he finished with a doctorate in theology and returned to a six-year-stint working for the pope's representative in Australia.[330] There must be something of substance behind the set smile. He then moved to Lismore as secretary to the bishop. Norman had a charmed life. He was never academic, read little, ignored radio and television and shunned newspapers. A man of duty and obligation, Norman filled his Sydney days with his Roman Church.

And Norman said his prayers. Each morning when we made it into the chapel by 6.30 am, there was Norman, off to the side, kneeling and apparently absorbed in discussions with his Maker. This spiritual communication compensated for the lack of serious discussion he had with humans. My friend, Speed, assured the rest of us students that when he raced down to the chapel soon after 6.00 am, Norman was already there kneeling quietly, saying his prayers.

Norman led a pious life and found meaning in the four great truths that formed and guided him through life: his belief in God, his belief in the one true Catholic Church which Christ had founded, his belief in the papacy and his belief in the Code of Canon Law. All else was extraneous to the meaning of life.

In 1966, I remember introducing students to Norman. I'm reasonably certain that those of us from outside the Sydney Archdiocese had not had the pleasure of meeting Norman on his previous visits. I was surprised when Norman's Sydney students at Springwood told me that after ordination they were not permitted to own a car, and had to either walk or ride a bike around their parishes. I recall Norman's permanent smile, incongruously combined with a cold and formal stiffness, his red socks and buckled shoes, and his failure to acknowledge the person who was introducing the students to him – I was the only one who did not meet him officially.

Norman had a most affected voice. He came from a poor background and I suspect Henry Higgins, a phonetics professor, the one who filled Eliza Doolittle's Cockney mouth with pebbles to rid her accent of London's East End, had worked on Norman's Glebe voice. George Bernard Shaw, who wrote the play *Pygmalion* on which *My fair lady* was based, borrowed the pebble story from Demosthenes who became a great Greek orator by practising with a mouthful of pebbles. Perhaps Norman, like Demosthenes, had a sword over his head to give him Discipline.

Norman was born under a lucky star. He had a habit of being in the right place at the right time – a man who accumulated honours and titles the way a philatelist collects stamps. According to T. P. Boland, who wrote his biography for the *Australian Dictionary of Biography*, Norman was nominated to become the bishop at Port Augusta in South Australia without ever working in a parish as either a curate or parish priest. In 1937 he was plucked from obscurity and appointed as coadjutor to Michael Kelly, Archbishop of Sydney, with right of succession. This was at a time when Rome wanted indigenous appointees to bishoprics. Norman had made valuable connections in Rome and in 1946 he became the first Australian-born cardinal. In 1969 he was knighted, becoming the first Cardinal to be knighted anywhere in the world since the Protestant Reformation! In 1970 he was the Australian of the Year.

For his sins, Edmund Campion, author, priest and historian, was forced to live in what he called Norman's 'heavy house'. It was here that Ed did his purgatory. Twice a day the clerical family gathered for meals:

> As at the court of Queen Victoria, conversation was orchestrated by the top person. Serious topics were never raised, except by an ingenuous visitor, and then not for long … The adamantine rule was never to mention another priest at table, lest you unwittingly said anything that could somehow discredit him. If table conversation was guarded and circumspect, overall the atmosphere of the house was bleak, watchful and inhumanly cautious, as if you were under house arrest.[331]

Norman was known for his frugality. He didn't have a car, until someone left him a Daimler, but before that his secretary, Father Ian Burns, drove him to Springwood in his own small Volkswagen. Norman sat uncomfortably in the front seat, deliberately pushed too far forward, leaving him squashed against the dashboard. He never complained and Ian didn't offer to push it back.[332]

Cardinal Norman Gilroy travelled to Rome in 1950 and stayed for six weeks. While there he ordained John Molony and his class to the subdiaconate. He was given a Vatican car and a chauffeur. The driver was a poor man who expected a decent tip from Norman. For his troubles, Norman gave him a box of chocolates.[333]

Norman knew he was important. When he interviewed his seminarians they first genuflected to him before kissing his ruby ring. When giving communion to the faithful, he held the consecrated host in the air, but then, before placing the host on the recipient's tongue, he offered them his ruby ring to kiss.[334]

Clericalism thrived in Sydney. Norman had no time for the lay apostolate that dominated the Mannix rule in Melbourne. Norman shared Pius X's view that 'the one duty of the multitude [i.e. the laity] is to allow themselves to be led, and like a docile flock, to follow the Pastors'.[335] If it was a choice between Catholic Action and Housie for Norman it was Housie every time. If it was a choice between the YCW and Housie it was Housie every time. If it was a choice between Santamaria and Housie it was definitely Housie every time. I have distinct memories of Sydney seminarians telling me that one of their first clerical tasks when ordained would be to organise the Housie/Bingo nights in their local parishes.

Norman and his predecessors made a bad mistake in separating their students for the priesthood into two groups, philosophers and theologians, and placing them geographically miles apart. Isolated in Springwood meant that the end result of our labours – ordination – was in the too distant future. We were too disconnected from the end.

Apart from our meetings with the spiritual director, our vocation for the priesthood was not mentioned. Despite being specially chosen, we were never made to feel welcome. We operated in a vacuum, doing time. We desperately needed practical involvement of some sort, but we were never given pastoral experience. Apprentice plumbers get to dig drains. Apprentice mechanics get to change oil. We didn't even meet priestly practitioners. In my nearly three years at Springwood, we had no guest speakers, no practical men who might explain to us their work as priests. We all knew what work priests did, but we needed to get a feel for it from those who practised it. The gap between those setting out on the path to ordination and those ordained was immense.

We needed to feel part of something, of belonging to a community of brothers. But there was no attempt by the authorities to even build community within our seminary. Even our attempts to build community with friends in the seminary were frowned on. There was a distinct lack of trust. We never worked in small groups. We never discussed our work formally. Ironically, while we were specially chosen – a privileged elite – at a human level we were not valued. Instead the authorities placed us under surveillance. When we complained about the quality of the food, we were told it improves after ordination. We marked time in the wilderness studying Thomism, learning to follow rules and to be obedient. We could have been training to be Latin-speaking prison guards.

We were, in general, young men of great good will. Standing outside another student's door in the corridor brought a dean hurrying down to see what mischief was going on. Only the brave and strong would see it through to the end. Some lost interest. Some became bored. Some sought female companionship. Some cracked and were sent home. Some, in typical Australian fashion, became resigned and said to themselves, 'Stuff the lot of them', and set their teeth in a determined fashion to beat the system.

At the end of the nineteenth century, the Church fumbled for a word to describe the modern global heresies and arrived at *modernism* – a useful word because of its vagueness. This was a wide net that could catch all kinds of clever butterflies, even the most loyal butterflies. Modernism placed the Church in a ghetto in which I grew up. Leo XIII locked himself away in the Vatican and peeped out to write *Rerum novarum*, forty-three years after *The communist manifesto*. The modern Catholic Church developed backwards in opposition to the world it was called to save. Darwin's theory of evolution of the species challenged the Church at its heart. What was at stake for the Church was its notion of salvation history, which involved the story of creation, fall and redemption. The barque of Peter drew up its anchor, floated out into the middle of the ocean, called on board all its adherents and turned its back on the shoreline – which goes a long way in explaining the values underlying the Springwood seminary and the formation I received in the 1960s. The threads of Modernism have a long history. They go back in a long thin line through the infamous *Syllabus of errors* (1864), the rejection of the French Revolution and the ideas of the eighteenth-century Enlightenment.

When I commenced training for the priesthood, ordained priests were still obliged to take an oath against modernism. Father Eugene Stockton, one of our lecturers in 1964, swore his oath in 1960. The modernist oath is evidence of the loyalty demanded by the papacy for its priests and is a symbol of papal rule that separated the Roman Church from the enlightened modern world.[336] The oath goes some way in explaining the Church's narcissism and isolation, and the failure of its bishops to respond as decent human beings to the sexual abuse by its clergy. All clergy, pastors, confessors, preachers, religious superiors, and professors in philosophical-theological seminaries were required to take the oath set out by Pius X in 1910. The swearing of the oath was abandoned sometime after the Second Vatican Council.

Reading the oath now, I can see that my old mate Donnelly would have been forced to cross his fingers and toes on the first clause, which states:

> … I profess that God, the origin and end of all things, can be known with certainty by the natural light of reason from the created world (see Rom.1:19), that is, from the visible works of creation, as a cause from its effects, and that, therefore, his existence can also be demonstrated.[337]

So what is this modernism that so upset Pius X in the early years of the twentieth century? The pope's attack was directed in particular at a group of Catholic scholars who published their work around the end of the nineteenth century and the beginning of the twentieth. These intellectuals, labelled as modernists, attempted to incorporate into Catholic life and thought new philosophies and critical studies of the Bible that had developed in the wake of the Enlightenment.[338] The reaction of the Church was to reject the new thinking outright and place bans on its own people who tried to incorporate such thinking.

But the Church's animosity to the new thinking went back much further than Pius X. The papacy had engaged vociferously with the world outside the Church following the French Revolution. Mark Chaves, Professor of Sociology, Religion, and Divinity at Duke University, North Carolina, argues that antimodernism has been a feature of Catholicism since the late eighteenth century. Chaves divides this antimodernism into three phases. The first phase ranged from the French Revolution to the end of the nineteenth century. The popes argued in this phase against the notion of liberal democracy, 'according to which the state must be free from control exercised by the Church'. The French Revolution defended notions of egalitarian political sovereignty, freedom of speech, of the press, and of the exercise of religion. There was also the issue of freedom of conscience. Pope Gregory XVI (1765–1846) abhorred the lot, but in particular the concept of liberty of conscience:

> From the evil-smelling spring of indifferentism flows the erroneous and absurd opinion – or rather, derangement – that freedom of conscience must be asserted and vindicated for everyone.

In the second phase, the papacy attacked the modern historical-critical method or higher biblical criticism of scriptures, and the biological evolutionary theories of Charles Darwin. The third phase came after the Second Vatican Council. The main papal target in this phase was women, especially the notion that women should enjoy full gender equality in the Catholic Church.[339]

I had no historical knowledge of modernism in 1966. What I did understand, and what I instinctively rejected at the time, without being able to articulate it, was the Church's fear of the world. In truth, I loved the world. It was that love that had led me to Springwood in the first place, along with my commitment to making it a better place for those who lived in it, but who didn't share in all the benefits it had to offer. It emerged that the Church and I were looking at two different worlds.

As I contemplate my future, Donnelly, a very clever butterfly, writes from Rome. April 1966. Donnelly had left behind the Australian bush and settled instead on the top of Janiculum Hill overlooking Saint Peter's Basilica in Rome – 500 metres away from the pope himself. Donnelly had found his rightful place.

Donnelly is a student at the Urban College of Propaganda Fide, established by Pope Urban VIII in 1627. This is a seminary for the likes of Donnelly – intelligent students from around the world, who will study for a doctorate in theology and on completion return to their countries and become leaders of their local churches.

Australia had been sending its best and brightest there since the end of the nineteenth century. As part of the students' intellectual development, the cosmopolitan nature of their environment will encourage them to imbibe deeply the universal, rather than the national, nature of the Catholic Church and its Roman foundations. And once back home, in case some were distracted by other matters and their Roman experience began to fade, they were obliged to write a report to *Prop*. Every three years they reported on their welfare and gave their impressions of the state of their local church.[340] The Roman system, like the legendary Lernaean Hydra, had many heads.

But all is not well with my friend. He has heard a rumour that I'm on my way and seeks to warn me. His letter, miraculously still in my keeping, is now a valuable primary source. Life at *Prop*, it seems, is less than ideal:

> The institution is more liberal in many respects than what we have learned to expect at home, and in many respects the Rector resembles Mgr. Veech – in other words he is a thorough gentleman. Both he and Mgr. Veech are a bit conservative in practice, but the latter is also what you might describe as a 'good old-fashioned liberal', whereas the rector here is nothing of the sort – he's a Roman product to the marrow of his bones. He (or some say it's the spiritual directors) sets the tone here, and this means in effect that one is simply not at ease with the staff.[341]

This morning I walked along the beach near my home at Brighton and thought about my writing and my life in the seminary. Suddenly I was surprised by a vivid image. Not all my images of the seminary are vivid. Some are fragile amalgams of fluffy white clouds that dissipate in thin air when I search them for meaning. This image was solid.

It is Sunday morning. In my room I am dressing for High Mass. Around my waist I clip on a red sash with four black press-studs. I press in the studs on my right side and then drag the sash around to my left where it hangs down below my knees. Next I place the white surplice on my desk, front down, and gather up the back into a roll held in the palms of my hands, throw it over my head and search for my left arm. It's all twisted around my shoulders and I straighten it out, pulling down at the back until the lace edges are level. I pick up my biretta and walk down to the chapel.

The image persists. I see two black soutanes. One of the soutanes is heavy and fits poorly, grabbing me under the arms. The other I wear most days is light and far too short. If I were serious I should have changed these soutanes in first year. On this Sunday I choose the heavy one. The surplice is recently washed and ironed by the nuns. Where did I come by this clothing, this biretta? I suspect that I procured them on the first day.

Then I see what looks like a small office with a counter. It's a shop of sorts. Behind the counter are two young men dressed as priests who tell me what I need and pass them over. I could reach out and touch them. One is the older brother of Vince, who cared for me in the infirmary when my leg became infected in first year. There are books on a shelf. Did any money change hands? I don't think so. Perhaps my clothes are on long-term credit. To be returned on my sudden departure.

I am in the chapel. I stand with the tenors at the back of the choir. We are on the gospel or left side of the chapel, just inside the back door. Donnelly sits and waits at the organ on my right close to the glass door. But not Donnelly. He's in Rome. So who played the organ in third year? I cannot remember. Walshy, our choirmaster, head up, hair immaculate, hums the Gregorian chant through closed mouth. I am very much part of the scene. A performer waiting for my cue.

20 October 2016

Dear Donnelly,

I saw you this morning when I was walking along the beach. You were smiling. I have a couple of questions for you. I've been reading Bertrand Russell, your mate and now mine, on Thomas Aquinas. Russell doesn't think much of Thomas as a philosopher. In fact he hardly rates him as a philosopher at all. The problem is, mate, it seems that Thomas knows the answers before he begins to philosophise. The answers are settled in Catholic doctrine. Thomas, it appears, uses reason as a prop when it suits, but when this doesn't work he refers back to revelation and Bob's your uncle.

This is too big a question for me, friend, but it raises a couple of even bigger questions. Does this mean that people who have faith can never do philosophy? And here's another question. Do you think Kant was right to argue that metaphysics is beyond us and we can never come to God via reason? It seems to me now that the God question comes down to faith. Do you remember telling me just that in 1965? But as you well know, old mate, Kant still thought we needed a God to believe in, if we were to lead moral lives. I don't believe that now. Many people live highly moral lives and don't appear to need God. Many God-believers lead immoral lives.

You're very quiet, old man. I haven't heard from you in fifty years. Tell me what you think.

Cheers

Kev

ps. Do you still play J. S. Bach?

pss. Do they have ants in Rome?

When I read Donnelly's letter in 1966, I realised that the Church was universal and seminaries were much the same around the world:

> On the material side, life is more comfortable here. We are permitted a whole host of petty satisfactions that were denied us at home. You can make a brew in your room; go out fairly readily; have a grog; watch TV (at very restricted times); stay in your room during recreation; talk at every meal except breakfast on class days; smoke (subject to restrictions of place); write as many letters as you like, and so on. But it should come as no surprise to you when I say that it is not so much an easy life we need as one that is psychologically and religiously fulfilling. And there's the rub.

> Without exception, students are handled by *organisation en masse*. The impersonality of the place is most depressing. Like Springwood, the Rule is designed for adolescents (or worse), and to some extent that is understandable; but unlike Springwood, this is carried to its absurdly logical conclusion, and it is not

even tacitly recognised that many people just do not fit into that stereotype. As an illustration, albeit an unimportant one, of what I mean: it is easy to get permission to go out here, but for some mysterious reason, almost impossible to get permission to eat out. Permission is given to eat out only with close relatives and Bishops. A similar situation at Springwood was the difficulty of getting out in the first place; one would not customarily be allowed out to contract business. But Mgr. Veech, recognising that there are certain commitments someone of my age would have, was quick to give me permission to visit the University to discuss scientific work with people there. Here, it is not recognised that the commitments of older people go far beyond their parents and bishops.

We had a spy system at Springwood and Donnelly had one in Rome. This universal seminary system is unnatural and profoundly sick:

> Then there is the prefecture. The prefects are nothing but spies, although the rector denies this. When the rector or a vice-rector sees you doing something contrary to the rule, he says nothing, just stores it up. And every few weeks the prefects are called up and asked to report on every student, the names being brought up in turn. Nothing is said to the students concerned; again it is just stored up. You have no chance to explain because no one ever accuses you; they just collect information. A few weeks ago, two students (who had a reason for being there) were seen emerging from my doorway by a vice-rector, and what do you think he did? He walked straight past them, straight past my room and knocked on the prefect's door, and then asked the prefect (not me) *who* lived in that particular room, and *whether* he knew that the students were there, and whether it had ever happened before? The same thing happens if you come back a bit late from being out: you walk past a vice-rector, who is almost invariably hanging around the front door, and he says *nothing*, which means that you get no chance to explain yourself.

Donnelly gets an injection from the Propaganda Nuns:

> At the philosophy house, the students were given tetanus injections in the seat by the nuns, according to the following procedure: Student comes into the presence of nun, dressed in soutane etc.; removes trousers under soutane; receives injection through the soutane pocket.

Donnelly's letter from Rome does not add to my peace of mind. I move closer to a decision. The seminary system is insane. The Romans are breaking down my old mate. Come home, Donnelly, tell me again how many chromosomes I have, play me some Bach, tell me again that Bertrand Russell is a genius. I'll forgive you for rejecting my offering of medieval holy water. Donnelly writes:

> The system at Springwood made for a certain amount of isolation between students. But it didn't have a patch on the system here. We remarked on the lack of a common room at home, but here you don't even have the equivalent of third philos class room, nor is there a rec hall. Apart from the official recreation of an afternoon, there are a couple of periods in which you are supposed to stand in a practically empty room and talk for about 20 minutes. When you are not doing these things, you can only spend your life in your room. This situation makes for much breaking of the rule prohibiting entry to other people's rooms because it is the only form of satisfactory social contact that can be had in the place – and now they are beginning to police that rule too. In short we live in a social vacuum. They even make rules about whom you can talk to and on what occasions, dividing the place into groups called cameratas and prohibiting any but restricted contact between them.
>
> Since Christianity is a social religion, and there is no social life here, there is a religious vacuum also. The only way you can get to exercise any form of personal apostolate (outside of these bloody interminable societies that do nothing but have meetings) and have any discussion on any matter worth discussing (including religion) is to break some rule or other. And liturgically the place is right off the map. They are always talking about community (the staff, I mean) as though all you have to do to get a community

is to regulate people to do required things in unison at required times, and prohibit any form of contact other than in prescribed activities. In short, I feel isolated from my fellow students, from the staff, from the priesthood, from the apostolate, and from God.

Jesus, Mary and Joseph! Donnelly, the best of us, is slowly breaking. The Church authorities have this all wrong. They have no idea what it means to be human.

Donnelly and I are late vocations, which means we have lived in the world before entering the seminary and in my case for some ten years. Unlike most of my friends here I am no innocent teenager just out of boarding school. The world of women and work has washed over me leaving me less exposed to the dangers of the clerical culture that informs my Springwood home.

My life experiences before Springwood should count for something in not falling prey to this narrow culture fixated on the next life. The Catholic ghetto in which I grew up cracked ajar when I left my Catholic primary school. The final two years of education at the local State High School introduced me to a new, intoxicating and challenging non-Catholic world. My emigrant memory has wandered, but I still recall the shock I experienced on listening to the undoubtedly exaggerated sexual exploits of my new adolescent schoolfriends, who neither understood nor feared the terrible consequences of sins against the sixth commandment and who took delight in stimulating my prurient curiosity.

On finishing school at fifteen I engaged with the world of work. Here I rubbed shoulders with people working in racing stables, timber yards and dairy farms. I carted hay with teams of men on long semi-trailers; I put on a tie and collected cash and sifted accounts surrounded by young women in offices. At seventeen I was secretary to the civically-minded trustees of the Terang Recreation Reserve, all non-Catholics. At an early age I experienced a sense of community and goodness outside the Church which puzzled me initially, but with the help of Joseph Cardijn (I was the first secretary of the local YCW), I became convinced we were all God's children. At eighteen I was in the army. Before I could vote I was handing out how to vote cards in federal and state elections. Falling in love with every new girl who came into the town became a glorious but painfully unsuccessful habit. I played cricket and football with my non-Catholic mates in the local teams. I frequently sang in the local dance band around the district. And while I remained loyal to my Catholic tribe, I was well out of the ghetto by the time I was twenty. At twenty-one I was tramping through paddocks in New South Wales and Victoria talking up anti-communism and collecting funds for B. A. Santamaria's National Catholic Rural Movement.

This seminary would, if it could, excise my last ten years. It would remake me in its clerical image, draining me of my natural compassion and empathy for others. Our emotional and social lives are sacrificed to a dry and fear-filled asceticism, which Holy Mother Church mistakenly thinks is holy. My life experiences have worked to unite the sacred and the secular. My new clerical calling, however, appears to rest on separating me, practically and symbolically, from the world which I love and where my apostolic endeavours as a priest will be conducted. The seminary system values more the office of priesthood than the missionary call of Jesus, that Jewish non-priest, who urges us to love one another as he loved us. The Church has never understood that in loving the world, in all its wonders and beauty, and especially in its pain and suffering, we simultaneously love its creator. My faith brought me to this seminary, but I belong in the world in ways that many there, including the lecturers, will never understand. I am coming to believe I'm bigger than the institution, but I must be vigilant. If Donnelly can crack, anyone can.

Although there is no conclusive evidence, I suspect that late vocations to the priesthood, men like Donnelly and me, were less likely to become sexual abusers of children and minors than those who entered the seminary direct from secondary school. The first John Jay report commissioned by the United States Bishops (2004) has some indicative evidence suggesting just that. John Jay analysed the 4,392 Catholic clerics who allegedly committed sexual abuse against minors in the years 1950–2002. More sexual abuse occurred in the 1970s than in any other decade under review. Some 10% of those priests ordained in the year 1970 were allegedly sexual abusers. The figure dropped to 8% for all those ordained in 1980.

Approximately 68% of American priests with allegations of abuse were ordained between 1950 and 1979. In considering this shorter period, when most of the abuse occurred, just on 80% of them were ordained between the ages of 25 and 29. Therefore many entered the seminary in their teens direct from secondary college. When considering the same sample group of 4,392 who sexually abused in the longer period, 1950–2002, some 76.3% of them were aged under 29 at the time of their ordination. What is interesting is this: if we compare those who were ordained in the age group 34–60, and who allegedly committed sexual abuse against minors in the period, 1950–2002, they totalled just 7.3%.[342]

The problem with all these figures is that we don't know the percentage of the under 29 group, or for that matter, the older group, in the total population of some 109,000 priests. For example, it is possible that some 80% of the men in the total population were ordained under the age of 29. If this were so then we shouldn't be surprised at the high percentage of the younger men in the smaller sample of 4,392. While the figures are interesting more work needs to be done. It is hoped that the Royal Commission into Institutional Responses to Child Sexual Abuse might provide further evidence on this point. If it can be shown that the young ordained are more likely to become sexual abusers than older men, then the teenage years of the young seminarians would be better spent growing up in the wide world before entering the seminary, or as Dr Michael Whelan would have it, doing their training in the world outside seminaries completely.

A decision has to be made. At the end of this year we all must go – somewhere. Most will go to Sydney and the seminary on the beach at Manly. Others will go to Rome. It would be easy for me to drift. I'm on the clerical treadmill. To jump off and begin again is frightening. I have made so many false starts. At the end of this year I will be thirty. By that age most people have settled on a career, marked out a future and have children. Many days I curl up tight as a snail hiding on the bottom of the big hole I've dug for myself. At other times I'm a balloon or a kite or Gerard Manley Hopkins' falcon swinging and swirling over old man bush at the thought of joining my Chevalier friends at universities in Sydney. But in the meantime I must sing. Third-year students sing the epistles in Latin at High Mass on Sundays. This priestly work is becoming serious. As a senior I'm asked to take my turn early in the year. I worry that I'll sound like a crooner, like Foxy's father, and that I'll make a mess of the Latin. When my turn comes, I head into the bush and sing the epistle. Old man bush is silent. He stands and listens but shows no interest. Occasionally he crackles in the hot sun. I could be howling at the moon for all he cares. I've made sure my epistle is short. When it's all over, I head back to the bush and sing a different song, a song full of promise and light with petals on a pool drifting. In the distance I hear a dog barking.

Perhaps, subconsciously, I begin exploring new possibilities. I discover H. Daniel-Rops. He has lived all this time in the library but only now do I appreciate his presence. Daniel-Rops' real name was Henri Petiot. I'm not sure why he used a pseudonym. All I know is in 1955 Pope Pius XII invested him with the order of the Grand Cross of Saint Gregory, which casts some doubt on the claim by some that Henri was an agnostic.

In my free time on Thursdays and Sunday afternoons I bury myself in the library with Daniel-Rops. He is a literary man with a social conscience, who writes music, short stories and novels, which explain why I find him so readable. His monumental work, written between the years 1948–65, is a history of the Christian religion in five volumes entitled *History of the Church of Christ*. I start with Volume Four, *The Protestant Reformation*, then Volume Five, *The Catholic Reformation*. What I read is a revelation. I had no idea history could be so interesting. Henri takes me back in time to other worlds and real people. I've heard of some of his people but they have meant nothing to me. This is personal. A sense of engagement, of wonder and excitement, suddenly and surprisingly emerges and challenges my old self. With anticipation I look forward to my meetings with Henri and his people who walk the streets of Paris.

One such person is Ignatius of Loyola, aged forty. According to Henri, he is an 'ageing scholar'. He 'limps through the narrow streets of La Montagne Sainte-Genevieve'. I am fascinated by the limp, dismayed by the ageing forty. I am already approaching thirty! Ignatius is:

> ... not one of those towering geniuses who move with sovereign grace among ideas and forms, and upon whom the gifts of intellect seem to have been conferred by destiny. In order to learn and to understand he needed patient research, conducted with modest means and suspicious of intuitive perception.[343]

Henri could be talking to me. I realise that if I leave and go to the university, history might be the only subject I can do. I have no science or mathematics. If I could write like Henri? Perhaps history is my future.

Monthly visits to see the spiritual director, for me at any rate, concerned the strength or otherwise of my vocation. Other students may well have focussed on their spiritual development, but my visits always came down to this question: 'Are you happy here?' For nearly three years I never once gave an unequivocal 'Yes'. I was filled with doubt. But there were times, certainly rare, when heart and mind came together and I imagined a future in Wagga as a priest with a degree of Sisyphus-contentment. For that is all there was.

I can identify those times precisely. Each year in August, the newly-ordained priests came back to Springwood, the alma mater of their teenage years and offered a Mass for us students and stayed with us overnight. These were happy times and I entered emotionally into the celebrations. At such moments I belonged to a tribe with a tradition, with a history and a clear sense of mission. I was profoundly aware of the achievement of these men – of the dedication and perseverance they exhibited, of the hardships and struggles they endured, of the doubts and fears they conquered and of the sacrifice of their youth they offered up in this bush-wilderness. The newly-ordained were joyous and proud men, and those same feelings of joy and pride filled our hearts too and I think there was a general feeling that if they could do it we could too. They had climbed their mountain and unlike Sisyphus they were now moving on.

Following their Mass there was a special blessing. We filed up to the altar and knelt while the newly-ordained placed both their hands on our heads, called us by name and then, following the blessing gave us their two anointed hands which we clasped in ours. This was especially joyous when there was a special connection. Then at the main meal, which was always held in the middle of the day, all the staff, led by Veechy, would enter at the front entrance of the refectory while we stood behind our chairs in anticipation, and then to thunderous applause, like conquering heroes, the newly-ordained men would enter separately, acknowledging our presence while we clapped and clapped.

Fifty years on I am conscious of only two such men. One belonged to our Wagga diocese. He was fair and tall, charismatic and charming, athletic and handsome. He sang the Mass with the confidence of a male peacock, his beautiful lyrical voice filling the chapel. I met him many times on my yearly visits to Wagga. He became a thief and a con-man, a criminal and an abuser of young men. How could this be possible? I have only sadness and two certainties – that he failed and that the institution that nurtured and formed him for eight years failed with him. Eight years of supervision and the authorities, especially chosen to observe him, failed to find a serious fault?

The other man is special, a model priest, a model citizen. I especially remember him because of his honourable career and because we both were students at Chevalier College. He became a bishop, one of the few in Australia worthy of that title. He is a man of faith, compassion and courage, an outspoken fighter for social justice, for the poor, for gays and lesbians, for refugees. He is an advocate for radical change in the Church. He questions mandatory celibacy and the low status of women in the Church. He supports ecumenism. I am honoured to be regarded as his friend.

But my time in this seminary is coming to an end. The emotional highs of the newly-ordained could not sustain my vocation. I've had contact with my priest friends from Chevalier College in Bowral. The Sacred Heart priests know I am restless at Springwood. They invite me to join them. They live in communities and try to convince me I would be happier with them. They say I am not suited to live on my own. They may be right. I am no lighthouse.

Chapter 19

Death

On Good Friday, I had made my way to the Grotto with its statue of Mary and walked the Stations of the Cross with the students for the last time. We were close enough to the road to hear the traffic. I have measured my years here by that day. I was conscious that this was the third and last time I would pray these stations. Next year I would either be at Manly studying theology or who knows where:

>Were you there when they crucified my Lord?
>Were you there when they crucified my Lord?
>Oh, sometimes it causes me to tremble, tremble, tremble
>Were you there when they crucified my Lord?

My cousin is killed in Terang, aged four. Kath leads her small boy, Gavin, and his older brother Paul onto the footpath in front of her house in Grey Street. They are going some few hundred yards up the street to spend time with their grandmother, Eileen, my mother's sister, a woman whom I love dearly. Later in the day, Eileen leads the two small boys back onto the footpath. She says goodbye and they run for home. A utility truck backs out from a drive and runs over Gavin killing him instantly. Eileen runs to his side and cradles his smashed head in her arms. She will tell me later that she lost whatever faith she had in God at that moment. On a Sunday afternoon I wrote a letter of sympathy to Kath and her husband Jack, Eileen's son. I would have made sympathetic comments, but I told them it was God's will and Gavin was safe in His arms. God forgive me.

I begin reading Boris Pasternak's *Doctor Zhivago*, sometime in the middle of 1966. I remember it now as a big heavy book, hardcover, difficult to read under the blankets while holding a torch. I think it had a yellow cover but I can't be sure. I am not even sure if it was mine. The English academic, Oliver Miles, went to visit Boris in 1958 with a friend of the Pasternak family and they talked for three hours. Miles became a British diplomat and remembers Pasternak sitting at an upper window looking out and seeing 'a large, shiny, black' car pulling up at his front gate, stopping a while then slowly driving off only to reappear shortly after and go through the process yet again. Stalin had provided homes for authors in a writers' commune. Here he kept an eye on them. Some writers quietly disappeared but Pasternak was lucky. Stalin died and those leaders who followed were 'beginning to lose their nerve'. As a joke, the writers referred to their commune as, *nye-Yasnaya Polyana*. *Yasnaya Polyana* translated into English as 'Clear Glade'. Pasternak's commune was known as 'not *Yasnaya Polyana*'.[344]

At Springwood our lockers are in the ablution block where we sing when we can. Mick Rohan has a locker next to me. Mick came to Springwood from school. He is a big, strong boy, handsome, gentle and friendly. His brother, Billy, also came to Springwood and is now ordained and in his first parish in Sydney. Billy falls in love with a young woman and plans his escape from the priesthood. On a holiday to the beach with four priestly mates, he folds his clothes neatly on the beach and walks into the surf. When his friends look for him, there is no sign. All that's left of Billy is his clothes on the sand. Billy has disappeared, believed drowned. After a frantic search that eventually involves the authorities, Billy is declared dead. Notices appear in the Sydney press and Requiem Masses are said for the repose of Billy's soul. His mates have Masses said around Sydney to release the young man's soul from Purgatory.

Mick is told of his brother's death and goes home immediately. After a week or two, Mick returns and we pass on our condolences. But the police are suspicious. Billy was a superb swimmer. They interview Billy's mother. His mother tells the police Billy borrowed her red case before he went on holidays. The police say no red case has been found. Billy has disappeared and taken his mum's red case. Eventually they track Billy down with his female friend.[345]

Cardinal Norman Gilroy, 'the smoothly dull', is shocked. Appearances are vital. Mick becomes the scapegoat. The presence of Mick at Springwood is untenable. He has, according to the Cardinal, the smell of his brother's scandal about him. He must go, but where? The obvious choice is to send Mick to Rome, but the Cardinal finds even Rome unsatisfactory. Too many Australians there. The Cardinal looks for a place in the world where no-one will know about Billy. He selects Genoa. So Mick says goodbye and departs, alone, to a seminary in Genoa. I never see him again.

Before the year is out my Auntie Poll, who saw clearly the error of my ways, and who waved me out of sight from her garden adjoining the rail tracks, will be dead. So will my darling father, who without a word fell down dead while washing the back walls of the verandah at home. The hose he held in his hand dropped to the ground with him. Let loose from his hand, it snaked and sprayed its water over him, but failed to revive him. This is how my mother found him. I never got to tell him how much I loved him.

Chapter 20

Unlike other men

Sitting in the second back seat of Saint Patrick's Cathedral, Ballarat, I become aware of what appears to be someone behind me crying. I cannot be certain. Crying is so disconcerting. Coming in the door of the Cathedral I noticed priests from the Ballarat diocese, many of whom I recognised, occupying the back seat. We are here to remember *The O'Keeffe Nine,* Irish priests, now all dead, who were recruited to the Ballarat diocese in the 1940s by Father Martin O'Keeffe. Yesterday we gathered to hear the main address in the Blainey Auditorium at the University of Ballarat delivered by my friend and mentor, Professor John Molony. The year is 2003 and the Ballarat clan has gathered. But some are missing. George Pell, from the Royal Oak Hotel, on the corner of South and Raglan Streets, has moved to Sydney as Archbishop and will be Cardinal Pell before the year is out. I never met George. Father Gerald Ridsdale is in jail. Monsignor John Day, paedophile and parish priest of Mildura for fifteen years, is long dead. The paedophile Christian Brothers of East Ballarat have moved out, some to jail. Father Paul David Ryan, paedophile, is no longer a priest in the diocese. This year a mother will report Ryan to *Towards healing,* the national Catholic Bishops' response scheme for managing the sexual abuse of priests. In 2006, Ryan will go to jail. The Royal Commission into Institutional Responses to Child Sexual Abuse is nearly ten years away. The dark truth of this diocese will be dragged into the light. We all learn then that when its bishops had a choice between the Church and its criminally-abusing priests or its innocent children, they chose the institutional Church over the victims. We should not be surprised. When the Royal Commission comes to town, this fence that rings the Cathedral will be festooned with coloured ribbons and balloons announcing to the world that the men and women of Ballarat have made their choice. They will stand with the children who were abused and raped and survived. It is too late for thirty-four of them to see the ribbons in their honour. They have taken their own lives.

Father Bill Melican preaches the homily. I remember him as the parish priest of Mortlake, a parish now synonymous with Ridsdale's sexual abuse of the children at Saint Colman's Primary School. The sniffles from behind have become sobbing. Someone needs comforting, but I dare not turn around. When the ceremony is over I recognise the priest who was crying – Father John McKinnon. I have known John for decades. We have been friends but never close. He returned from his studies in Rome at the same time as I left the YCW to work for the National Catholic Rural Movement. I remember John – childlike in his innocence, enthusiasm, honesty and openness. Outside in the late autumn afternoon I approach him and we talk. Eventually I make a personal observation: 'You were upset.' I don't expect an explanation. People reserve such explanations for those they love. But he did offer this. Something exciting was happening in the diocese when he returned from Rome at the end of the 1950s. There was a vision, Catholic Action was flourishing, and clerical and lay leadership was at its zenith. He told me about visits with one of his best mates in the priesthood to lay apostolate groups – the guitars, the singing, the enthusiasm, the work of changing the world in which we lived, the satisfaction felt from success. His priestly guitar-playing mate left Ballarat in the 1960s and married. There were others, clerical and lay. All left town. Bill Melican's homily had brought all the good times back. Somewhere along the way it fell apart. I spoke later to Molony and suggested he talk with John McKinnon. After the 1960s, when everything was on the up, it suddenly collapsed. McKinnon was crying for what might have been.

Father John McKinnon is asked to state his name. He will validate the argument running through this story. He was sworn in on 14 December 2015, before the Royal Commission into Institutional Responses to Child Sexual Abuse meeting in Melbourne. He was questioned by Mr Angus Stewart.

Towards the end of the questions, McKinnon makes an extraordinary statement. He tells Stewart the Church needs help:

You see, I think how on earth are we going to change the culture? I think the church would never have done a Royal Commission on itself, and even if it did, I'm not sure whether it could have run one.

We need people from outside looking in, I think. It's so hard, when you're part of a culture to recognise what you're – what it's like. I think that we need help, but it will have to be from help that we don't want, in a sense. Help that's hard for us to face.

I just wonder whether we almost need to – this is just me wondering – go to a stage where we've sort of almost faced – we've got to face the wall before we bounce back in a realistic way. But I hope this helps us. I really do.[346]

This, of course is heresy but McKinnon is a truth-teller. He thinks out loud. If he struggles to say what he means it is because, as he said, he is 'wondering'. He is as I remember him. McKinnon is a most unusual witness. At times he appears to be talking to himself, as if he has forgotten where he is and as if he is talking with a group of us, old friends around the table in Canberra at Molony's, or at Fatima House in Ballarat in the old days when we thought we belonged to something big. What shone through in December 2015 was a complete absence of guile and his transparent goodness.

Mr Stewart wants McKinnon to explain to him the workings of the College of Consultors who advised Bishop Ron Mulkearns, the Bishop of Ballarat, on the placement of priests in the diocese. McKinnon served on this committee from 1986–1997. That is why he is here. The College of Consultors is appointed by the bishop. The Church is a monarchical and paternalistic society. Bishop Mulkearns owes his loyalty to the Pope in Rome who traces back his office two thousand years to the time of Christ, not to the State of Victoria or the Commonwealth of Australia where he was born and lives. The Commission comes from outside the Church. It is here to demonstrate its authority. It represents the Commonwealth and the people of Australia. It threatens the Church's autonomy. Mr Stewart wants to know if the Consultors ever discussed the sexual abuse of children when making their decisions.

The mistake most normal people make in asking such questions is to assume the clerical caste in the Catholic Church are like other men. They are not. Or that in a meeting between a bishop and his priests, it is a meeting of equals where participants share their views. They do not. The Church is not democratic. The Church is at once authoritarian and hierarchical. Bishops belong to the episcopal order and are successors to the original apostles who received their mission direct from Christ. Only bishops are the true and authentic teachers of the faith. The Second Vatican Council reminded bishops to regard their priests as sons and friends and be ready to listen to them, but in this family some sons never become real adults. Within the hierarchy, priests are merely 'connected' to the episcopal order and regarded as 'co-workers', but they work under the authority of their Bishop and they 'share in his ministry to a lesser degree'. The language may have softened, but Canon VI, promulgated at the Council of Trent in the sixteenth century, still explains the essential relationship between the two:

> If anyone saith, that bishop [sic] are not superior to priests; or that they have not the power of confirming and ordaining; or, that the power which they possess is common to them and to priests ... let him be anathema.[347]

Catholics are taught that their bishops and priests are removed from all other kinds of priests in other religions. Catholics are taught that their priests are set apart from all other human beings because in their sacred office they have the unique power to change bread and wine into the body and blood of Christ. Cardinal Ratzinger (later Pope Benedict XVI) instructed the Anglican/Episcopalian priests in 1998 that any sacraments they administered were 'void'.[348] The Catholic Church believes itself to be unique. Its clergy suffer from exceptionalism. Mr Stewart will question Father McKinnon on how this unique, mystical body, answerable to no-one but the pope, operated in the Ballarat diocese.

Catholic culture is responsible for the failure of its bishops to act decisively against their clergy who sexually abused children. Catholic culture is, in part, responsible for the crimes and sins of its clergy. John McKinnon will highlight the problems of the culture. On display will be the rigid hierarchical structure of the Church, the extraordinary religious authority vested in the office of bishop, the secretive nature of the institution, the psychosexual immaturity of many of its celibate clergy, and their fear of intimacy and sharing their innermost feelings with their colleagues. These men were trained to live like lighthouses, on the edge of the world, shining their light, living within themselves with their God who will reward them in another life. This Church culture makes it virtually impossible for the Consultors' meeting to function productively. McKinnon quickly blames the clerical culture for the failure of the meetings, especially the priests' attitude to the bishop:

> As I look at myself, I would say our attitude to the bishop, I think – and this would have been strengthened, deepened, by the subculture that we were part of, the clerical culture – we had a deep respect for the bishop. The whole authority thing in the church, has been emphasised, emphasised, emphasised. Just even the titles, 'My Lord' and 'your eminent' [sic], even 'Father'. I suppose, they're titles that don't encourage growing up, it seems to me and I think that's a real problem, I really do.[349]

McKinnon tells Angus Stewart that the meetings of the Consultors were 'eminently forgettable'. They lacked a 'proper process'. If there was an agenda, McKinnon didn't see it. Discussions 'went round and round'. The end result was 'frustration'. The Bishop (i.e. Mulkearns), said McKinnon, 'was not a good chairman'.[350] The Commission is less interested in the quality of the meetings than what was discussed. Stewart pushed McKinnon as to whether sexual abuse was ever discussed:

> I don't recall; I doubt it, I don't think so. I'm not sure whether anything came up during that time I was a Consultor. My memory would be – I can't remember it anyhow. I'm inclined to think, no. There'd be no discussion as such anyhow, because he wouldn't tell us if it was an offence against minors. We were just told in that case that someone would be moved and the Bishop would have somewhere in mind where a fellow would be moved, so we'd normally just go along with that, save a bit of time discussing it really.[351]

McKinnon tells Stewart that if the Bishop felt something was confidential then he 'kept it confidential'. Reading the transcript it is clear that while Consultors had the right to speak up, they understood when to remain quiet. Some things are never spoken about. Sexual abuse by the clergy was one.

McKinnon explains that the Bishop gave a clear impression about when to not ask questions:

> But I'd also make the point ... that somehow or other – you know, this doesn't excuse this at all – but somehow or other the power of the culture I think was such that, if the Bishop gave the impression that he wasn't going to say anything, we didn't push him, and I think that's a failure on our part.[352]

It is clear that, in Ballarat at least, there was never any real query from the Consultors as to why priests were moved from parish to parish. The Bishop wasn't prepared to say and nobody asked why:

> ... and we'd just go along because we had no reason to query him, we just didn't know what the problem was; it could have been a number of problems other than paedophilia.

Incredibly, in all the eleven years McKinnon was on the Consultors' committee, Mulkearns never once gave paedophilia as a reason for moving a priest.[353]

McKinnon is preaching to his small flock in the tiny Mallee church in Minyip. It's the early 1990s and Ridsdale has recently been sent to jail. McKinnon has read it in the press. McKinnon supports his Bishop. There is some ambiguity in the transcript here, but McKinnon gives the impression to his congregation that the Bishop did not know about Ridsdale's behaviour. After Mass, one of his parishioners challenges McKinnon. Her son was 'offended against' and they told the Bishop. McKinnon is upset and arranges to confront the Bishop. He tells the Bishop he has met a parishioner who said he (the Bishop) did know. Mr Stewart becomes very interested at this point:

> *Question:* 'Just to clarify, by which you mean, you said to the Bishop, you said you didn't know but someone's told me that you did know.'
>
> *Answer:* 'Yeah, and he said, "I didn't say I didn't know". He's a real lawyer. He did say, "What I said was it's not true to say I didn't know and did nothing". He said he did what he could, I suppose at that stage, I don't know. I gather he sent him to counselling and all that sort of stuff and then eventually to New Mexico.'[354]

Of course Mulkearns did know about Ridsdale's offences. Some five years *before* McKinnon spoke in Minyip, the Bishop had written to Ridsdale (April 1988) requesting him to 'step down'. He did this without consulting the Consultors' Committee.[355] The management of this Church is dysfunctional. Stewart asked McKinnon if he ever discussed Ridsdale, and in particular his offending against children. 'Not really,' said McKinnon.

McKinnon next tells Stewart about the lack of maturity amongst the Australian clergy. His rough statistics (he is remembering the figures) follow the same pattern as overseas studies. Following seven or eight years of study in seminaries, the newly-ordained men enter the world of real people inadequately prepared.

Realising there was a problem with the formation of the clergy, in 1985 the Catholic bishops established a Ministry to Priests. Priests from around Australia were invited to a centre in Canberra for a three-month period of what we might call professional development. The course concentrated on spiritual and intellectual development. In 1988 McKinnon was working on this Ministry to Priests at the national and diocesan level. Emotional development and, in particular, issues relating to sexual maturity were left to in-house training in each diocese. Lack of support by the clergy led to the early demise of this Ministry to Priests.

Mr Stewart appears surprised at this early demise of professional development. McKinnon explains:

> I think we're all hard to move, I think. We don't see the need of it or, if we do see the need of it, we might be scared of it and – I don't know. It's hard. It's probably part of that emotional difficulty we have, emotional development difficulty, that self-knowledge is not all that great and the ability to share where we're at is not all that great. I think that's part of the whole culture that has to be somehow or other – I don't know ... (indistinct).[356]

McKinnon tells the Commission of a survey of priests that was done at the time. Some 1300 priests around Australia filled out questionnaires organised by the national group running the Canberra House. McKinnon told the Commission that priests 'were about 6 per cent or so less developed, less emotionally developed' than the control group. McKinnon divided the

1300 into three groups. One-third was emotionally dependent, particularly on their bishop and authority in general. About half of this one-third would like to become more mature but lacked 'the wherewithal, the courage or the – I don't know, whatever it was, the assistance to grow'. The other half had problems with relationships, with intimacy and with leadership. McKinnon concluded that at least one-third of the priests who filled out the questionnaire were in his word, 'struggling'.

The second group comprising about one-third had a greater sense of their own identity. They tended to be motivated by law and order. Authority was important to them. The final group of one-third were reasonably integrated. This group could see beyond the law and were able to interpret its spirit and recognise the values the laws were there to protect. This group was striving to form their individual consciences, although McKinnon estimated that at least a half of them had not yet succeeded. They lacked the confidence to take the final step. McKinnon did not open up the vexed issue of freedom of conscience in an organisation whose members are expected to obey the teachings of its clerical leaders.[357]

Stewart makes the observation that the priests are not an entirely mature body of men. McKinnon replied that it is a 'sad fact'. Stewart links this professional development and the problem of the sexual abuse of minors by priests, and wonders what steps were taken to help resolve the problem. McKinnon made it clear that no steps were taken. From his memory the issue of sexual abuse was never discussed. Stewart appears nonplussed: 'When you say it wasn't talked about what do you mean?' McKinnon replies that it was 'Pushed under the carpet'. Stewart replied:

> So what you are saying, as I understand it, is a program was developed to help priests but it didn't talk about the problems of sexuality and the difficulties that can arise for some priests who become sexual offenders.[358]

McKinnon struggles to reply. Mr Stewart struggles to understand. This Church is different. This is not the Boy Scouts Association, the Salvation Army or even the Anglican Church. McKinnon tells him that seminaries never discussed celibacy. Intimacy and friendships with others was viewed with suspicion.

McKinnon finds it hard to explain the fear of intimacy that leads to the failure of many priests to share their innermost thoughts with each other. He identifies a problem with their development as human persons. He explains that priests have been trained to not form intimate and loving relationships and this impacts on the proper development of their personalities. He wanders around a point concerning 'cultural immaturity'. Eventually he settles on celibacy as a problem. He wonders whether their early entrance to the seminary meant they missed the normal incentive to grow:

> I just think part of the celibacy thing is such that, particularly if a fellow goes to the seminary from school, as we used to in our days, college – and then we get ordained and then we go out into our parish, in the meantime, most fellows would have had the opportunity to cope with falling in love and negotiating relationships, and some would have grown and would have their own families and so on, and again developing that capacity, that sensitivity in a child and sense of the sacredness of the child.[359]

The truth-teller wanders far from the straight and narrow when he tells Stewart that women should be invited to join Consultors' Committees. Women, he says, are instinctively more sensitive than men in such matters of child abuse. Asked if he thinks matters had improved in the area of the sensitivity of priests to the issue of sexual abuse, McKinnon was less than positive:

> I hope that the – I'd say today we're so much more alert to paedophilia that at least they'd be open to that. I don't, I wouldn't have any doubt about that at all. You wouldn't have to be very emotionally, I don't think developed to be sensitive to that, that's a big deal. But whether we feel it the same way as a woman or even the father of a family, I don't know. I hope we do. I think we can, but I don't think – we haven't had that opportunity to – for our capacity for intimacy and generativity to develop as fellows usually would have.
>
> I presume – I hope it's developed, I hope it's developed in myself, but it's a different path we have to follow and I don't know whether everyone does. I think the normal path is falling in love and negotiating relationships and having a family, I think that's a wonderfully, or can be anyhow, wonderfully maturing thing that we miss out on.[360]

Towards the end of the questions, Commissioner Murray intervenes. Murray tells McKinnon that this whole question of culture and sexual abuse in the Church is a 'quagmire'. He puts it to McKinnon that his evidence is 'essentially' saying that the issues of child sexual abuse cannot be dealt with separately from the issues of Catholic culture and Catholic attitudes to sexuality. Murray then asks, 'Is that right?' The truth-teller replies, 'Well, I think there's a big overlap, I do; yes, I do.' He is aware of what he is claiming. He continues:

> You see, again, it is hard for me to know what's being got across in the seminary these days. I think back to the 1950s, and it was most inadequate then. But I do feel that, whatever formation we got, was a formation in, what's the law, and does this break the law, and that sort of stuff. We didn't – we weren't prompted to raise the other question, why is it wrong? What's the effect on people? I don't think we were helped much to address those issues, and I think they're the crucial confidence issues and the crucial things that enable you to grow.[361]

When McKinnon is done, Mr Stewart, on behalf of the Commission, thanks him. McKinnon goes to speak but only manages three words, 'I'm only a ...' The final word in his sentence was missed, but Mr Stewart replies:

> Well, you're an intelligent, experienced man who's been through decades of Catholic experience in the priesthood, so your remarks in that context are, of course, of use to the Royal Commission.

McKinnon replied, 'I wouldn't like to think that I'm the guru, that's all.'[362]

Michael Morwood was the deacon at Ron Mulkearns' episcopal consecration in late 1968. He was Bishop Mulkearns' first ordinant to priesthood in 1969. After nearly thirty years of priesthood with the Missionaries of the Sacred Heart Order, Morwood left to become a widely read and respected author on spiritual matters in Australia and America. Michael Morwood is Ron Mulkearns' cousin. A few weeks before Mulkearns died on 4 April 2016, Morwood wrote a passionate plea on his cousin's behalf.

Walking a tightwire, Morwood hangs in the air, urging his readers to see the story behind the story of his cousin, the Bishop of Ballarat. This is no easy task. Most commentators and others have made up their minds about Ronald Mulkearns. To argue a case for the Bishop will require extraordinary skill. For those whose hearts are cold and minds set, they are unlikely to look up to the balancing act on the tight wire.

Mulkearns' leadership of the Ballarat diocese was disastrous. He knew as early as 1972 about Ridsdale's behaviour. It took another twenty-one years before Ridsdale was arrested and jailed. In the intervening years, Mulkearns did little more than consult psychologists while Ridsdale raped, abused and assaulted his way around the diocese as Mulkearns moved him from one parish to another.

Yet Morwood steps out on the wire:

> I want to stand with him and honour him while also wanting to stand compassionately, sorrowfully and respectfully with people who have been hurt by his decisions and actions in the Ballarat sexual abuse scandal. My cousin is and always has been a thoroughly decent man. There is not an ounce of evil intent in him. I do not wish to excuse any of his decisions and actions that have caused immense pain to so many people, but I do want to expose the great injustice and hypocrisy that is being cloaked over as this and other cases of bishops handling sexual abuse are investigated.

There is tragedy here. Standing simultaneously with the condemned man and the innocent, those who were betrayed by the one condemned, will be misconceived and seen by many as contradictory, inappropriate or much worse. Morwood's argument, however, is neither contradictory nor inappropriate. It is essential to understanding how a good man like Ron Mulkearns, with 'no ounce of evil intent in him', behaved so badly. This is not to excuse or condone what he did, but, rather, to seek understanding.

If Mulkearns was the only Catholic bishop who behaved badly, the only one who placed the reputation of the Church before the victims, then Morwood has no argument. The fault would lie solely with Mulkearns. But his cousin is not alone. He stands in solidarity with bishops in Australia and around the world who behaved just as he did. The problem is systemic and cultural. There must be a story behind the story and it is not a story about certain individuals behaving badly.

Morwood invites us to look beyond the person named Ron Mulkearns. He wants us to see Ron in a bigger context, in the culture that formed him. This Ron is family, the one loved by those close to him. This Ron is the priest whose conscience was formed by and in the institution that led him to the episcopacy. This Ron was the one *groomed,* above everything else in his life, to be loyal to the Church he devoted his life to – this is the Ron snared in circumstances beyond his ability and experience to solve. Nothing in Ron's training prepared him to deal with this. Morwood enjoins us all to draw on our better selves.

The story behind the story is the story of the Roman mould of the Australian Catholic Church. It is the story of the Roman culture of the Australian Church that reached its apogee during the twentieth century at the height of the sexual abuse scandal. It is the story of a culture that can be immediately defined as clerical and triumphal. It is the story of a monarchical culture that helped to bring down Bishop Ronald Mulkearns, and it is the story that explains why Catholic bishops behaved uniformly around the world in response to the sex scandal, or as Francis Sullivan of the Truth, Justice and Healing Council would have it: 'It was as if it [i.e. consistent behaviour of the bishops] had been built into their DNA.'[363]

The modern story that impinges on the issue of clerical sexual abuse and the failure of the bishops to report the crimes of their clergy to civil authorities began in 1922 with the release of Pope Pius XI's decree *Crimen sollicitationis*. The decree applied to the ancient crime of soliciting sex in the confessional as well as homosexuality, bestiality and abuse of children by clerics. The decree required that all investigations by the Church of clerical abuse must be carried out in strict confidentiality 'in all things and with all persons'.

The penalty for breaching confidentiality was automatic excommunication: secrecy was at the heart of the process. It was seen by the Vatican as so important that:

> ... the automatic excommunication for reporting to the police the evidence that the Church had uncovered about the sex crimes

of its priests against children could only be lifted by the pope personally.

Secrecy applied not only to what bishops had discovered, but to the very process itself. *Crimen sollicitationis* was not to be published or commented on by canon lawyers. The few copies that were printed for bishops were to be kept in a locked safe where they and their chancellors alone had the key. As Tapsell writes: 'The success of the venture depended on the outside world not knowing about it.' The secret was given a name: the *Secret of the Holy Office*.[364]

The *Secret of the Holy Office* persisted through the twentieth century. In 1962, Pope John XXIII reissued *Crimen sollicitationis* with some minor changes and in 1974, Pope Paul VI, in his decree *Secreta continere* renamed the secret as the *Pontifical Secret*. Saint John Paul II issued *Motu proprio sacrementorum sanctitatis tutela* in 1997. The Pope wrote that the Pontifical Secret as outlined in *Secreta continere* remained in place. He also required bishops to send results of their preliminary inquiries under canon 1717 in respect of child sexual abuse to the Congregation for the Doctrine of the Faith, which would instruct them on what to do.[365]

Kieran Tapsell, in considerable detail, outlines how Bishop Mulkearns consistently followed the Church's Canon Law – emanating from Rome – in respect to clerical sexual abuse for the period he was Bishop of Ballarat. Mulkearns not only followed the 'proper meaning of the words' in Canon Law, 'but the interpretation that the Vatican itself had placed on them'. Importantly, the *Victorian Parliamentary Inquiry Report* (2012) agrees. That *Report* concluded Mulkearns had dealt with complaints of sexual abuse in the strictest confidentiality and had destroyed documents in accordance with the policy laid down by *Crimen sollicitationis*.[366] Ironically, in commenting on the craven criticism made by the current Victorian Church leaders, determined to distance themselves from Bishop Mulkearns and the Archbishop of Melbourne, Sir Frank Little, the Parliamentary Inquiry found that:

> ... while personal errors of judgement were made, it is unfair to allow the full blame to rest with those individuals, given that they were acting in accordance with Catholic Church policy.[367]

This is the story behind the story.

We live in the age of the individual. Individuals must stand and fall on their own. External influences on behaviour – systems, societies and cultures – read like excuses. The Nuremburg defence will not do. But it was never that simple. Conscience is a lonely thing, a pliable thing, plasticine in the hands of children. Some of what it tells us is instinctual and we know it to be true, but much of is nurtured and refined. Conscience rubs up against and is shaped by our experiences in the real world. The institution Ron was born into knows this better than most. It has never been one to promote the supremacy of individual consciences.

The Church nurtured and refined Ron's conscience from his childhood. Following his seminary training, it educated him in Rome. Ron held a doctorate in Canon Law. He was one of the founders of the Canon Law Society of Australia and New Zealand. He was the first chairman of the Special Issues Committee set up by the Australian Catholic Bishops Conference to find a better way of dealing with priests who abused children.[368] His Church has its own set of laws dating back centuries, which, historically, have frequently collided with the civil laws of the state. As far as Ron was concerned, his work as bishop involved doing at least one thing: following Rome's instructions reflected in the Church's Canon Law. If anyone was to follow the strict letter of the law it was Ron. With virtually no pastoral experience, Ron became the Co-Adjutor Bishop of Ballarat in 1968.

Ron knew one other thing instinctively. Rome was *the boss*. His young cousin asked him about celibacy once. At the time, Ron was a member of a Vatican Commission for Priestly Life:

> 'Was it [i.e. celibacy] ever on the agenda?'
> 'Yes, regularly.'
> 'What happened?' asked Morwood.
> 'The Vatican officials always removed it from the agenda.'
> 'Why don't you object?'
> Ron replied, 'Well, they're the boss.'

The sexual abuse scandal surrounding Mulkearns' leadership resembles a Greek tragedy. The Greek gods messed with humans. Everyone was a loser. Those Greeks not directly involved looked on aghast at mysterious events outside their control. Outcomes left them despairing at the human condition while, paradoxically, convincing them such outcomes were somehow just and necessary.

Morwood knows all this, yet his family loyalties, his sense of an injustice done and the hypocrisy of the institution which hides behind Ron, pushes him out onto the wire. But unfortunately for Morwood, tragedy for many of us is irrelevant, too clever by half, too complex. Tragedy clouds the issue and demands our compassion.

Modern bishops are not free men. Morwood believes they leave their 'intellectual integrity at the door'. Before becoming a bishop, they place on record their opposition to the ordination of women and to any change in the Church's teachings on contraceptive practices. Bishops:

> ... have to sign onto absolute surrender of intellect to what the Church believes and teaches – and that includes such questionable issues as humanity emerging into a state of Paradise, the literalness of the infancy and resurrection accounts in the gospels, the physical resurrection of Jesus, and that Jesus actually ordained and set up a male clerical Church before he died ...

Morwood argues that the 'real issue' in this whole scandal is not just Ron's shocking lack of judgement and reckless disregard for the safety of children, but:

> the intellectual dishonesty, the hypocrisy, the violence and the moral bankruptcy of Institutional Roman Catholicism, held together by secrecy, by bullying and by silencing – and until recent years, rewarding those who engaged in these tactics to safeguard the Church's reputation.

Alone, out on the wire Morwood keeps his balance. But guilt cannot be levelled solely at the Church. Ron, too, is guilty. Morwood knows that. In what sense, then, is Ron guilty? Morwood says he is guilty of 'acting in accord with what the Institutional powers asked of him'. He is guilty, writes Morwood, because he placed his faith in the 'sacredness' of the institution that made him. He is guilty because he was 'blinded' by his loyalty and 'acted misguidedly'. And 'he acted, relying on the advice he trusted according to what he thought was right. And he now stands condemned for his decisions.'

All that is the case but I would put it another way. Ron Mulkearns is condemned not just because he was blinded by loyalty to his Church. Loyalty takes us only so far. Ron is condemned because his failings were personal. Ron sacrificed too much of himself to the Church. In giving so much he sacrificed something of his humanity, that something that makes him a man. Morwood might well argue the Church moulded Ron like that and he is right to do so. But therein lies the tragedy. If we don't hold onto something personal, to that which makes us free, to that which makes us what and who we are, but rather something made in the image of an institution, then we are lost.

What upsets Morwood is the injustice of it all. He denounces the failure of every priest who privately disagrees with aspects of the Church's teaching but won't speak out for fear of being silenced. He attacks those older priests who remain silent for fear of losing their pension. He castigates the academic theologians and moral theology professors who fear more the loss of their teaching jobs than speaking the truth. He pillories those bishops, those 'yes-men', who bully and silence and intimidate; those men who ensure no informed scholarly voices are raised in their dioceses. His most bitter criticism is directed to a Cardinal, a man renowned for his 'bullying and silencing tactics', a man who now reaps his reward from Rome.

Morwood recalls the Cardinal's hypocrisy before the Royal Commission. He was:

> ... awesome to behold and it pinpoints something that needs attention in this sad story: the institution gets off scot-free. It is not brought to trial to examination, and ultimately to rightful condemnation. Not only that, it can, in the words of this cardinal at the Royal Commission, pompously condemn Ron from the high moral ground, see itself as pure and innocent as Snow White, and not look in the mirror and see the harm it wreaks with the intellectual dishonesty and hypocrisy at every level of Church life.

In his evidence before the Royal Commission, Cardinal George Pell was

Unlike other men 269

asked if Mulkearns was just 'one bad apple'. Pell replied, 'Unfortunately, I would have to say that I can't nominate another bishop whose actions are so grave and inexplicable.' Later on in his evidence he said he was 'deceived' by Mulkearns. This refers to the alleged failure of Mulkearns to explain to Pell as a Consultor why Ridsdale was constantly shifted from one parish to another. Pell said that Mulkearns's handling of Ridsdale was a 'catastrophe'.[369] Pell is a true Roman. By March 2016, when Pell gave his evidence, he surely knew Mulkearns was following Roman rules. Pell's critical comments about Mulkearns came some two years after the Victorian Inquiry found that Mulkearns had followed the Church's Canon Law and Church policy. 'Inexplicable' indeed.

Pell was never about to criticise Rome at the Royal Commission. He displayed no compassion or empathy for his one-time bishop caught between Rome and Ridsdale. Saint John Paul II promulgated the new Code of Canon Law in 1983. The 1983 Code extended the pastoral approach to sex-abusing priests. Thus, it required bishops to attempt reform of priests before subjecting them to a canonical trial for dismissal. As for paedophile priests like Ridsdale, the 1983 Code introduced a *Catch 22* defence: a priest could not be dismissed for paedophilia because he was a paedophile, that is, he could not help himself.[370] Mulkearns was trapped.

Morwood approaches the end of the wire. He makes one more point. Ron Mulkearns would never think of betraying the institution to which he devoted his life. Yet that institution betrayed him. It instructed him how to act and now it washes its hands of him. As far as the Church is concerned, Ron is an embarrassment and he will be buried accordingly.

When Mulkearns appeared before the Royal Commission in February 2016, he was 85 years of age and very sick. Much of what he said was incoherent. He had forgotten more than he remembered. He read nothing in preparation for the Commissioners. He couldn't remember ever discussing the sins and crimes of the paedophile priests in his dioceses with them personally. The evidence suggests any discussions he ever had with anyone about sexual abuse occurred with the psychologists who advised him. He couldn't remember ever discussing these issues with his Consultors.

When asked why he retired early he said, 'I wasn't handling myself very well in the sense that I was not doing the job as well as I felt I should be doing'. He then went on to apologise for his decisions as bishop: 'And I'd like to say, if I may, that I'm terribly sorry that I didn't do things differently in my time, but I didn't really know what to do or how to do it.'[371] Counsel assisting the Commissioners asked him if 'differently' meant 'seriously'. Mulkearns replied, 'Well, yes, I suppose that is true. I did want to take it all seriously, and so, in those days, it's a long time ago, but we didn't really know quite how to deal with these things, or I didn't'.

> Question: 'Bishop, the church has known for centuries that the sodomy of small boys and the rape of small girls was wrong.'
>
> Answer: 'Sure.'
>
> Question: 'You knew it was wrong, didn't you?'
>
> Answer: 'Oh, yes, yes.'
>
> Question: 'It had always been a crime, hadn't it?'
>
> Answer: 'I don't know really.'

Bishop Mulkearns died a little over one month after appearing before the Commission.

Bishop Mulkearns' funeral Mass in April 2016 was a small private affair held at Nazareth House in the Nursing Home Chapel, where he had spent the last eight months of his life. A month later the Bishop of Ballarat, Paul Bird, invited the priests and people of the diocese to a Memorial Mass in Saint Patrick's Cathedral to offer prayers for their late bishop. Adverse reaction to the proposal was such that Bishop Bird, fearing protests, decided to cancel such a public event. Survivors of sexual abuse in the diocese agreed with the cancellation. Mulkearns is the first Ballarat Bishop not to be buried in a crypt in the Cathedral:

> No more prayers now. For mortal men
> There is no escape from the doom we must endure.[372]

In his will, Mulkeans left virtually the whole of his assets to the diocese of Ballarat. His beachside home near Fairhaven, on the Great Ocean Road, was valued at approximately $2.1 million. There was some $40,000 in cash. What the Church didn't wish to keep was to be given to his only brother, Geoffrey.

Media reports said the house was given to the Bishop by his father. Bishop Paul Bird told the media that the money from Mulkearns' assets would be set aside to help abuse victims. To the very end, Ronald Mulkearns gave everything he was and everything he possessed to the Church that made him. And, as predicted, they didn't accept it.

Chapter 21

Begin again

Up in the mountains I contemplate my future. I worry about my debt to Bishop Henschke. I worry about what my family and friends back home will say if I leave. Most of them are delighted that I have at last found my calling. I wonder if I have left my run too late. Will I meet someone to marry? Previous attempts were not successful. Am I too old to start at the university? How can I study with no money? Perhaps it's easier to stay.

On Sunday nights, I talk with my friend Father Bede Heather. Relationships between students and staff were not close which may have been seminary policy. It wasn't simply that we operated at different levels but the fact they were priests and we were not. They kept their distance. It may have had something to do with the mystique surrounding the priesthood – something in their training. We were all beings as Thomas made clear, but priestly-beings, I suspect, felt they were beings over and above the rest of us.

With the exception of Bede, I am not close to any of the staff. I get on well with most of them but none is my friend. Bede gives me confidence. When I discuss my future, he never says what I should do but rather, 'Well Kev, I'm certain you will work it out all in good time.' Bede is teaching us Greek. It is very basic and he says that some of us may never find it useful in later studies, but for those who go to Rome and become interested in scriptural studies, a knowledge of Greek is important. I learn the Greek alphabet but my heart is not in it.

In my small room looking out onto the bush I worry about an event in Terang that occurred during the last Christmas break. It could help me decide my future. I was asked to drive a number of young girls home from their basketball game. They were dressed in their short frocks for basketball. One, whom I knew well, sat next to me in the front seat. She sat close, too close. I was very conscious of her body touching mine, her bare legs. I was horrified at my reaction. Back in the seminary, I told my spiritual director about the incident. I told him that celibacy was too much for me. I was completely innocent, but the thought of living a celibate life with such temptations was something I did not wish to contemplate. I can't remember now what he said, but he obviously calmed me down. I got on with my celibate life, but there was a new resolve that I was not suited for the priesthood. That I remember this incident fifty years on says something of its significance.

I could suffer much of the madness of the seminary that irritated Donnelly, but not celibacy. The year after I left Saint Columba's, Pope Paul VI released his encyclical *Sacerdotalis caelibatus*. Paul wrote to defend mandatory celibacy. According to Paul, the priestly life had 'a special advantage' in that it gave one 'a special aura of the otherworldly'. The priestly life, claimed the pope, gave to the faithful a glimpse of eternal life following the resurrection where there is neither marriage nor people given in marriage and where all live like angels.[373] Such an argument could not be offered today.

The seminary system failed, to a large degree, my best mates in the seminary. These young men were ten years my junior. They were encouraged to enter the seminary direct from their final year at boarding schools. After two or in some cases three years at Springwood, they were given the opportunity of studying at Propaganda Fide in Rome. They were thrilled with the idea and suggested I should go with them. They knew my bishop had asked me to consider doing a shortened course of theology at the Beda in Rome. I told them I was unsure about my future. 'Go for the trip, Kev.' I love these young men. They are too young to be here, making these decisions. They have never had a look at the world. Probably never fallen in love. Never been rejected. Never had a little blonde kid run faster than his little legs can carry him and throw his arms around their necks and hold on as if they are the most important person in the world. Do they appreciate the difficulties of celibacy? If I'm skating on life, my friends are skimming over it on jet skis without a worry in the world. They all go to Rome. One leaves shortly before ordination. The rest are ordained. They all leave the priesthood shortly after returning to Australia.

Veechy, the one who according to Geraghty, 'often toppled over the edge of sanity', calms me down and keeps me sane. He promises me a future, but it is not one wearing a black dress and a white collar. Veechy knows Napoleon like a brother. Because of him I continue to buy every new biography of Napoleon. Bonaparte is a Corsican with a heavy accent that brings derision in Paris. 'Ah, gentlemen, a remarkable man – baptised and confirmed in the Catholic faith.' Veechy's cheeks huff and puff and I know the smile well enough to recognise the irony. The successful French army has defeated the enemies of the Revolution. It begins the long walk to Moscow. Most walk, others ride horses. This is a one-way-walk for most. Napoleon rides a small grey horse. He always rides small horses. The army stretches out for miles and Napoleon rides well back from the front. The horses snort and throw their heads at each other, bridles and bits jingle jangle. The army is relaxed. Napoleon talks with the men. He is one of them. Then they stop. They look ahead to see what the problem is. Nothing. Still they wait. Napoleon is wanted up at the front. He heads off slowly and his men make way for him. He is a military genius and they know it. The men at the front of the line have stopped before a narrow bridge, about four horses wide. Someone thinks they saw movement on the other side. Perhaps a glint of steel. Should they cross? Napoleon looks across the water but all is still. He digs his horse in the ribs and they move onto the bridge. Slowly the two warriors begin, horse and rider, out onto the bridge, unhurried. The French army waits and watches. Two thirds of the way across, Napoleon turns in the saddle and beckons his men to follow. This is why they will walk with him to the gates of Moscow.

When Napoleon destroys what is left of the French Revolution and becomes Emperor, he invites the pope to crown him. He will be the first French Emperor in a thousand years. The pope, Pius VII, is delighted and remembers earlier popes and coronations. The pope suggests a crowning on Christmas Day 1804, as Charlemagne did in 800, but Napoleon refuses that date. Too much religious symbolism. Before the coronation there is much talk. Napoleon tells the clerical group that the greatest day in his life was the day he made his first communion. Veechy huffs and puffs and bursts out laughing. In *Notre Dame Cathedral*, the pope picks up the crown and moves to place it on the Emperor's head. But Napoleon stands and takes the crown from the pope and places it on his own head.

Veechy's stories have lived with me for fifty years. Many years later, when I am teaching the French Revolution and Napoleon, I retell my students Veechy's stories. They listen intently and believe their teacher. At the time, I cannot verify them. They're good stories and it may encourage them to read more. That is what happened to me.

Perhaps I should pray to Napoleon for courage. With pressure mounting about where I will go at the end of the year, I enter into serious discussions with my spiritual Director, Michael Kelly. His argument is much the same as my earlier Director, Ted Shepherd. When I think of it now, the argument to stay and become a priest circled around one issue – God's will. From the perspective of the spiritual directors, it is God's will that I should stay. But God's will is a slippery argument. How do they know what is God's will for me? How do I know what is God's will for me?

Father Kelly explains that God's will must be discerned or interpreted. God does not whisper messages in my ear. There is no direct communication. This is a very silent God. But, and this worries me, giving advice to people like me is their business. This is what they do; this is what they are good at. Unlike Napoleon, I have always been one to seek advice from those in authority. While the ultimate decision is mine this director will help me discern God's will. We go over it again. Father Kelly explains that discernment must involve an objective assessment of my life both before I entered the seminary and my efforts inside the seminary. He outlines the known facts. I am not a teenager, I am an older man, I have spent time out in the world, I have a record of working for the Church in Catholic Action, I am spiritually inclined, I have not married, and therefore, objectively at least, my life experiences point to a serious vocation to the priesthood. He next argues I have overcome a deficiency in my education, faced the difficulties of going back to secondary school with a classroom of young boys and have successfully completed nearly three years at Saint Columba's. Michael Kelly concludes that God is telling me that it appears I have a vocation. This is discernment. Why would I leave now? I have overcome so many difficulties to get this far. I recognise the logic, but I know I have never settled. Father Kelly advises me that if I still feel the same in a month's time then perhaps I should leave.

I realise now I was not well served by Father Michael Kelly or Father Ted Shepherd. I hold nothing against them. They were doing their best. Naturally they wanted me to stay, but they were not manipulative or dishonest. The problem was they framed the question of my leaving in such a way that it looked as if I was rejecting the highest offer God could make to any man – to be one of his chosen ones, namely, his priest – one who would stand at the altar, change bread and wine into the body and blood of Christ and offer once again his sacrifice on Calvary to his heavenly Father. To reject such an offer was preposterous. In a sense I was turning away from a divine vocation. I was turning away from God.

The director's question to me was, 'What is God's plan for you?' Even if God did have a plan for me, and at the time I probably believed he did, it was too difficult for me to answer. My spiritual advisers certainly believed that God had a clear and detailed plan for me, which brooked no alternatives and which I, somehow, had to discern. In other words, there was *one* plan and I had to conclude, after weighing up the facts, what it was.

I now think their question to me should have been, 'What is the best thing for you to do?' Or, put another way, 'What will make you happy?' These were the only questions I could answer with any certainty. My advisers should have stressed my freedom to choose. They should have said, 'God wants you to choose', not 'What does God want you to do?' Because of the elite nature of the priesthood, an especially reserved vocation for the chosen, I was placed under great pressure to get it right. Their question meant that I was forced to read the mind of God. But surely staying or leaving was not that sort of question. I was not making a moral choice. In this case, there was no law set down by either God or the Church for me to follow. There was no right or wrong answer to the question of my vocation.

It seems to me now that this question of my vocation in life should have been a question left for me to answer *without* bringing God into the equation. In a real sense, God was not directly or even indirectly involved in my answer. They should have advised me that God would be happy with whatever decision I made. Whether I was to become a poet, a pastry cook or a priest was my choice. My vocation was to love him in whatever career I chose. As an adult being I possessed the dignity of a human person with free will. I should have been advised that I had the right to choose based on that dignity. Despite a certain relaxed pragmatism for much of my time in the seminary, I worried about the possible link between leaving and rejecting the offer God was apparently making. My spiritual directors left me with the idea that God had written his mission statement for me and included in it was his desire for me to be one of his special ones – a priest in the One, True Church. Such an idea was damaging to my psychological well-being. Life is difficult enough without reading the mind of God.[374]

My way of looking at a priestly vocation now appears to be sharply at odds with the views of John Molony in his autobiographical *Luther's pine*. For John, the Catholic priesthood traces its roots back through the Jewish Bible. John's argument is that the individual person does not choose to be a priest, but rather God chooses the person. His evidence comes from the *Epistle to the Hebrews,* where the writer claims that a priest of the New Testament must not, 'claim this honour for himself but that, like Christ, he is also "called by God, as Aaron was"'. At ordination, he becomes 'a priest of the order of Melchizedek, and for ever'.

And again, but more strongly, when John acted as the master of ceremonies for some of his friends, who were ordained shortly before him, he writes:

> During the ordination, at which I was a master of ceremonies, it dawned on me that God had chosen these entirely normal young men with their varying gifts and lack of same because He wanted them as His priests. That they had anticipated God and chosen the priesthood on their own behalf seemed preposterous.[375]

I waited for a month and told Father Kelly I wanted to leave. Those leaden embryonic words, protected and hidden inside me for years were suddenly out in the night air, vibrant and alive, light as petals on a pool, and my world suddenly changed.

I have, in my mind's eye, a few images of those last days. The first is walking back to my room, down the corridor from the director's office, out into the night and up the stairs to my room. I felt light, a huge weight lifted now that the decision was made. In the end it was easy. Already I was planning for the future. The second image I have is sitting on a rock high up in the bush looking down into a gorge and talking to a friend. Down below are the tops of tall grey gums. I hear the sounds of male whip birds calling to their mates. Their shrill calls crack and split the air and I am reminded of my father. When we were young he would crack his stock whip around Mum and us kids. The sharp crack came before the whip wrapped gently around us. My friend asks me what I will do outside. I want to get to know my father better. *I hardly know him after all these years. I have taken him for granted. I want to engage with him, man to man.* The third image I have is half a dozen of my best friends sitting on a floor in a room on the top floor. I can't remember the time of day, but I remember the warmth, the friendship, the talk about the future and the general feeling of optimism. We were saying goodbye. The seminary never succeeded in destroying our human feelings for each other. The fourth image I have is sitting in Doc Joiner's classroom a few days before I left. We are doing an examination. I didn't answer his questions but I wrote numerous pages about my past and future life. I recalled the last ten years especially and the difficult decisions I had already made. If I had done it before I could do it again. I concluded the greatest virtue was not prudence, but courage, mental courage.

I wrote to my parents telling them I was leaving. My brother, Gerard, tells the story. He drove into the back yard at home and saw my father sitting in his car. Walking over to speak, he saw my father look up and begin to cry. My father didn't cry, at least not in front of his children. Thinking something terrible had happened, Gerard hesitated to speak. My father said, 'Kevin is coming home.' Gerard said, 'Then why are you crying? Do you feel ashamed?' 'No, no,' my father said, 'because he stayed so long.'

After saying goodbye to Veechy at the foot of the stairs, I made my way to the front of the building. A part of Veechy I take with me. Then out of the cloisters, under the tower and into the light where Bede's car was waiting. We left Jimmy Lawrence's house on the left, the Grotto and the Stations of the Cross on the right, and rolled out between the sandstone heritage gate a mile down the track and into the world. This day was nearly five years in the making. I begin again.

In the end it was clear the seminary and I worshipped different Gods. God can never be gender specific, but my seminary God was gender specific. He was male, cold, distant and aloof. The seminary God was a judgmental God, who demanded my obedience and submission. He enveloped me not in his love but in his rules, and I demonstrated my love for him when I obeyed his rules. The seminary God played rugby, and banned white curtains. He forbade communication with those who washed and cleaned and cooked for us. He was fearful of the very world he had created and he viewed my love for my friends with suspicion. The seminary God was misogynist, jealous and selfish who sought my devotion wholly for himself.

My God was female. She was sweet and warm, and she loved the world she had begun and the people who were created in her image. She was as sweet and warm as the stationmaster's daughter. My God wore mini-skirts, had streaks of grey in her hair and went out of her way to find me. When I asked her for help she always replied, 'Of course.' My God stood in vegetable gardens and waved me goodbye. She stood in the middle of the road with tears in her eyes, waving a white handkerchief because I was leaving her. Sometimes my God stood on the road wearing a pink dressing gown, and made me hot curries when I came home for Christmas. My God was calm and gentle. She wore a green cardigan, had soft hands, and whispered in the ear of a nervy horse to calm her. My God wore blue overalls and worked in a factory. She voted for the Labor Party and was a member of a union. My God was everywhere, even in the most unlikely places, even in the seminary. My God huffed and puffed, carried a white handkerchief like Pavarotti, told stories and inspired me to learn more. She sang in the ablution block with her friends and she helped me carry my guitar into the bush. My God had red hair, played Bach and knew how many chromosomes I had. She knew that people who needed people were the luckiest people in the world.[376]

In Sydney, I stayed for a week with John Traill, his wife and children on the north shore at Pymble. John had worked for Santamaria's Rural Movement and I knew him years ago. 'Stay as long as you like,' he said. On that first night John showed me his library. 'I can read one of these Penguins in a night,' this big man says. Already a barrister he will become a Queen's Counsel. I asked him if he had a copy of Flaubert's *Madame Bovary*. John looked at me and queried Flaubert's authorship. 'It's Flaubert,' I said. He didn't know that Veechy and I shared Emma as our secret lover. That night I met Emma for the first time – no one-night stand, but a slow and easy introduction. Emma and I have the rest of our lives.

The next morning I travel with John on the train into the city. We grasp overhead straps in a crowded train of dark-suited workers from the North Shore. Over the bridge and I see the sailing roof-ribs of the new Opera House. He pushes twenty dollars into my hand – new money. I missed the change to decimal currency. 'You might need it,' he says. Still skating on life but that will change. The scarlet letter, burnt into my forehead, has gone. Before he goes, he says, 'We'll talk about your future tonight.' With John anything is possible, and with Emma Bovary in my coat pocket I believe him.

Chapter 22

Deo gratias

In 1970, my old classmates, who saw it to the end, were ordained priests. In the same year, as if in concert, Margaret Murray, aka Lover, and I were married in Melbourne. We wrote some of the prayers. Below is a verse of the Post Communion prayer I wrote. This is what I was like in 1970:

In each beginning there is an end.
In every change something is gained and something is lost.
For this is the rhythm of life.
Today a new beginning has been made
and with all the spontaneity and gaiety of beginners we set out.

On summer mornings she wakes first. She said forty-seven years ago that she loved me and would stay with me forever and she has.

'Quick, quick, look at the sun,' she says.

I open slowly to the new day. The sky is on fire. It fills our bedroom. Busy old sun.

'Do you see it, dear old man?'

Thank you Lover. 'Yes.' Thank you. Thank you. 'Yes. Yes.'

Endnotes

1. Alex Miller, *The simplest words: A storyteller's journey*, Allen & Unwin, Crows Nest, 2015, p.15.
2. Chris Geraghty, *Cassocks in the wilderness: Remembering the seminary at Springwood*, Spectrum Publications, Melbourne, 2001, p.19:
   A dove with snowy wing
   Resplendent with rosy red neck
   Seeks a starry place
   Away from the yellow, cloistered world.
3. Quoted by Francis Sullivan, *What have we learned? What must be done? The Royal Commission and the challenges for the Catholic Church*, ABC Religion and Ethics, 23 October 2015, p.3, www.abc.net/religion/articles/2015/10/23/4337562.htm.
4. Ibid.
5. Katarina M. Schuth OSF, 'America, seminaries and the sexual abuse crisis', *American Magazine*, 22 March 2004, http://americamagazine.org/issue/478/article/seminaries-and-sexual-abuse-crisis, pp.1–2.
6. Gail Furness, Opening address, Royal Commission into Institutional Responses to Child Sexual Abuse, Case 50, 6 February 2017, www.businessinsider.com.au/here-is-the-shocking-opening-address-to-the-royal-commission-about-child-abuse-in-the-catholic-church-2017-2. The total number of sexual abuse claims between January 1980 and February 2015 was 4,444. The total number of identified alleged perpetrators was 1,880. Over 500 unknown people were identified as alleged perpetrators. It cannot be determined whether any of those people whose identity is unknown were identified in a separate claim. There are a number of problems using claims as the method of numbering clerical abuse. No system is perfect. Claims don't prove a person guilty. Claims require investigation and substantiation. In this case, however, there is such an imbalance of power between the claimant and the accused, such powerlessness versus prestige, that it is most unlikely claims would be made lightly. Embarrassment and fear are involved. Extraordinary courage is required to make a claim, even 33 years after the alleged event – the average time it took for claims to be made. The number of claims doesn't equal the number of alleged offenders; one individual can have any number of claims against him.
7. Ibid.
8. Dr Michael Whelan, Royal Commission into Institutional Responses to Child Sexual Abuse, Transcript (242), 6 February 2017, p.24770. The 'empire' metaphor used to help describe Church since Constantine and influence culture should be replaced by the 'pilgrim' metaphor introduced at the Second Vatican Council.

9. Between 1975 and 2008, the world's Catholics increased by 64%. Numbers to the priesthood increased by 1%. The French Church has closed half its parishes in recent years. Its priestly numbers halved between 1965 and 2006. www.futurechurch.org/future-of-priestly-ministry/optional-celibacy/facts-aboutpriestly-shortage-optional-celibacy-and. Ordinations to the priesthood in the United States declined from 1527 in 1960 to 454 in 2005, i.e. 29.7% of the 1960 figure. A report presented to the United States Conference of Catholic Bishops by the John Jay College Research Team, The causes and context of sexual abuse of minors by Catholic priests in the United States, 1950–2010, 2011. p.37. www.usccb.org/issues-and-action/child-and-youth-protection/upload/The-Causes-and-Content-of-Sexual-Abuse-of-Minors-by-Catholic-Priests-in-the-United-States-1950-2010. Ordinations from Corpus Christi College, Melbourne, which trains priests for Victoria and Tasmania, had 33 men ordained in 1969 and 3 in 2015. There were 49 entrants to the seminary in 1969 and 11 in 2015. catholicview.typepad.com/catholic_view/priestseminarian-demographics/ 4 May 2015. Attendances at weekly Mass in Australia are down from a peak of 74% in 1954 to 10.6% in 2011. Peter Wilkinson, Catholica, 6 September 2013, www.catholicia.com.au/gc4/pw/005_pw_print.php.
10. Michael Whelan, Royal Commission into Institutional Responses to Child Sexual Abuse, Transcript (242), Case 50, 6 February 2017, p.24764, no.27.
11. I thank Dr David Ranson for validating the title of this chapter. David was a witness at the Royal Commission into Institutional Responses to Child Sexual Abuse, Transcript (242), 6 February 2017. The Commissioners asked David to explain his PhD thesis. In so doing he outlined an historical and conceptual framework that made sense of my deeply felt alienation in the seminary. I realise now my individual difficulties were merely part of a changing paradigm. I was worshipping a different God, but I was not alone, and fifty years on I am grateful for that understanding.
12. Stephen Sondheim, *Send in the clowns,* from *A little night music,* 1973.
13. Philip Toynbee, *End of a journey: An autobiographical journal 1979–81,* Bloomsbury, London, 1988, p.7.
14. Saint Matthew's Gospel 25:35–40.
15. Chris Geraghty, *The priest factory: A manly vision of triumph, 1958–1962 and beyond,* Spectrum Publications, Richmond, 2003, p.12. Both the 1917 and 1983 Canon Law refer to impediments to the priesthood, but nothing refers directly to the importance or otherwise of testicles. Law 1041.5 refers to one who has attempted suicide, or one who has mutilated oneself or another gravely or maliciously. Castration is mentioned along with mutilation of hand or foot. But the point seems to be self-infliction. See also: Garry Wills, *Why priests? A failed tradition,* Viking, Penguin Group, New York, 2013, p.234, on early formula for ordination of priests and deacons: 'with no doubt about his genitals'. There is some evidence that popes, when proclaimed in the 15th century, sat on a pierced chair where a junior clergy groped them to ensure they had testicles. John Julius Norwich, *The popes: A history,* Vintage Books, London, pp.63–5.

16. Geraghty, *The priest factory*, p.74.
17. www.iep.utm.edu/buber/. Martin Buber, *Between man and man*, translated by Ronald Gregor-Smith with an introduction by Maurice Friedman, Routledge, London and New York, 2002, Introduction, pp.xi-xx. www.en.wikipedia.org/wiki/Martin-Buber. Stephen Trombley, *A short history of Western thought*, Atlantic Books, London, 2011, p.214.
18. Nasha Bita and Chris Merritt, *The Australian*, 12 July 2008 (online), www.theaustralian.com.au/archive/news/visit-proves-a-payout-blessing/sory-e6frg606-1111116892207. David Marr, *Sydney Morning Herald*, 29 January 2005, www.smh.com.au/news/National/The-limit-of-the-law/2005/01/28/1106850111190.htm. Andrew Bolt, *Herald Sun*, 11 July 2008, www.heraldsun.com.au/blogs/andrew-bolt/making-a-martyr-of-the catholic-church/news-story/b4d4b503d48e02586e15265f211aa398.
19. Royal College of Psychiatrists, United Kingdom, 2007. Submission to the Church of England's *Listening Exercise on Human Sexuality*. www.rcpsych.ac.uk/workingpsychiatry/specialinterestgroups/gaylesbian/submissiontothecafe.aspx.
20. Marie Keenan, Royal Commission into Institutional Responses to Child Sexual Abuse. Transcript (Day 242), 6 February 2017, p.24729, no.9–15, www.childabuseroyalcommission.gov.au/case-study/261be84b-bec0-4440-b294-57d3e7de1234/case-study-50,february-2017,-sydney.
21. Pope Francis, www.reuters.com/us-pope-celibacy.
22. Interview with Richard Sipe, www.awrsipe.com/interviews/2012-11-05-FAQ.html.
23. John Jay (2011), p.74. Garry Kearns, 'Looking into the dark', *Dublin Review of Books*, Issue 77, April 2016, p.5, http://www.drb.ie/essays/looking-into-the-dark.
24. Richard Sipe interview with Andrew West, *What explains the Catholic Church's silence on child sexual abuse?*, 1 March 2017, Radio National, www.abc.net.au/programs/religionandethicsreport/what-explains-the-catholic-chirch's-silence-on-child-sexual-abu/8314992.
25. Interview with Richard Sipe, Dr Laurent Schley, Luxemburg, 11 January 2011, www.awrsipe.com/interviews/2011-01-11-LUXEMBURG.htm.
26. Marie Keenan, Royal Commission into Institutional Responses to Child Sexual Abuse. Transcript (Day 242), 6 February 2017, p.24725, no.8 and no.27–34, www.childabuseroyalcommission.gov.au/case-study/261be84b-bec0-4440-b294-57d3e7de1234/case-study-50,february-2017,-sydney.
27. Donald B. Cozzens, *The changing face of the priesthood*, The Liturgical Press, Collegeville, Minnesota, 2000, p.25.
28. Anne Manne, *The life of I: The new culture of narcissism*, Melbourne University Press, Carlton, 2014, pp.57–9.
29. Louise Milligan, *Cardinal: The rise and fall of George Pell*, Melbourne University Publishing, 2017, p.93.
30. Maurice Friedman, introduction to Martin Buber, *Between man and man*, p.xvi.

31. Bertrand Russell, *A History of Western philosophy*, Routledge, London, 2000, pp.50, 56.
32. Eugene C. Kennedy and Victor J. Heckler, *The Catholic priest in the United States: Psychological investigations,* United States Catholic Conference, Washington DC, 1971, pp.8–11. William Grimes, Obituary for Eugene Kennedy, 'Ex-priest foresaw the Catholic sex scandals', *The Age*, Melbourne, 23 June 2015, p.34.
33. Wills, *Why priests?*, pp.117–57.
34. Ibid, p.25.
35. Ibid, p.80.
36. Kennedy and Heckler, pp.51–2.
37. John Jay (2011) has been criticised for ignoring the official age of children in the States, i.e. thirteen.
38. John Jay (2011), pp.2–3, 5, 118.
39. National Review Board for the Protection of Children and Young People, *A report on the crisis in the Catholic Church in the United States,* Washington, 27 February 2004, pp.7–8.
40. Marie Keenan, Royal Commission into Institutional Responses to Child Sexual Abuse. Transcript (Day 242), 6 February 2017, p.24730, no.13–19. www.childabuseroyalcommission.gov.au/case-study/261be84b-bec0-4440-b294-57d3e7de1234/case-study-50,february-2017,-sydney.
41. Kennedy and Heckler, pp.178–9, 202–3, 213.
42. Marie Keenan, Royal Commission into Institutional Responses to Child Sexual Abuse. Transcript (Day 242), 6 February 2017, p.24726, no.1–34. www.childabuseroyalcommission.gov.au/case-study/261be84b-bec0-4440-b294-57d3e7de1234/case-study-50,february-2017,-sydney.
43. Thomas P. Doyle, A. W. R. Sipe, Patrick J. Wall, *Sex, priests, and secret codes*: *The Catholic Church's 2000-year paper trail of sexual abuse*, Volt Press, Los Angeles, 2006, p.278. The word 'culture' in the quote does not refer to Church culture.
44. A. W. Richard Sipe, *Sex, priests, and power: Anatomy of a crisis*, Routledge, New York, 2014 edition, p.12.
45. John Jay (2004), p.6.
46. Michael Proeve PhD, Catia Malvaso BPsyh (Hons) and Paul DelFabbro, PhD, University of Adelaide, *Evidence and frameworks for understanding perpetrators of institutional child sexual abuse: A report commissioned and funded by the Royal Commission into Institutional Responses to Child Sexual Abuse*, 29 September 2016, p.7, http://childabuseroyalcommission.gov.au/policyandresearch/our-research/published-research/evidence-and-frameworks-for-understanding-perpra.
47. John Jay (2011), p.48, p.119. See also, M. Glasser (deceased), I. Kolvin, D. Campbell, A. Glasser, I. Leitch, & S. Farrelly, review article, 'Cycle of child sexual abuse: links between being a victim and becoming a perpetrator', *The British journal of psychiatry*, December 2001 in *Psych*, vol. 179, Issue 6. http://bjp.rcpsych.org/content/179/6/482.

48. Marie Keenan, Royal Commission into Institutional Responses to Child Sexual Abuse, Transcript (Day 242), 6 February 2017, p.24728, no.21–38. www.childabuseroyalcommission.gov.au/case-study/261be84b-bec0-4440-b294-57d3e7de1234/case-study-50,february-2017,-sydney.
49. Kennedy and Heckler, p.8.
50. Ibid, pp.9, 11.
51. John Cornwell, *The dark box: A secret history of confession*, Profile Books, London, 2014, pp.164–5.
52. Kennedy and Heckler, p.9.
53. John Jay (2004), p.27.
54. Furness, Opening Address, Case 50, 6 February 2017, www.businessinsider.com.au/here-is-the-shocking-opening-address-to-the-royal-commission-about-child-abuse-in-the-catholic-church-2017-2.
55. John Jay (2011), pp.65–9.
56. Ibid, p.74.
57. Conrad Baars, MD, *The role of the Church in the causation, treatment and prevention of the crisis in the priesthood*, unpublished, 1971.
58. Doyle, Sipe and Wall, pp.57–8.
59. Kennedy and Heckler, p.11.
60. Ibid, p.11.
61. Sipe address at Santa Clara University, 11 May 2012: http://www.awrsipe.com/Comments/2012-05-11-sexual-abuse-by-priests.htm.
62. John Jay (2011), p.68.
63. Ibid, p.98.
64. Patrick Parkinson, *Child sexual abuse and the churches: A story of moral failure? Part Two*, pp.2, 5, www.abc.net.au/religion/articles/2013/10/25/3877072.htm.
65. Michael Proeve PhD, Catia Malvaso BPsyh (Hons) and Paul DelFabbro, PhD, University of Adelaide, p.8.
66. Geoffrey Robertson, *The case of the pope: Vatican accountability for human rights abuse*, Penguin, Camberwell, 2010, p.6.
67. Parkinson, Part One, p.5.
68. Ibid, p.4. Note that these statistics refer to priests who were *convicted* of sexual offences from one seminary, and should not to be confused with national figures of *claims* against priests.
69. Ibid, p.5.
70. Ibid, p.6.
71. Parkinson, Victorian Parliamentary Inquiry into the handling of child abuse by religious and other organisations, before the Family and Community Development Committee, 19 October 2012, p.2, www.parliament.vic.gov.au/images/stories/committees/fedc/inquires/57th/Child-Abuse-Inquiry/Transcripts/Prof_Parkinson_19-Oct-12.pdf.
72. Sipe, *Frequently asked questions*, www.awrsipe.co./interviews/2012-11-05-FAQ.html. *Interview with Richard Sipe* by Luxembourg's Alliance of Hu-

manists, Atheists and Agnostics, www.aha.lu/index.php?option=com_content&view=article&id=129. Sipe, Preliminary Expert Report, www.awrsipe.com/reports/sipe_report.htm.
73. Furness, Opening Address, Case 50, 6 February 2017.
74. Francis D. Murphy, Helen Buckley and Larain Joyce, *The Ferns report*, presented by the Ferns Inquiry to the Minister for Health and Children (Dublin: Government Publications, October 2005), Chapter 2, 'Child sexual abuse and abusers', pp.13–4, www.bishop-accountability.org/Ferns/.
75. Hans Küng, *Can we save the Catholic Church?*, William Collins, London, 2013, p.20.
76. Geoffrey Robertson, p.20. Jamie Doward, *Guardian*, 24 April, 2005, www.theguardian.com/world/2005/apr/24/children.childprotection. Joseph Ratzinger as Prefect of the Congregation for the Doctrine of the Faith, http://en.wikipedia.org/wiki/Joseph_Ratzinger_as_Prefect_of_the_Congregation_for_the_Doctrine_of_the_Faith.
77. Robertson, pp.20, 214. John Jay (2004) pp.4, 161–2.
78. Michael Whelan, Royal Commission into Institutional Responses, Transcript (242), Case 50, 6 February 2017, p.24767. Whelan told the Commission: 'One thing we could do is have more transparency about the appointment of bishops and the involvement of the lay faithful in that process...' Whelan also told the Commission, 'that more women should be involved at all levels of decision making and ministry within the Church'.
79. George Pell, Royal Commission into Institutional Responses to Child Sexual Abuse, Transcript (159), Case 35, 29 February 2016, p.16186.
80. C. M. H. Clark, *A history of Australia, Vol. VI: The old dead tree and the young green tree, 1916–1935*, Melbourne University Press, Carlton, 1987, pp.221, 417, 440.
81. Geraghty, *Cassocks*, p.xiii. Paul Crittenden, *Changing orders: Scenes of clerical and academic life*, Brandl and Schlesinger, Blackheath, NSW, 2008, pp.81–2.
82a. Geraghty, *Cassocks*, p.30.
82b. Ibid, p.86.
83. Geoffrey Robinson, email to author, 21 April 2017. Permission to use Robinson's name, email 28 April 2017. I have other impeccable sources who wish to remain anonymous.
84. Geraghty, *Cassocks*, pp.29, 43; pp.65–6, 180.
85. Crittenden, pp.89–90, 105–6.
86. Tom Moore, 'No regrets', in Paul Casey (ed.), *Where did all the young men go? Life stories from 1960s' student Catholic priests*, FeedARead.com. Publishing, 2015, p.277.
87. Ibid, pp.24, 56, 137, 221, 238, 276–7, 395, 446, 474, 493–4, 517.
88. Geraghty, *The priest factory*, p.52. Frank Devoy, *Where did all the young men go?* p.494. Gospel of Saint Mark 3:31–33.
89. Tom Keneally, Interview with Robin Hughes for *Australian Biography*, September 2002, Tape 4, www.australianbiography.gov.au/keneally/interview9.

90. Vasily Grossman, *A writer at war*, edited and translated by Antony Beevor and Luba Vinogradova, Pimlico, London, 2006, p.261.
91. Vasily Grossman, 'The Sistine Madonna' in *The road*, Maclehose Press, Quercus, London, 2010, pp.181–92.
92. Saint Paul, Letter to Philippians 3:10.
93. T. S. Eliot, 'The love song of J. Alfred Prufrock', in *Selected poems*, Faber, London, 1980 reprint, p.14.
94. Geraghty, *Cassocks*, p.109.
95. Geraghty, *The priest factory*, pp.52–4. Interview with Betty King, 21 February 2015. Interview with Bill Armstrong, 20 February 2015.
96. Karen Armstrong, *The gospel according to woman*, Fount, London, 1986, p.9.
97. Hans Küng, p.306.
98. Geoffrey Robinson, *For Christ's sake: End sexual abuse in the Catholic Church ... for good*, JohnGarratt Publishing, Mulgrave, 2013, p.72.
99. Furness, Opening Address, Case 50, 6 February 2017, p.26, www.businessinsider.com.au/here-is-the-shocking-opening-address-to-the-royal-commission-about-child-abuse-in-the-catholic-church-2017-2.
100. Robinson, p.5.
101. Armstrong, p.5.
102. Stephany Evans Steggall, *Interestingly enough... The life of Tom Keneally*, Nero, Collingwood, 2015, pp.48–9. Reference to 'silly old bugger': Interview by Robin Hughes.
103. Steggall, p.147.
104. Ibid, p.49.
105. Tom Keneally, interviewed by Robin Hughes. The priest concerned was Father Con Keogh who had a mental breakdown and was removed from Springwood. Steggall, p.46.
106. Tatha Wiley, *Original sin: Origins, developments, contemporary meanings*, Paulist Press, New York, 2002, p.155. John Selby Spong, *Re-claiming the Bible for a non-religious world*, HarperCollins, New York, pp.361–2.
107. Wiley, p.155. 1 Timothy 2:12–14.
108. Wiley, p.156. Elizabeth Abbott, *A history of celibacy*, De Cappo Press, Cambridge, MA, 2001, claims that Tertullian's 'Gateway to the Devil' refers to the female vagina, pp.49, 436.
109. Wiley, p.31.
110. Armstrong, pp.98, 172.
111. Augustine (354–430); John Chrysostom (347–407); Jerome (c.345–420). Philip Kennedy, *A modern introduction to theology: New questions for old beliefs*, I. B. Tauris, New York, 2006, pp.203–6.
112. Armstrong, p.22.
113. Ibid, p.59.
114. Abbott, pp.49–50. Wiley, pp.171–5.
115. Philip Kennedy, p.204. Clement of Alexandria (c.150–215).
116. Armstrong, pp.35–6.

117. Wiley, p.167.
118. Philip Kennedy, pp.205–6.
119. Armstrong, pp.7–8, 24–5, 263–4.
120. Council of Trent (1563), *Canons on the sacrament of Matrimony*, Canon 10, http://www.ewtn.com/library/COUNCILS/TRENT 24.
121. Cornwell, *The dark box*, p.142.
122. *Gaudium et spes*, Part 11, Chapter 1, no.48.
123. Furness, Opening Address, Case 50, 6 February 2017, p.11, www.businessinsider.com.au/here-is-the-shocking-opening-address-to-the-royal-commission-about-child-abuse-in-the-catholic-church-2017-2.
124. Schuth, p.1.
125. Wiley, p.167.
126. David Kertzer, *Prisoner of the Vatican: The pope's secret plot to capture Rome from the new Italian State*, Houghton Miffin Company, Boston, 2004, pp.29–32, 65, 80, 94–9, 160, 165–73, 198–206.
127. G. K. Chesterton, *St Thomas Aquinas*, Hodder and Stoughton Ltd, London, 1952 reprint, pp.47–51.
128. Richard Tarnas, *The passion of the Western world: Understanding the ideas that have shaped our world view*, Pimlico, London, 1991, p.279. A. C. Grayling, *Descartes: The life and times of a genius*, Walker Publishing Co., New York, 2005, pp.237–8. Grayling argues that Descartes believed that the existence of God could be proven from Descartes' own existence.
129. Leo XIII, *Aeterni Petris*, 1879, no.7, www.Vatican.VA/.
130. Geraghty, *Cassocks*, p.110.
131. Tarnas, p.180.
132. Etienne Gilson (1884–1978). Joseph Komonchak, 'Thomism and the Second Vatican Council', *The Catholic University of America*, p.11, Jakomonchak.files.wordpress.com/2011/08/08/Thomism-at-Vatican-11, p.11.
133. Ibid, p.8. Marie Dominique Chenu (1895–1990).
134. Komonchak, p.2.
135. Maritain, *St Thomas Aquinas*, Chapter IV.
136. Paul Lakeland, *The liberation of the laity: In search of an accountable Church*, Continuum, New York, 2002, pp.31–2.
137. Fyodor Dostoevsky, *The Brothers Karamazov*, Vintage Classics, London, 2004, p.255.
138. Komonchak, pp.8–9.
139. Lakeland, p.48.
140. Quote by Gerald A. McCool, in *From unity to pluralism: The internal evolution of Thomism*, New York: Fordham University Press, 1989, p.230, cited in Joseph Komonchak, *Thomism and the Second Vatican Council*.
141. My recreation of Veech's story, which I can't remember in detail, with the help of Joseph Frank, *Dostoevsky: A writer in his time*, Princeton University Press, Princeton, 2010, pp.172–80.
142. Interview with Peter Donoughue, 18 June 2014.

143. Christopher Geraghty, *Dancing with the Devil: A journey from the pulpit to the bench,* Spectrum Publications, Richmond, 2012, pp.44–5, 212.
144. Crittenden, pp.210, 215.
145. Geraghty, *Cassocks,* p.167.
146. Geraghty, *Dancing,* p.45.
147. John Burnheim, *To reason why: From religion to philosophy and beyond,* Darlington Press, Sydney, 2011, p.35.
148. Yves Congar, *My journal of the Council,* ATF Theology, Adelaide, 2012, p.770.
149. Geraghty, *Cassocks,* p.28.
150. Mark Twain, *The adventures of Huckleberry Twain,* Penguin Classics, London, 1985, pp.245–6. Geraghty, *Cassocks,* pp.28, 97.
151. 'Rickety-rackety', in honour of my grandson, Ryan Peoples. Ryan loved rhyming words and taught me 'rickety-rackety', as well as 'snacky-wacky' (eating time). All this aged four.
152. *Terang Express,* 21 February 1964, p.1.
153. My poem with an idea borrowed from Miguel de Cervantes' *Don Quixote.*
154. John Wyngaards, *The priesthood of the faithful,* www.womenpriests.org/scripture/baptism.asp.
155. Truth, Justice and Healing Council, *Activity report,* Kingston, ACT, December 2014, p.23.
156. Ibid, p.23.
157. John Jay (2011), p.76.
158. Ibid, p.102. For the same loyalty to their priests, *The Ferns report,* Chapter 2, p.20, www.bishop-accountability.org/Ferns/.
159. Kearns, p.1.
160. Colm Tóibín, *London Review of Books,* vol.27, no.23, 1 December 2005, p.5, http://www.Lrb.co.uk/v27/n23/colm-tóibín /at-st-peters.
161. Kearns, p.4.
162. Cornwell, *The dark box,* p.163.
163. Furness, Royal Commission, Case 50: Diocese of Wollongong, 11.7% alleged perpetrators; Diocese of Lismore, 13.9%; Diocese of Port Pirie, 14.1%; Sandhurst, 14.7%; and Sale, 15.1%.
164. *Report by Commission of Investigation into Catholic Archdiocese of Dublin,* 1975–2004, (2009) Part 1, Chapter 1, Overview, p.2.
165. Ibid, pp.3–4.
166. Thomas P. Doyle, A. W. Richard Sipe and Patrick J. Wall, *Sex, priests, and secret codes,* p.ix.
167. Tóibín, p.4.
168. Catriona Crowe, 'On the Ferns Report', *The Dublin Review,* Issue 22, Spring 2006, p.8, https://thedublinreview.com/ferns-report/.
169. Tóibín, p.5.
170. Ibid, p.5.
171. Ibid, p.6.
172. www.futurechurch.org/future-of-priestly-ministry/optional-celibacy/

facts-aboutpriestly-shortage-optional-celibacy-and. Patrick Counihan, 'Only 13 Students sign up for the priesthood in Ireland', 25 August 2014, http://www.irishcentral.com/news/Only-13-students-sign-up-for-the. Michael Kelly, 'Irish priestly vocations in worrying decline', *The Catholic World Report*, 30 October 2012, www.catholicworldreport.com/Itm/1706/irish_priestly_vocations_in_worrying_decline.aspx.

173. Francis Henschke, Bishop of Wagga Wagga, letter to author, 27 March 1962.
174. Albert Camus, *The myth of Sisyphus: An absurd reasoning*, translated from French by Justin O'Brien, 1955, p.78. sharepoint.mlva.net/teachers/HectorP/SoPol/Documents.
175. Viktor Frankl, http://www.rjgeib.com/thoughts/frankl/frankl.html.
176. Statistics from the annual *Official Directory of the Catholic Church in Australia*.
177. Geraghty, *The priest factory*, p.21. enwikisource.org/wiki/Catholic_Encyclopedia_(1913)/Archdiocese_of_Sydney; article written by Denis F. O'Haran.
178. Geraghty, *The priest factory*, p.5; Patrick O'Farrell, *The Catholic Church and community: An Australian history*, New South Wales University Press, Sydney, pp.225, 231, 356–7.
179. Alexander Pope, 'The Dunciad', in *Alexander Pope*, with an introduction by John Bailey, Book 3, Thomas Nelson and Sons Ltd, London and Edinburgh, n.d., p.284.
180. John Molony, *Luther's pine: An autobiography*, Pandanus Books, Canberra, 2004, p.109.
181. Ibid, pp.124–9.
182. Ibid, p.14.
183. Interview 30 May 2015 with Father Mike Wheeler, parish priest of Wheelers Hill.
184. 'born bad' taken from John Boyce, *Born bad: Original sin and the Making of the Western World*, Black Inc., Collingwood, 2014. Council of Trent, Decree on Reformation, Twenty-Third Session, Chapter XVIII. www.history.hanover.edu/texts/trent/ct23.html. See also Geraghty, *Cassocks*, p.17.
185. Doyle, Sipe and Wall, p.35.
186. Ibid, pp.36, 234.
187. Ibid, pp.35–6.
188. Geraghty, *Cassocks*, pp.31–2.
189. Ibid, pp.32–36, 101.
190. Tóibín, p.2.
191. John Cornwell, *Seminary boy*, Harper Perennial, London, 2007, pp.25, 29.
192. Ibid, pp.45, 102–3, 127.
193. Pius X, *Notre Charge Apostolique* (Our Apostolic Mandate), www.catholicculture.org/cultrue/library/view.cfm. This document disbanded the French movement *Le Sillon*.
194. Cornwell, *The dark box*, p.79. Eamon Duffy, *Saints and sinners: A history of the popes*, Yale University Press, New Haven and London, third edition, 2006, p.320. Owen Chadwick, *A history of the popes, 1830–1914* (Oxford History of the Christian Church, Oxford University Press, New York, 2003), writes that

Pius X was the son of the village secretary, p.341. Carlo Falconi, *The popes in the 20th century*, Weidendfeld and Nicolson, London, 1967, says Pius was the 'bailiff's little son', p.17.
195. Cornwell, *The dark box*, p.87.
196. Ibid, pp.86–7. *Pieni l'animo*, Encyclical of Pope Pius X, promulgated on 28 July 1906, no.4, www.papalencyclicals.net/Pius10/p10clr.htm.
197. Marie Keenan, Royal Commission into Institutional Responses to Child Sexual Abuse, Transcript (Day 242), 6 February 2017, p.24727, no.23–33, www.childabuseroyalcommission.gov.au/case-study/261be84b-bec0-4440-b294-57d3e7de1234/case-study-50,february-2017,-sydney.
198. Cornwell, *The dark box*, p.87.
199. Geraghty, *The priest factory*, p.255.
200. Crittenden, p.167.
201. B. A. Santamaria (1915–1998) was Australia's most famous – some would say infamous – lay Catholic. His employment of the methods of Catholic Action were strictly political.
202. Luigi Sturzo (1871–1959), founder of *Partito Popolare*. John N. Molony, *The emergence of political Catholicism in Italy: Partito Popolare, 1919–1926*, Croom Helm, London, 1977, p.133. Richard Webster, *Christian democracy in Italy, 1860–1960*, Hollis and Carter, London, 1961, pp.78–9. D. A. Benchy, *Church and State in Fascist Italy*, Oxford University Press, London, 1970, p.501.
203. Wills, *Papal sin*, pp.65–8. Küng, pp.194–7.
204. Congar, p.808.
205. Cozzens, p.x.
206. Küng, p.121.
207. Second Vatican Council *Decree on Priestly Training (Optatam totius)*, proclaimed 28 October 1965, 'The Urgent Fostering of Priestly Vocations', 3, http://www.vatican.va/archive/hist_councils/ii_vatican_council/documents.
208. Ibid, Part V, *The revision of ecclesiastical studies*, no.13–18; Part VI, *The promotion of strictly pastoral training*, no.19–20. www.etwn.com/library/COUNCILS/V2ALL.
209. Story by David Foster Wallace (1962–2008), moreintelligentlife.com/story/david-foster-wallace-in-his-own-words.
210. Robert Zaretsky, *Albert Camus: Elements of a life*, Cornwell University Press, Ithaca and London, 2010, p.1.
211. Bernard Malamud, *The fixer*, Penguin, Ringwood, 1966, p.159.
212. Andrew Roberts, *Napoleon the Great*, Allen Lane, London, 2014, pp.146, 500.
213. Alfred Cobban, *A history of modern France, Volume 1: 1715–1799*, Pelican, Ringwood, 1963, p.172. George Rude, *Revolutionary Europe, 1783–1815*, Collins, London, 1964, pp.116–8. http://en.wikipedia.org/wiki/Charles_Maurie_de_Talleyrand. *The Prince de Talleyrand and the Duchesse de Dino at the Chateau de Rochecotte* (copy with author).
214. A variation of my favourite Bruce Dawe poem, 'Soliloquy for one dead', in *Condolences of the season*, Cheshire, 1971, p.3.

215. John Molony, *By Wendouree*, Connor Court, Ballan, 2010, p.122. Molony, *Luther's pine*, pp.186, 235.
216. Molony, *By Wendouree*, p.86.
217. Interview with author, 16 May 2014.
218. Sipe, Interview by Luxembourg Alliance of Humanists, Atheists and Agnostics, www.aha.lu/index.php?option=com_content&view=article&id=129.
219. Cornwell, *The dark box*, pp.141–9.
220. Father Tom Doyle, Transcript (243) Royal Commission into Institutions Responses to Child Sexual Abuse, Case 50, 7 February 2017, p.24817, no.30–38a.
221. John Jay (2011), p.2.
222. Ibid, pp.3, 118.
223. *The Ferns report*, Chapter 3, The Catholic Church, p.36, www.bishop-accountability.org/Ferns/.
224. John Jay (2011), p.34.
225. Schuth, p.2.
226. John Jay (2011), pp.4, 118.
227. Sullivan, *What have we learned?*, p.2.
228. Doyle, Royal Commission into Institutions Responses to Child Sexual Abuse, Transcript (243) Case 50, 7 February 2017, p.24818, no.27–36.
229. Doyle, Sipe and Wall, p.4.
230. Cornwell, *The dark box*, p.33.
231. Ibid, pp.45–6.
232. Ibid, pp.14, 43, 51–2 and Chapter 10. Richard McBrien, 'Questions surrounding the John Jay Report', *National Catholic Reporter*, 27 June 2011, http://ncronline.org/blogs/essays-theology/questions-surrounding.joh.   Thomas Doyle, *A very short history of sexual abuse in the Catholic Church*, www.crusadeagainstclergyabuse.com/htm/AShortHistoryhtm.
233. Richard McBrien, 'Questions surrounding the John Jay Report', p.13.
234. Thomas C. Fox, 'Richard Sipe on the John Jay report', *National Catholic Reporter*, 19 May 2011, www.ncronline.org/blogs/ncr-today/richard-sipe-john-jay-report.
235. www.themediareport.com/hot-topics/rev-thomas-p-doyle-o-p.
236. Doyle, Royal Commission into Institutional Responses to Child Sexual Abuse, Case 50, Transcript (243), 7 February 2017, p.24821, no.6–44.
237. Thomas P. Doyle, *Sexual abuse in the Catholic Church: A decade of crisis, 2002–2012: A radical look at today and tomorrow*, 11 May 2012, pp.7–8, www.awrsipe.com/doyle/2012/SantaClara-May.15,2012c[5].pdf.
238. Parkinson, Part One, p.16.
239. Robertson, p.166.
240. Parkinson, p.16.
241. Kearns, p.4.
242. James Franklin, 'Gerald Ridsdale, pedophile priest, in his own words', *Australian Catholic Historical Society*, 36 (2015), pp.219–30.
243. http://en.wikipedia.org/wiki/Pedophilia.

244. John Jay (2011), p.124.
245. www.awrsipe.co/interviews/2012-11=05-FAQ.html.
246. John Jay (2011), pp.11, 34–5, 53–5. John Jay's figures are not to be trusted here. John Jay uses 10 years of age rather than the official age of 13 (2011 report pp,10–11, 55).
247. Cozzens, p.124.
248. John Jay (2004) does not distinguish between boys and girls. The majority of victims were aged between 11 and 17. 50.7% of all individuals who made allegations of abuse were between the ages of 11–14. John Jay notes that it is often difficult for victims to remember the exact age they were when abused. Claims are often made many years after the actual event. Further, just 84% of those surveyed included the date of age when first abused. www.usccb.org/issues-and-action/child-and-youth-protection/upload/The-Nature-and-Scope-of-Sexual-Abuse-of-Minors-by-Catholic-Priests-and-Deacons-in-the-United-States-1950–2002.pdf, p.70.
249. Furness, Opening Address, Case 50, 6 February 2017, p.11, www.businessinsider.com.au/here-is-the-shocking-opening-address-to-the-royal-commission-about-child-abuse-in-the-catholic-church-2017-2. Desmond Cahill, Royal Melbourne Institute of Technology, private email, 7 February 2017.
250. John Jay (2011), p.9.
251. Furness, Opening Address, Case 50, 6 February 2017, p.11, www.businessinsider.com.au/here-is-the-shocking-opening-address-to-the-royal-commission-about-child-abuse-in-the-catholic-church-2017-2.
252. Ibid, p.100.
253. William A. Donohue, President Catholic League for Religious and Civil Rights, *John Jay Study on sexual abuse: A critical analysis*, www.catholicleague.org/wp-content/uploads/2011/05/John-Jay-Report-1-27-12-Update.pdf. Rachel Zoll, Study: 'Gays not to blame for pedophile priests', 18 May 2011, http://www.edgemedianetwork.com/news///119731.
254. Sipe, *Sex, priests, and power*, p.ix. Glenn Wilson and Qazi Rahman, *Born gay: The psychobiology of sex orientation*, Peter Owen, London, 2005, pp.16–22. The number of gays in the community at any one time is a complex question. The answer depends on how being gay is determined. The popular notion that one in ten people is gay is incorrect and based on flawed research by Kinsey in 1948 and 1953. The Wilson and Qazi figure is based on how people respond emotionally to sexual stimuli, rather than what people say or do.
255. John Jay (2011), pp.4, 38, 62.
256. Doyle, *Clergy sexual abuse in the Catholic Church reflections, 1984–2010*, pp.3, 5, 11, www.awrsipe.com/Doyle/2010/20/2010-08-27-reflections.htm. Garry Wills, *The future of the Catholic Church with Pope Francis*, Viking, 2015, New York, pp.185–99, for an excellent chapter on the Church's dependence on an outmoded theory of natural law.
257. Doyle, *A radical look at today and tomorrow*, p.5.
258. Cozzens, p.123.

259. Sean D. Sammons, see foreword to Stephen Rossetti, *Slayer of the soul*, quoted by Cozzens, p.123.
260. Richard Holloway, *Leaving Alexandria*, Text Publishing, Melbourne, 2012, pp.177–8.
261. Kearns, p.5.
262. Ibid, p.5. Gerald Ridsdale, Australia's most prolific paedophile offender, had precisely the same difficulties with impure thoughts, masturbation, and healthy relationships with adults. James Franklin, 'Gerald Ridsdale', pp.221, 229.
263. Timothy Jones, 'Paedophile priests are criminals, not sinners', *The Age*, 27 May 2015, p.45.
264. Cornwell, *The dark box*, pp.194–5.
265. Kearns, pp.5–6.
266. Cornwell, *The dark box*, p.162.
267. Sipe, *Sex, priests, and power*, p.140.
268. *The Ferns report*, Chapter 2, 'Child sexual abuse and abusers', 2005, pp.14–6.
269. Sipe, *Sex, priests and power*, pp.30–1.
270. Cornwell, *The dark box*, p.188.
271. John Jay (2011), p.113.
272. Ibid, pp.105–115, for section on excuses and justification.
273. *Roger Landry*, www.catholiceducation/org/en/culture/catholic-contributions/pope-francis-and-the-reform-of=the-laity; Robert Mickens, *National Catholic Reporter*, 24 November 2014, www.ncronline.org/blogs/roman-observer/true-and-false-reform-roman-curia.
274. Cornwell, *The dark box*, p.154.
275. Robertson, p.6. Hans Küng, p.303. Bishop Geoffrey Robinson argues that celibacy itself is not the problem, but obligatory celibacy is an issue, Robinson, p.17.
276. Cornwell, *The dark box*, pp.195–6.
277. Sipe, *Interview with Sipe*, www.awrsipe.com/interviews/2012/11-05.
278. Abbott, pp.104–5. *Catholic Encyclopedia*, www.newadvent.org: www.nndb.com/people.
279. *Catholic Encyclopedia*, www.newadvent.org/cathen/03481a.htm.
280. Wills, *Papal sin*, p.133.
281. Ibid., p.133.
282. Küng, p.122.
283. Ibid, p.123.
284. http://en.wikipedia.org/wiki/Total_institution. www.markfoster.net/neurelitism/totalinstitution.pdf. Article by Erving Goffman, 'The characteristics of total institutions', reprinted from presentation in April 1957, in *Organisation and society*, is.muni.cz/el/1423/podzim2009/SOC139/um/soc139_16_Goffman.pdf.
285. David Jary and Julia Jary, *Collins dictionary of sociology*, HarperCollins, Glasgow, 1991, p.663.
286. John Thavis, *The Vatican diaries: A behind-the-scenes look at the power, personalities and politics at the heart of the Catholic Church*, Penguin, London, 2013, p.14.

287. Brendan Ryan, 'Mother and daughter', in *Travelling through the family*, Hunter, Melbourne, 2012, p.47.
288. Tarnas, p.336. George Berkeley (1685–1753).
289. John Cowburn SJ, *Love*, Marquette University Press, Milwaukee, 2003, quote from Menninger's *Love against hate*, p.212.
290. Phone interview, 14 March 2015, with Chris Geraghty, who commenced lecturing at Springwood in 1967.
291. Geraghty, *Dancing*, p.52.
292. John Molony, *The Roman mould of the Australian Catholic Church*, Melbourne University Press, Carlton, 1969.
293. Stephen Trombley, *A short history of Western thought*, Atlantic Books, London, 2011, p.141.
294. Crittenden, p.20.
295. Samuel Beckett, last two lines of *The unnameable*, www.samuel-beckett/unameable.html.
296. Molony, email to author, 1 August 2014.
297. Despite the media publicity given to the Ballarat Diocese, the number of claims against alleged perpetrators was 8.7%, just above the national average of 7.9%. One priest, Gerald Ridsdale, accounted for a great many claims. Some 199 priests served in the Ballarat diocese between the years 1950 and 2010. Ridsdale was one of seventeen who were identified as alleged perpetrators. Apart from these seventeen, the disgrace in the Ballarat Diocese must be shared with the failure of authorities to stop Ridsdale, in particular Bishop Mulkearns and his Consultors. Exhibits for Case Study 50, 6 February 2017, Exhibit Number 50-0001, Day 242. See also Exhibit Number 50-0008, *Explanation document, proportion of alleged perpetrators*, Gail Furness, Day 250, 16 February 2017. www.childabuseroyalcommission.gov.au/case-study/261be84b-bec0-4440-b294-57d3e7de1234/case-study-50,february-2017,-sydney.
298. Doyle, Sipe and Wall, *Sex, priests and secret codes*, pp.5, 14.
299. The priest was Father Bob Maguire. Milligan, *Cardinal*, pp.91–2.
300. David Marr, *The prince: faith, abuse and George Pell*, Quarterly Essay, Black Inc, Collingwood, pp.11–12, 70–72. Broken Rites Australia, *A Church report contains allegations about George Pell abusing an altar boy in 1961–62*, www.brokenrites.org.au/drupal/node/36. Witness Statement of Cardinal George Pell, 24 February 2014, to Royal Commission into Institutional Responses to Child Sexual Abuses, Towards Healing Stat. 0169.001.0013_R https://kangaroocourtofaustralia.files.wordpress.com/2014/03/cardinal-george-pell-witness-statement.pdf.
301. Royal Commission into Institutional Responses, Case Study 28, Transcript Day C134, 7 December 2015, p.C14165, www.childabuseroyalcommission.gov.au/case.../case-study-28-february-2016-ballarat.
302. Marr, p.41.
303. Martin McKenzie-Murray, *The Saturday Paper*, 5–11 November 2016, https://www.thesaturdaypaper.com.au/news/religin/2016/11/05/geo.

304. Submissions of Counsel Assisting, 10 June 2016, Case Study 28, Ballarat, Submission-of-Counsel Assisting pdf, Gail Furness, SC, Angus Stewart, SC, Stephen Free, p.81, no.392. http://www.childabuseroyalcommission.gov.au.
305. Ibid, p.81, no.390.
306. Ibid, p.82, no.397; p.88, no.431.
307. Ibid, p.91, no.448.
308. Ibid, p.90, no.440.
309. Ibid, p.81, no.389.
310. Martin McKenzie Murray, *The Saturday Paper*, 5–11 November 2016. Tessa Akerman, Pia Akerman and Rebecca Urban, *The Australian*, 1 November 2016, p.1.
311. Submissions of Counsel Assisting, 10 June 2016, Case Study 28, Ballarat, Submission-of-Counsel Assisting pdf, Gail Furness, SC, Angus Stewart, SC, Stephen Free, p.299, no.1652; p.301, no.1660; p.301, no.1661, http://www.childabuseroyalcommission.gov.au.
312. Ibid, p.282, no.1550, 1551, 1552.
313. *The official year book of the Catholic Church of Australia and Papua-New-Guinea, New Zealand and the Pacific Islands, 1969–70*, E. J. Dwyer, Sydney, pp.166–78, 202–5. The Archdiocese of Melbourne had 20 religious orders working in parishes.
314. Submissions-of-Counsel Assisting, p.308, no.1701.
315. Ibid, p.199, no.1060.
316. Royal Commission Transcript (209), 14 September 2016, Case No 44, Evidence of Bishop Bede Heather, no.21110–21111.
317. Submission of Counsel Assisting, 10 June 2016, Case Study 28, p.303, no.1675.
318. Ibid, p.303, no.1671.
319. Ibid, pp.302–3, no.1669. There is some confusion between Ridsdale being appointed as administrator and later as parish priest. Pell was not involved with the first decision. 'Removed' must refer back to Inglewood.
320. Ibid, p.305, no.1683.
321. Ibid, p.211, nos.1132, 1133, 1139.
322. Ibid, pp.188–9, no.998–999, 1001, 1003, 1004.
323. Ibid, p.307, no.1698.
324. Ibid, p.308, no.1702–1703.
325. Ibid, p.310, no.1714.
326. Ibid, p.310, no.1716.
327. Ibid, p.307, no.1699–1700.
328. Ibid, p.315, no.1735–1736.
329. Melissa Cunningham, *The Courier*, 9 December 2015, http://www.thecourier.com.au/story/3549125/priest-admits-he-knew.
330. T. P. Boland, *Dictionary of biography*, Vol. 14, Melbourne University Press, 1996. Gilroy had powerful clerical friends in Rome: Bruce Duncan, *From ghetto to crusade: A study of the social and political thought of Catholic opinion-makers in Sydney during the 1930s*, 1987 Doctoral Thesis, University of Sydney, digital copy online, The Sydney eScholarship Repository, p.194.

331. Edmund Campion, *A place in the city: Living around the cathedral, from the mysteries to the wider world*, Penguin, Ringwood, 1994, p.4.
332. Geraghty, *Dancing*, p.48.
333. Molony, email to author, 1 August 2014.
334. Geraghty, *The priest factory*, pp.89–90.
335. Pius X, *Vehementer Nos*, 1906, No.8, w2.vatican.va/content/piusX/en/encyclicals/documents/hf_p_10_en_11021906_vehementer.nos.html.
336. Küng, p.5.
337. www.papalencyclicals.net/Pius10/p10moath.htm.
338. Philip Kennedy, p.36.
339. Ibid, pp.35–7.
340. Molony, *Luther's pine*, pp.134, 169, 172.
341. Bob Donnelly, letter to author, 5 April 1966, p.1.
342. John Jay (2004), pp.5, 27, 41.
343. H. Daniel-Rops, *The Catholic Reformation: History of the Church of Christ*, Vol. 5, first published in France by Librairie Artheme Fayard, 1955, translation J. M. Dent & Sons, London, and E.P. Dutton & Co., New York, 1962, pp.40–1.
344. Oliver Miles, letter in *London Review of Books*, London, 9 October 2014, p.4.
345. Geraghty, story of Billy's escape sent to author by email, 11 August 2014.
346. Father John Stuart McKinnon, Royal Commission, Case 28, Transcript (C139), 14 December 2015, p.C14727.
347. Second Vatican Council, *Christus Dominus*, proclaimed by Pope Paul VI, 28 October 1965, no.16. Decree on Ministry and Life of Priests, *Presbyterorum Ordinins*, promulgated by Pope Paul VI, 7 December 1965, no.2. www.vatican.va/archive/hist_councils/documents/vat-ii_deecree_19651028_christus-dominus_en.htm www.thecounciloftrent.com/ch23.htm.
348. Wills, *Why priests*, pp.2–3.
349. Father John Stuart McKinnon, Australian Royal Commission, Case 28, Transcript (C139), 14 December 2015, p.C14725. See also Furness, Transcript (242), Case 50, 6 February 2017, p.24767, no.37–44, on the powerlessness of some priests with their bishops.
350. Ibid, p.C14717 (McKinnon).
351. Ibid, p.C14718.
352. Ibid, p.C14736.
353. Ibid, pC14731.
354. Ibid, p.C14731.
355. Father B. P. McDermott, Royal Commission, Case 28, Transcript (C139), 14 December 2015, pp.C14756–C14757.
356. McKinnon, p.C14726.
357. Ibid, pp.C14724–14725.
358. Ibid, p.C14726.
359. Ibid, p.C14736.
360. Ibid, p.C14737.
361. Ibid, p.C14739.

362. Ibid, p.C14739.
363. Francis Sullivan in article by Kieran Tapsell 'A Response to Francis Sullivan', in John Menadue Blog, *Pearls and irritations*, 17 March 2017, johnmenadue.com/?p=9780.
364. Kieran Tapsell, *Potiphar's wife: The Vatican's secret and child sexual abuse*, ATF Press, Adelaide, 2014, p.53.
365. Ibid, pp.16, 27.
366. Ibid, p.210.
367. *Betrayal of trust*, Victorian Parliamentary Inquiry, November 2013, 7.3.3, p.166, www.parliament.vic.gov.au/images/stories/committees/fedc/inquires/57th/Child_Abuse_Inquiry_into_Handling_of_Abuse_Volume_1_FINAL_web.pdf.
368. Ibid, p.46.
369. Cardinal George Pell, evidence before Royal Commission, Case 28, Transcript (160), 1 March 2016, pp.16278, 16280. Transcript (159) 29 February 2016, p.16200, www.smh.com.au/national/cardinal-george-pell-blames-former-bishop-for-letting-abuse-fester-20160301-gn71uj.html.
370. Tapsell, p.18.
371. Michael Morwood, *Catholica*, 5 April 2016, www.catholica.com.au/gc2/mm/011_mm_print.php. Shannon Deery, 5 September 2016, www.heraldsun.com.au/news/victoria/former-catholic-bishop-ronald-mulkearns-leaves-most-of-2.1m-estate-to-church/news/story www.abc.net.au/news/2016-09-06/assets-from-bishop-mulkearns-to.../7818984. Bishop Mulkearns, *Royal Commission*, transcript (C153), Case 28, 25 February 2016, p.C16136.
372. Sophocles, 'Antigone', in *The three Theban plays: Antigone, Oedipus the king, Oedipus at Colonus*, translated by Robert Fagles, Penguin Classics, Camberwell, 1984, p.127.
373. Wills, *Papal sin*, pp.184–5.
374. John Cowburn SJ, *Free will, predestination and determinism*, Marquette University Press, Milwaukee, Wisconsin, 2008, pp.233–9.
375. Molony, *Luther's pine*, pp.267, 269.
376. God, by definition, is genderless. My female God is a reaction to the machismo God I met in the seminary.

Index

A

Abbott, Elizabeth, 289 n.108, 289 n.114, 296 n.278

Abelard, Peter, 78

Aboriginal land, 58-9

Activity document in response to the Royal Commission into Institutional Responses to Child Sexual Abuse, 116-7

Adam (biblical figure), 69

Adams, David (pseudonym), 58

Adventures of Huckleberry Finn, The (Mark Twain), 100

Aeterni Patris (1879), 75, 80-1, 86

altar servers, girls as, 178

Ambrose, Saint, 219

American Psychiatric Association, 177

Anaximander, 19

Anderson, John, 98

Anglican Church, 260
  priesthood of, 256
  sexual abuse in, 41-2

Anselm of Canterbury, 78

Antichrist, 139

antimodernism, 238

Apollo Bay, 226, 228

Aquinas, Thomas, see Thomas Aquinas

Aristotle, 19, 36, 47, 71, 72, 77, 78, 82, 100, 109

Armstrong, Bill, 65, 289 n.95

Armstrong, Karen, 72, 289 n.96, 289 n.101, 289 n.110, 289 n.112, 289 n.113, 289 n.116, 290 n.119

army, see National Service

Augustine, Saint, 20, 69-70, 71, 129, 219

Auschwitz, 130, 144

Australian bush, 1, 17, 20, 21, 46, 47, 53, 56, 57, 58-9, 60, 61, 77, 86, 95-6, 104, 138, 142, 160, 163-4, 195, 201, 204, 206, 207, 209, 221, 232, 238, 246-7, 248, 272, 278, 279

Australian Catholic Bishops Conference, 221, 266

Australian Labor Party (ALP), 101, 102, 279

authoritarianism, 2, 169, 172

B

Baars, Dr Conrad, 38-9

Ballarat, Diocese of, 219, 222-31, 253-5, 256, 257-9
  see also Mulkearns, Bishop Ronald

Balzac, de Honore, 15, 162

Beckett, Samuel, 206

Benedict XV, Pope, 83, 144

Benedict XVI, Pope, 6, 147
  see also Ratzinger, Cardinal Joseph

Bergoglio, Cardinal Jorge Mario, see Francis, Pope

Berkeley, George, 198, 205

Best, Brother Robert, 223

Bird, Bishop Paul, 270-1

bishops
  failure to act on abuse, 24, 264
  secrecy regarding abuse cases, 170-1, 264-5, 267
  subservient to Vatican, 267

see also Catholic hierarchy
Blake, Terry, 94, 232
Blue Mountains, 29, 59, 76, 81
   National Park, 13, 180
Bok, Yakov Shepsovich (fictional character), 150
Boniface, Pope, 15
Borromeo, Saint Charles, 172
Boswell, James, 204-5
Bourke, Maureen and Pat, 57, 123, 125, 207-9
Bovary, Emma (fictional character), 63, 204-5, 280
Bowral, 13, 53, 212, 249
Boyce, John, 292 n.184
Boylan, Eugene, 199
BPF, Mrs (pseudonym), 228
BPL, Mr (pseudonym), 228-9
British Journal of Psychiatry, 34
Broken Rites, 221, 297 n.300
Bryant, Father Eric, 230-1
Buber, Martin, 20, 21, 26, 36, 285 n.17, 285 n.30
Burnheim, John, 98
Burns, Father Ian, 163, 212, 234
bush, the, see Australian bush

C

Calwell, Arthur, 101
Campion, Edmund, 234
Camus, Albert, 128, 130, 148
Canon Law, 83, 139, 174-5, 178
   and civil law, 175, 178
   in Australian Church, 174
   misuse of, 3
   sexual abuse in, 119, 174-5
Cardijn, Cardinal Joseph, 64, 98-9, 133, 244

Carroll, Father Noel ('Say'), 63, 99-100, 106, 199, 211
Carroll, Shirley, 65
Catch 22 defence, 269
Cathedral Colleges, 134
Catholic Action, 12, 133, 149, 220, 235, 254, 275
Catholic Church
   as founded by Jesus Christ, 173
   change in paradigm, 144-5
   dualism in, 185
   high levels of clerical sexual abuse in, 39-42, 44, 166-7
   otherworldly, 2, 12, 186, 273
   structural change in, 44-5
   systemic issues in, 35, 42, 171, 179, 182, 264
   see also Holy Mother Church; One True Church
Catholic culture, 3, 171, 174, 187-9
   arising from Church's self-understanding, 45
   as a cause of clerical sexual abuse, 3, 33, 35, 113, 179, 183-4, 187, 256-7, 262
   hindering Church action on abuse, 3, 113, 171, 256
   triumphalism, 2, 3, 47, 143, 264
   see also clericalism; misogyny and the Church; sex
Catholic Enquiry Centre (CEC), 229, 230-1
Catholic hierarchy, 171, 256-7, 267
   self-image of, and sex abuse crisis, 179
   own sexual failures and hiding of abuse cases, 24
   secrecy regarding abuse cases, 170-1, 172-3, 264-5
   see also bishops
Catholic priests
   as 'lighthouses', 5, 17, 26, 47, 249, 257

issues with intimacy, 35-6, 37, 185, 257, 260
link between psychosexual/emotional immaturity and sexual activity, 38-9
married, 191
mission as salvation of souls, 140, 149-50
need for intimate friendships, 25-6, 36, 37
see also clerical sexual abuse of minors; clericalism

Catholic Right, 102

celibacy, 23-4, 134-5, 147, 149, 166, 170, 190, 261, 266, 273
and clericalism, 193
and lack of empathy, 181-2
and misogyny, 66, 73
as charism, 190
as factor in sexual abuse, 24-5, 168, 187
cause of psychological damage, 26
history of, 191
Jesus as model of, 190
mandatory, 2, 22, 23-4, 26, 38, 67, 117, 145, 149, 168, 179, 182, 184, 190-1, 193, 249, 273, 296 n.275
means of institutional control, 166, 193-5
non-compliance with, 24, 167
superior to marriage, 72-73, 135, 192-3
Virgin Mary as model of, 53-4

Center for Applied Research in the Apostolate (CARA), 44

Cerutty, Percy, 110

Cervantes, Miguel de, 109

Charter for the Protection of Children and Young People, 32

Chaves, Mark, 237-8

Chenu, Marie-Dominique, 82-6

Chevalier College, 13, 89, 124, 149, 205, 212, 217, 232, 246, 249

Christ, see Jesus

Christian Brothers, 6, 219, 223, 234, 253

Chrysostom, Saint John, 30, 70, 71

Church, see Catholic Church

Church Councils, see Council of Elvira; Council of Trent; First Vatican Council; Second Vatican Council

Clancy, Canon, 120, 122

Clement of Alexandria, 71

clerical culture, see clericalism

clerical sexual abuse of minors, 183
abusers who were themselves abused, 4, 33-5
and lack of empathy, 180-2, 185, 186
as betrayal of laity, 117-8
comparison of diocesan and order priests, 36
distinguished from paedophiliac behaviour, 4, 177-8, 183
existential threat to Church, 5-6
in history, 171-2
mandatory reporting of, 174-5
parents wanting to protect abusive priests, 117
predominately of males, 178
response of bishops, 3
statistics on, 4-5, 33, 43, 43-4, 119, 177-8

clericalism, 2, 30, 36, 140, 147, 149, 169, 172, 186, 193, 235
and celibacy, 188, 193
and lack of empathy, 181-2
and misogyny, 65, 73, 188
and power, 117
and sexual abuse, 113, 116-7, 175
at odds with Jesus, 30-1

block to Church reform, 38, 44
central to Catholic culture, 116
cultic priesthood, 115-6, 118
historical development of, 30-1
Code of Canon Law (1917), 83
College of Consultors, Diocese of Ballarat, 222-3, 225-6, 227, 228, 229-230, 255, 257-8, 259, 261
Collins, Father Donal, 120-1
Commission of Investigation into the Catholic Archdiocese of Dublin (2009), 119
communism, 10, 11, 142, 144, 145, 199-200, 245
confession/confessional, 11, 31, 123, 170, 180, 184, 187
and sexual abuse, 36, 120, 172, 264
Congar, Yves, 82, 98-9
Congregation of the Faith (CDF), 43, 265, 288 n.76
approach to sexual abuse cases, 174-5
Conheady, Eddie, 106-7
conscience, 260, 266
examination of, 48
freedom of, 238, 260
of Bishop Mulkearns, 264, 266
of priests, 188-9, 260
conscription, 6, 102, 165
contraception, 72, 143, 267
Copernicus, Nicolaus, 75
Copleston, Father Frederick, 19, 97-8
Cornwall Inquiry, Canada, 173
Cornwell, John, 35-6, 180, 183, 188-9
seminary experiences, 137-8
Corpus Christi College, Werribee, 132-3, 220, 284 n.9
compared with Saint Columba's Seminary, Springwood, 132-3

Council Fathers
Council of Trent, 134, 202
Second Vatican Council, 73, 142, 145, 191

Council of Elvira (309), 219
Council of Trent, 1, 20, 73, 80, 140, 147, 172, 256
and seminary life, 134-5, 140, 183, 202
on marriage and celibacy, 73, 134-5
Cowburn, John, 297 n.289, 300 n.374
Cozzen, Donald B., 25-6, 36, 181, 293 n.205, 295 n.247
Crimen sollicitationis (1922), 264-5
Crittenden, Paul, 51, 92-3, 293 n.200, 297 n.294
cultic priesthood, see clericalism
culture, definitions of, 2
culture of Catholic Church, see Catholic culture
Cuthbert, Betty, 110

D

Damian, Saint Peter, 172
Daniel-Rops, Henri, 247-8
Darwin, Charles, 236, 238
Davey, Father Brendan, 224
Day, Monsignor John, 253
Deans of Discipline, 1, 18, 49, 50, 105, 126, 132, 148, 203, 206
Decree on Reformation, 134
Decree on the Priesthood (1965), 190-1, 299 n.347
Decree on the Priestly Training (1965), 145-6
Democratic Labor Party (DLP), 101

Descartes, Rene, 75, 77-9, 80
Devoy, Frank, 52, 288 n.88
discipline, 35, 134, 140, 190, 195
  see also Deans of Discipline
Doctor Zhivago (Boris Pasternak), 14, 251
Donnelly, Bob
  at Springwood, 21, 59, 87, 88, 94-5, 127, 159-60, 199-201, 205, 209, 232, 237
  in Rome, 238-9, 240-44, 245, 273
Donohue, William A., 295 n.253
Dostoevsky, Fyodor, 84, 86, 90-1
Dowlan, Brother Edward, 223-5
Doyle, Father James, 120, 122
Doyle, Father Thomas P., 179, 286 n.43, 287 n.58, 291 n.166, 292 n.185, 294 n.220, 294 n.228, 294 n.229, 294 n.232, 297 n.298
  criticism of John Jay reports, 173-4
Dublin, Archdiocese of, 119
Dulcinea del Toboso (fictional character), 109
Dunne, Monsignor Charles, 16, 49-52, 53, 67
Duns Scotus, John, 78

E

Edenhope, 225, 226, 227, 228
Enlightenment, The, 76-6, 236, 237
ephebophilia, 177-8
Eve (biblical figure), 69, 71

F

Farrell, Brother, 223
Fascism, 144
Fathers of the Church, 71-2

Ferns (Ireland), Diocese of, 120, 122, 168, 173, 288 n.74
Ferns report (2005), 120, 122, 291 n.158, 296 n.268
Finkelhood, Dr David, 39
First Cause, 87, 200
First Vatican Council, 142, 147
  on priestly celibacy, 190-1
Fiscalini, Monsignor Leo, 225, 228-9
Fitzgerald, Brother, 223
Flaubert, Gustave, 15, 280
Fletcher, Father Frank, 212
Foley, Martin, 221
Fortune, Father Sean, 120-1, 122
Fox, Ian ('Foxy'), 60-1, 108, 246
Francis, Pope, 24, 186
Frankl, Viktor, 127, 129-30
Franklin, James, 294 n.242, 296, n.262
French Revolution, The, 75, 93-4, 160, 237-8, 274-5
Furness, Gail, SC, 25, 43, 66, 178, 226, 283 n.6, 287 n.54, 290 n.123, 295 n.249, 295 n.251

G

Gagen, Father Brian, 212
Galileo (Galilei), 75, 144
gay clergy, see homosexual clergy
gay marriage, 65, 73
Geraghty, Chris, 16, 50, 51, 52, 67, 92-3, 95, 135-7, 138, 204, 274, 288 n.88, 289 nn.94-5, 290 n.130, 291 n.146, 291 nn.149-50, 292 nn.177-8, 292 n.184, 293 n.199, 297 nn.290-1, 299 n.332, 299 n.334, 299 n.345
Gillard, Julia, 5

Gilroy, Norman, Cardinal Archbishop of Sydney, 16, 52, 64, 95, 102, 132, 138, 142, 163, 204, 212, 232-5, 252
Gleeson, Father J. H., 106
Goffman, Erving, 195-6, 197
Gordon, Adam Lindsay, 208
Greek tragedy, 266-7
Green family, 53
Green, Timothy, 224
Gregory VII, Pope, 191
Gregory XVI, Pope, 238
Grennan, Father, 120
Grossman, Vasily, 54-6

H

Heather, Bishop Bede, 14, 125, 162-3, 198, 272
Heckler, Victor J., see Kennedy, Eugene & Victor J. Keckler
Henschke, Bishop Francis, 9, 13, 123-4, 218, 233, 272
Heraclitus, 19, 27
Herlihy, Bishop Donal, 121
hierarchy, see Catholic Church hierarchy
History of Western philosophy (Bertrand Russell), 200, 286 n.31
Holy Mother Church, 75, 104, 134, 245
homosexual clergy, 21, 22, 38, 178, 184, 229, 230, 264
homosexuality, 21, 22, 23, 184, 295 n.254
confused with paedophilia, 23, 184, 229-30
homosocial, Church as, 25, 166-7
Hopkins, Gerard Manley, 246

Hoyos, Cardinal Dario Castrillón, 175
Humanae vitae (1968), 143
Humbert, Cardinal, 192
Hume, David, 79

I

Ignatius of Loyola, Saint, 247
Inglewood, 226, 228, 298 n.319
Innocent II, Pope, 191, 192-3
intimacy
and priests, 35-6, 37, 185, 257, 260
fear of, as predictor of child molesters, 37
intimacy deficits in sex offenders and priests, 37
Ireland
clerical sexual abuse in, 118-22
see also Commission of Investigation into the Catholic Archdiocese of Dublin; Dublin, Archdiocese of; *Ferns report*; Ferns (Ireland), Diocese of

J

Jenolan Caves, 29
Jerome, Saint, 63, 68, 70-1
Jesus (Christ), 2, 6, 12, 19, 30-1, 52, 53, 54, 56, 57, 65, 72, 84, 86, 87, 90, 108, 117, 129, 140, 143, 149, 150, 160, 168, 173, 183, 187, 190, 191, 192, 203, 205, 233, 245, 255, 256, 267, 276, 277
John Jay College of Criminal Justice reports
32-3, 34, 37, 168-71, 174, 177, 178, 185-6, 245, 284 n.9, 285 n.23, 286 n.47, 287 n.53, 295 n.244, 295 n.248, 295 n.253, 296

n.272, 299 n.342
criticism of, 33, 168-71, 172, 186, 286 n.37
see also Doyle, Father Thomas; Sipe, Richard
John Paul II, Pope, 6, 24, 43, 147, 175, 185, 265, 269
John XXIII, Pope, 49, 139, 142, 265
John, Saint, 129
Johnson, Samuel, 204-5
Joiner, Dr George ('Doc'), 29, 48, 94, 95-7, 98, 106, 136-7, 165, 193, 200, 202, 206, 211, 278

K

K&H, see Kennedy, Eugene & Victor J. Heckler
Kant, Immanuel, 21, 79-80, 241
Keenan, Dr Marie, 25, 32-3, 35, 180-2, 185, 285 n.20, 286 n.42, 293 n.197
Kelly, Archbishop Michael, 234
Kelly, Father Michael, 14, 275-6, 277
Kelly, Ned, 209
Keneally, Tom, 66-9, 148
Kennedy, Eugene & Victor J. Heckler, v, 29, 31-33, 35, 36, 37, 38, 39, 178
Kennedy, Eugene, 29, 30, 39
see also Kennedy, Eugene & Victor J. Heckler
Kennedy, Philip, 289 n.111, 289 n.115, 290 n.118, 299 nn.338-9
Kenny, Sister Nuala, 2
King, Betty, 65
Kohut, Heinz, 26
Küng, Hans, 43, 145, 186, 193, 289 n.97, 293 n.203, 296 n.275, 299 n.336

L

Lawrence, D. H., 47
Lawrence, Jimmy, 211
lay apostolate/spirituality, at odds with seminary formation, 12-3
Lee, Kevin, 148
Leo IX, Pope, 191, 192
Leo XIII, Pope, 75, 76, 79, 80-1, 86, 139, 144, 236
Leonard, Monsignor John, 65
Lermontov, Mikhail, 89
Liberalism, 75, 76, 139
liberation movements, 6, 170
Liggett, Ray, 29, 100
Little, Archbishop Sir Frank, 265

M

Madame Bovary (Gustave Flaubert), 15, 63, 204-5, 280
Madden, Monsignor James, 64-5, 68, 165
Maguire, Father Bob, 26, 297 n.299
Majella, Saint Gerard, 10
Malamud, Bernard, 150
Manly (Saint Patrick's College), 16, 23, 30, 49, 52, 58, 64-5, 68, 88, 92, 97, 131-2, 142, 146, 165, 246, 250
Manne, Anne, 285 n.28
Mannix, Archbishop Dr Daniel, 49, 132, 133, 235
Marist Brothers, 135, 181
Marist Fathers (Society of Mary), 36
Marr, David, 222, 285 n.18, 297 n.300, 297 n.302
marriage
  Church antipathy to, 72-3
  gay marriage, 65, 73

Marx, Karl, 92
Mary, Blessed Virgin, 10-1, 53-6, 57, 71, 137, 138, 190, 232, 250
  Our Lady of Fatima, 10
Mass attendance, 6, 284 n.9
Matthew, Saint, 12, 190
Mayne, Father Charlie, 132
McClellan, Peter, QC, 175-6
McKenzie, Monsignor, 225, 230
McKinnon, Father John, 254-5, 256-62
McMahon, Mary, 63
Mecham, Father Frank, 50, 63, 88-9
Meersman, Maria, 64-5
Melchizedek, 115, 277
Melican, Father Bill, 254
Menzies, Robert, 101, 102
Meredith, Father George, 136
Merton, Thomas, 199
metaphysics, 78, 81, 85, 241
Miles, Oliver, 251
Milligan, Louise, 26, 297 n.299
Ministry to Priests, 259
misogyny and the Church, 65-6, 69-74
  and sexual abuse, 66
  exclusion of women from leadership, 66
  linked to celibacy, 66
  see also sex; women
Missionaries of the Sacred Heart (MSC), 13, 212, 249, 262
Modernism, 144, 236-8
Modernist oath, 237
Molony, John, 9, 95, 104-5, 132, 133, 162, 163, 212, 220, 235, 253, 254, 255, 277, 292 nn.180-2, 293 n.202, 297 n.292, 299 n.333, 299 n.340

Monk, Ray, 200
Moran, Cardinal Patrick Francis, 131-2, 138, 204
Mortlake, 227-30, 254
Morwood, Michael, 262
  defence of Bishop Mulkearns, 262-9
Motu proprio sacrementorum sanctitatis tutela (1997), 265
Mulhearn, Geoff, 49
Mulkearns, Bishop Ronald, 222-3, 225-6, 228, 255, 257-9, 262-71, 297 n.297
Murphy Report (2009), see Commission of Investigation into the Catholic Archdiocese of Dublin
Murphy, Father Paddy, 52
Murphy, Francis D., 122, 288 n. 74
Murray, Commissioner, 262
Murray, Margaret, 281
Mussolini, Benito, 144
Myers-Briggs, 211

N

Nangle, Brother Paul, 224
Napoleon, Bonaparte, 93-4, 160, 274-5
narcissism, 21, 180, 181, 285 n.28
  and the Church, 174, 180, 181, 183, 184-5, 186-7, 237
National Catholic Girls' Movement, 64-5
National Catholic Rural Movement, 57, 144, 245, 280
National Committee for Professional Standards, 221
National Review Board (2002), 32
National Service, 60, 165
  compared to seminary, 195-7

Nationalism, 75-6
natural law, 36, 167, 179, 295 n.256
Neo-Thomism, 86
Norwich, John Julius, 284 n.15
Notre Dame Cathedral, 274

O

O'Brien, Monsignor, 225
O'Collins, Bishop James P., 9, 12, 176, 222
O'Gorman, Colm, 121
O'Keeffe Nine, The, 253
O'Keeffe, Father Martin, 253
O'Keeffe, Monsignor, 225
O'Neill, Father George, 133
One True Church, 11, 43, 173, 179, 187, 203, 277
Origen, 69-70, 71
original sin, 44, 53, 69-70, 74, 94, 134
Our Lady, see Mary, Blessed Virgin

P

paedophilia, 176-7
  Catch 22 defence, 269
  definition of, 4, 173, 177
  seminaries as breeding ground for, 68
  see also clerical sexual abuse of minors; ephebophilia; homosexuality
parents wanting to protect abusive priests, 117
Parkinson, Professor Patrick, 40-2, 174-5, 294 n.240
Parmenides, 28
Pascal's wager, 56

Pasternak, Boris, 14, 251
Paul III, Pope, 172
Paul VI, Pope, 145, 146, 192, 265, 273, 299 n.347
Paul, Saint, 23, 30, 126, 173
Pavarotti, Luciano, 15, 89, 279
Pell, Cardinal George, 26, 44-5, 223, 253, 297 n.300
  and Royal Commission into Institutional Responses to Child Abuse, 5, 44-5, 222, 223-5, 226-7, 229-31, 268-9
  'Big George', 220-1
  footballer, 220
  on structural change in the Church, 44-5
  Southwell enquiry, 220-2
Peoples, Kevin
  Ballarat, 218-9, 220, 253-4
  Catholic Action, 12, 149, 275
  celibacy, 193, 273
  dressing for High Mass, 211, 239
  family life, 10-1, 124, 129
  France, 93-4, 161-2
  Good Friday and Easter, 57, 209, 250
  his God, 20, 87, 138, 149, 279, 284 n.11
  leaving seminary, 14-6, 277-80
  life before seminary, 244-5
  marriage, 281
  mission and Kingdom, 150
  music, 60-1, 105, 108, 111, 123, 124, 127, 148, 160-1, 165, 195, 201, 209-10, 213-4, 240, 244-5, 246-7, 251, 279
  National Service, 195-7, 244
  priestly vocation, 9, 12, 58, 123-4, 129, 248, 249, , 272-3, 275-7
  Saint Columba's Seminary, 1, 6, 13, 14, 16, 17, 23, 27-8, 29-30, 46-9, 50-1, 53, 56-61, 62, 75-6,

81-2, 87, 88-92, 93, 94-8, 99-100, 101-2, 103-4, 123-7, 129, 148-9, 159-60, 162-4, 165, 197-8, 199-205, 206-12, 232-3, 235-6, 237, 238-244, 245, 246-9, 250, 251-2, 272-9
Terang, 105-9, 115, 213-4, 272-3
women, 9, 53, 62-4, 109, 123, 129, 213, 244
Young Christian Workers, 11, 15, 98-9, 106, 110, 149, 150, 163, 218, 219, 244
see also Peoples family; Sisyphus

Peoples family (author's relatives), 53
Anne (aunt), 53, 60
Beryl (aunt), 53
Bill (father), 10, 46, 108, 207, 208-9, 217, 218, 252, 278
Brian 'Blondie' (cousin), 107-8
Eileen (aunt), 217, 250
Gavin (cousin), 250
Gerard (brother), 213, 278
Ina (mother), 10-1, 17, 53, 62, 125, 143, 148, 197, 208, 209, 217, 218, 252, 278
John 'Rusty' (cousin), 207-8, 217
Kath (cousin), 250
Peg (sister), 10, 188, 213
Polly 'Poll' (aunt), 10, 11-2, 53, 217, 252

Peter D., 92, 108, 124-5

Peter H., 125-6, 165, 207

Peter, Saint, 30, 126

Pican, Bishop Pierre, 175

Pius IV, Pope, 172

Pius IX, Pope, 55, 75, 76

Pius V, Pope, 134

Pius VII, Pope, 174

Pius X, Pope, 75, 79, 138-41, 144, 148, 186, 235, 237
reform of seminaries, 140-1, 186, 202

Pius XI, Pope, 144, 264

Pius XII, Pope, 49, 144, 247

Plato, 14, 47, 72, 109, 110, 125, 201, 205
Plato's Forms, 77, 106, 205

police, 118, 183, 208, 221, 251
reporting clerical abuse to, 174-5, 176, 264-5
Victoria Police, 41

Pontifical Secret, see Secret of the Holy Office

Pope as Vicar of Christ, 173, 203

Pope, Alexander, 132

Presocratics, 19, 27-8, 80

priests, see Catholic priests

Propaganda Fide College, Rome, 92, 95, 162, 233, 273
Bob Donnelly at, 238, 241-4

Protestant Reformation, see Reformation, the

Puckapunyal ('Pucka'), 195-7

Pushkin, Alexander, 89

R

Raphael, 54-5

Ratzinger, Cardinal Joseph, 43, 256
see also Benedict XVI, Pope

Reformation, The, 5, 72, 134, 234

Ridsdale, Father Gerald, 175-6, 222-3, 225, 226, 227-31, 253, 258-9, 263, 269, 296 n.262, 297 n.297, 298 n.319

Robertson, Geoffrey, QC, 40, 175, 288 nn.76-7, 294 n.239, 296 n.275

Robinson, Bishop Geoffrey, 49-50, 65-6, 296 n.275

Rohan, Billy, 251

Rohan, Mick, 251

Rollo, Mrs, 109, 127
Ross family, 219
Ross, Jim, 99, 218-9
Rowley, Kev, 108
Royal Commission into Institutional Responses to Child Sexual Abuse (2013), 4, 5, 7, 25, 34, 40, 42, 43, 44-5, 66, 113, 116, 163, 173, 175-6, 178, 215, 222, 223-5, 226-7, 228-31, 246, 253, 254-62, 268-70
Rural Movement, see National Catholic Rural Movement
Russell, Bertrand, 28, 200, 201, 240, 243
Ryan, Brendan, 198
Ryan, Dave, 127
Ryan, Father Paul David, 253
Ryan, Father Paul, 163

S

Sacerdotalis caelibatus (1967), 192, 273
Saint Alipius Parish, Ballarat, 219, 222-3
Saint Colman's Primary School, Mortlake, 228, 254
Saint Columba's Seminary, Springwood
   administration of, 202-3
   bias against science, 18-9
   biology classes, 94, 136-7
   compared with Corpus Christi Seminary, Werribee, 132-3
   compared with Propaganda Fide College, Rome, 239, 241-4
   educational practice, 97-8
   fear of intimacy and friendship, 1, 26, 180
   food, 127, 193, 196, 203, 236
   spy system, 242
   teaching of philosophy, 18-9, 27-8, 81-2, 87, 88-9
   understanding of God, 20-2, 27, 279
Saint Patrick's College, see Manly
Saint Patrick's Secondary College, Ballarat, 137, 224
Saint Peter's College, Wexford, Ireland, 120-1, 137
Sale, Diocese of, 5, 291 n.163
Salesians of Don Bosco, 36
Sandhurst, Diocese of, 5, 163, 291 n.163
Santamaria, B. A., 12, 57, 101, 199, 220, 245
   see also National Catholic Rural Movement
Santamaria's Rural Movement, see National Catholic Rural Movement
Satan, 185, 192
Schillebeeckx, Edward, 82
Scholasticism, 78-9, 97
Scott, Phillip, 220-2
Second Lateran Council, 191
Second Vatican Council, 3, 6, 25, 74, 86, 98, 142, 145, 147, 165, 237, 238, 256, 283 n.8
   and priestly celibacy, 190-1
   and seminary life, 3, 145-7
   and Thomism, 86, 146
   life prior to, 3, 38, 47, 167, 169
   on marriage and sex, 73
Secret of the Holy Office, 265
Secreta continere (1974), 265
seminaries, 131-3
   and young boys, 133-8
   as breeding grounds for paedophiles, 68
   lack of sex education, 136-7

mental health issues, 68
minor, 135, 136-7, 145-6
poor screening, 3, 13, 32, 33
sex abuse within, 33

seminary training, 261
and discipline, 2, 35, 134, 140, 190, 195
and lack of sexual development, 3, 22, 32, 35, 38, 39, 136, 261
and obedience, 1, 2, 27, 59, 67, 68, 99, 117, 133, 140, 203, 236, 279
curriculum, 38, 167, 203, 204
failure to prepare for celibacy, 3, 67-8, 135
flawed, 3, 31-2
linked to sexual abuse, 32
see also Saint Columba's Seminary, Springwood

sex
Catholic approach to, 167, 192-3, 210
linked with sin, 67-8
linked with women and sin, 65, 66, 69, 71-3, 134, 192-3, 196
obsession with sex and sin, 3, 25, 31, 136, 167, 186, 196, 219

sexual abuse of minors
in general population, 34, 41, 177
see also clerical sexual abuse of minors; paedophilia

Shepherd, Father Ted, 59, 123, 275, 276

Sher, Mr, QC, 221

Sipe, Richard, 23-24, 33-4, 39, 42, 44, 177, 178, 181, 183, 286 n.43, 287 n.58, 291 n.166, 292 n.185-7, 294 n.229, 296 n.296, 297 n.298
criticism of John Jay reports, 33, 172-3, 178
on Church as homosocial society, 166-7, 178
on clerical celibacy, 24-5, 166-7, 184, 190

on high levels of abuse in Catholic Church, 42
on priests sexually abused as children, 33

Sisters of Our Lady Help of Christians, 62-3

Sisyphus, 28, 123, 127-9, 205, 232, 248

Smith Lecture 2013, 40-2

Smith, John, 126

Socialism, 139

Socrates, 201, 205-6

Southwell, Alex, QC, 220-2

Special Issues Committee, 266

Speed (pseudonym), 197-8, 205, 209, 233

Springwood Golf Course, 206-7

Springwood, see Saint Columba's Seminary

Stockton, Father Eugene, 59, 61, 237

Strangman, Father Paul, 212

Sturzo, Luigi, 144

Suing the Pope, 122

Sullivan, Francis, 113, 171, 264, 283 nn.3-4

Syllabus of errors (1864), 236

Synod of Bishops, Rome (1971), 38

T

Talleyrand, Charles-Maurice de, 160-2

Tannhauser (Richard Wagner), 105, 213

Tapsell, Kieran, 30, 265, 300 n.363, 300 n.370

Teilhard de Chardin, Pierre, 199

Terruwe, Dr Anna, 38-9

Tertullian, 69, 71

Thavis, John, 296 n.286

Index 313

Thérèse of Lisieux, Saint, 10, 137
Thomas à Kempis, 137
Thomas Aquinas, Saint, 1, 19, 47, 76-7, 78, 79, 81-3, 86, 87, 97, 109, 146, 148, 198, 201, 240, 272
  and Canon Law, 8
  on God, 77, 80
  on women, 71
  Vatican version of, 82-3, 85, 86
  see also Thomism
Thomism, 19, 76, 80, 82-4, 86, 88, 146, 212, 236
Tóibín, Colm, 120, 122, 291 n.160, 291 n.169-71, 292 n.190
Tolstoy, Leo, 91
Toomey, Father Kevin, 64-5
total institution, concept of, 195-6, 197
Towards healing (1996), 40, 50, 221, 253
Toynbee, Phillip, 11
Traill, John, 279-80
Treblinka, 55, 144
Trent, see Council of Trent
Truth, Justice and Healing Council, 4-5, 113, 171, 264
Twain, Mark, 100

U

United States Conference of Catholic Bishops, 38, 168, 171, 245, 284 n.9
Urban College of Propaganda Fide, see Propaganda Fide College, Rome
Urban VIII, Pope, 238

V

Vatican Commission for Priestly Life, 266

Vatican I, see First Vatican Council
Vatican II, see Second Vatican Council
Vatican, the
  as quasi-State, 175
  failure to assist civil investigations of abuse, 43
Veech, Monsignor Thomas McNiven ('Veechy'), 15-7, 20, 49, 50, 58, 63, 92-4, 96, 99, 103-4, 106, 107, 108, 124, 126, 127, 144, 164, 199, 202-4, 207-8, 210, 232, 239, 242, 248, 274-5, 278, 280
  and Dostoevsky, 90-1
  and Samuel Johnson, 204-5
  and Talleyrand, 160-2
  and Tolstoy, 91
  as lecturer, 89
  oral examination, 103-4
  request to play golf, 206-7
Vicar of Christ, see Pope
Victorian Government's Parliamentary Inquiry, v, 41-2, 265
Vietnam war, 6, 102, 165, 199
virginity, esteemed by Church, 73, 147, 167, 186, 191, 219
  see also celibacy
vocation(s)
  devaluation of marriage as, 72, 145
  late, to priesthood, 244, 245
  priestly, 3, 6, 12, 47, 54, 81, 131, 140, 143, 145, 147, 187, 235, 276
Von Trapp Family singers, 64

W

W (pseudonym), 22-3
Wagga Wagga, Diocese of, 9, 123, 132, 218, 233, 248, 249
Wagner, Richard, 105, 213, 214
Wallace, David Foster, 147
Walsh, Father John ('Walshy'), 18-19,

27, 50, 87, 89, 105, 148, 164, 206, 209, 240
Warrnambool, 63, 212, 226, 228-9
Welladsen, Des ('Barney'), 163-5, 197
Whelan, Dr Michael, 7, 246, 283 n.8, 288 n.78
Whitlam, Gough, 101, 102
Wholohan, Father Len ('Lenny'), 14-5, 101-2, 124, 127, 207
Wiley, Tatha, 74, 289 nn.106-9, 289 n.114, 290 n.117, 290 n.125
William of Ockham, 78
Williamson, Greg, 94
Wills, Garry, 187, 284 n.15, 286 nn.33-5, 293 n.203, 295 n.256, 296 nn.280-1, 299 n.348, 300 n.373

Wilson, Jimmy, 65
women
    Church opposes gender equality, 238
    ordination of, 44, 267
    see also misogyny and the Church; sex
Wyngaards, John, 291 n.154

Y

YCW, see Young Christian Workers
Yeats, W. B., 46, 47
Young Christian Workers (YCW), 9, 11, 15, 64-5, 98-9, 106, 110, 133, 149, 150, 163, 218, 219, 235, 244, 254

www.ingramcontent.com/pod-product-compliance
Lightning Source LLC
Chambersburg PA
CBHW020048170426
43199CB00009B/211